BUILDING SCALE MODEL

ELECTRIC-POWERED BOATS

Gordon Longworth

BUILDING SCALE MODEL ELECTRIC-POWERED BOATS

THE CROWOOD PRESS

First published in 2022 by
The Crowood Press Ltd
Ramsbury, Marlborough
Wiltshire SN8 2HR

enquiries@crowood.com

www.crowood.com

British Library Cataloguing-in-Publication Data
A catalogue record for this book is available from the British Library.

ISBN 978 0 7198 4116 3

Acknowledgements
I would like to say a heart-felt 'thank you' to my wife Lesley. Firstly, for the enthusiasm and confidence that she showed with her encouragement in convincing me to write this book. But perhaps more importantly, in her endless forbearance when cleaning spilt glue off my clothes, mending a hole created by a sanding disc, or helping to find an essential lost brass nut on the workshop floor. Not to mention the strong smell of solvents or paint pervading the house on occasions, which she suffered without complaint.

Also may I offer my thanks to all the members, too numerous to mention, of Etherow Model Boat Club, near Marple, Stockport, for your comradeship, and your help and guidance over the years: you have all given me so much pleasure.

Finally, my thanks to the Component Shop for their permission to reproduce the images and information on pages 74–5, 98, and 107–8, as well as for their advice and excellent service over the years.

Typeset by Chennai Publishing Services
Cover design by Sergey Tsvetkov
Printed and bound in India by Replika Press Pvt. Ltd.

Contents

Introduction

I have often found that the attitude held in the old days to the 'Wild West' cowboy era – when no matter how fast someone was with a gun there would always be someone faster – is analogous to that found in the world of model boat building. For no matter how good or skilled you are at making and detailing your model, there will always be someone who will come along, who in your eyes has greater ability.

However, never, ever, be discouraged by this, but look instead at how they did it, what materials were used, and how it was designed, and learn from it, and try to raise your own standards: that way you will simply get better next time. Because that stunningly detailed model you see before you, which you look at with envy and amazement, and which you know you can never emulate, may quite easily have been built by a professional model maker, or may have taken a dedicated enthusiast many years to construct, or may even have been built by a team with a diverse range of skills.

Every modeller I have ever met has always, without exception, been only too pleased to share their experience and knowledge, so the first thing you need to learn once you have taken the second step on that most satisfying road of building and sailing models is – to ask questions.

I say 'second step' because you will more than likely have built something simpler before this as a first step. It may have been a model aircraft years ago; it may have been last year after you watched someone sailing on a local lake; or perhaps you want a grandchild to enjoy the same pleasure that you obtained in the past, when you took those initial steps all those years ago.

However, model boats didn't start with the complex control systems that we can enjoy today, but which seem so baffling. They probably started with a dim and distant ancestor of Winnie the Pooh playing a Neanderthal version of 'Pooh sticks' in a stream – but I bet they obtained the same pleasure and satisfaction out of the experience that we do!

Making model boats is not a new thing – even King Tutankhamun had a few secreted away in his underground tomb. They were models of the simple single-sail open craft that plied their way up and down the River Nile. However, we will never know if King Tut ever played with them whilst he dodged the ever-present ferocious Nile crocodiles that frequented the river at that time. I think the models were there for a much more important role: as representative solar boats to carry his spirit with the god Amun-Ra through the sky each night.

The subject for the model I am currently making is from a wall engraving over a thousand years earlier than King Tut – so there are plenty of ideas to choose from.

Now, annoyingly, I have just fallen into the usual trap of saying 'played' – intimating that we are dealing with 'toys' or something of little significance. The quickest way to upset any modeller is to call their model a 'toy', be it a boat, or an aircraft, or a railway layout – for they are much more than that: they are scale model replicas, some working with many moving parts, some highly detailed

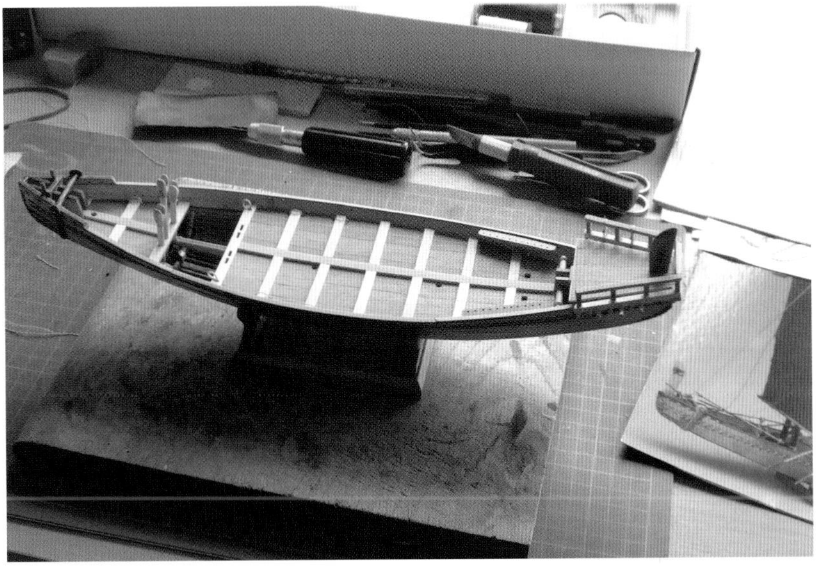

A small static model of the royal barge of the ancient Egyptian Pharoah Sahure, dated 2428BC. Ships such as this sailed to many lands bringing back myrrh, electrum and ebony wood for thousands of years.

static displays – many are pure works of art that will have taken many years to build.

But as I said at the start, don't be discouraged if your efforts are not as good in your eyes as someone else's – as likely as not they will still be better than some. Beauty is in the eyes of the beholder, is it not? The important thing is that you try. If you can honestly admit to yourself that you have done the best you are capable of, then that is perfectly acceptable. If, however, you are not satisfied with your efforts, then next time you will have a yardstick to aim at, to do better.

My intention in this book is to encourage you to take that second step. Arguably you already have, or you wouldn't be reading this – so let's call it a third step. I want to try to offer some pointers to ensure that the interest you already have is not blunted by having taken on a model that is either too simple, and doesn't satisfy you, or is too complex, when you become utterly disenchanted and bored, such that it will end up on a shelf – forgotten, and never to be finished.

I know from past experience of being handed part-finished models that something like half of the lovely old sailing-ship kits that are bought are never completed. Making the hull is the easy part – assembling all the masts, sails and rigging requires an inordinate amount of time and patience, and not a little skill. This is a great shame, as many of these kits can cost hundreds of pounds. Consequently, I do not propose to cover sailing ships here, although many of the more modern craft that we will look at do still have masts and rigging to some extent.

Here I should issue a word of caution: there are from time-to-time magazines advertised on television where a model can be built over a period of time following steps in a monthly magazine, with a few components for the model supplied with it each month. Apart from the fact that this may take perhaps three years to complete, it will cost far more than buying a kit outright – so that yet again, many are never finished and the modeller is totally discouraged. However, if you want to take your time and not have the initial cost layout, then that is also fine: it is simply another avenue into the hobby, if you have the patience.

I was lucky enough to grow up in South Devon, where the sea and ships are part of everyday life – so watching fishing trawlers and other watercraft come and go (and being on them) was as natural to me as breathing. However, my working life drove me to the North of England, many miles from the sea, so perhaps my pleasure in making models derives from a subconscious desire to re-create that feeling of being back by the sea.

What actually motivates someone to want to make a model boat is often hard to define. Perhaps it's down to an experience in their past. It could be something emotional – say, meeting a partner on a cruise – or a time in the Royal Navy, or the Merchant Navy, or wanting to re-create the golden age of sail.

Certainly many models will have a tale to tell. It can be seen in the love and care that goes into the construction. It shows in the careful detailing, in the patience and skill in construction, and in the involvement in time and money. All these testify to something much more than just wood, plastic, paint and glue. And only ask a modeller about their boat if you have plenty of time to spare, because once they start, they will never stop!

But whatever it is that motivates you to want to build a replica scale-model boat is not so important. What *is* important is that you choose something within your capabilities and that you can complete. This isn't simply down to your personal skills, it's also down to the environment in which you propose to build the model. Many models are built on the kitchen table, but if there are young toddlers about with inquisitive fingers, then sharp knives, glue and paint are perhaps not the ideal playthings for them to grab!

Having said that, I do feel that there are two age groups that are likely to be drawn into modelling. The first comprises young teenagers, who have the most inquisitive and fertile of minds, but not the wherewithal to purchase the materials; however, although loving grandparents may naturally want to encourage a grandchild, all I have said earlier should be considered before they go out and buy something that could easily put off a young mind for life. On the other hand it may perhaps put them on the road to a very fruitful career.

The second group is by far the largest, and comprises older people – though sadly mainly men – so why not women, who in my experience usually have greater dexterity and more patience? These individuals have retired and want to enjoy a hobby that uses hands-on skills and knowledge learned throughout their working life, or maybe they want to try something different now that they have the time. However, no matter what age or gender you are, I hope these pages will succeed in guiding you along a very rewarding and enjoyable path.

Most readers will already have made some kind of simpler model, as likely as not in a kit. And before we go any further, let's just define what we mean by a 'kit', and the pros and cons associated with it. There are literally thousands of them, all types of craft, at different scales and detailing, where everything is provided by the kit manufacturer, except glue and paint.

Then there is something called a 'semi-kit', which provides a basic hull and maybe some moulded superstructure; everything else you have to make. Alternatively you can buy a virtually finished model, the only extras necessary being the battery and the radio-control system.

Lastly there is the 'scratch-built' boat, and arguably this is the most challenging type of model, perhaps best left until you have some experience with kits. This is because you simply start with an idea, research it for any existing plans, and then make or adapt everything. However, there is no question that this is also the most rewarding type of model.

We will also discuss which type of model is best suited to the person who will build it. Is the hull big enough to take all the electronics, motors and batteries that we want to have in it? What type of radio control will we use? How many radio channels will we need? How heavy will it be? Will it fit into the car? Where will we be able to sail it? Where can we find more information? What restrictions are there, if any, to using open water?

These are all questions that will be covered in the next few chapters, and hopefully by the time you reach the end of this book, many of the pitfalls that put people off this exciting and rewarding pastime will have been avoided, and you will have learned a great deal. And likely as not, later you will get to know some really friendly, like-minded enthusiasts, who will be only too willing to offer help and guidance along the way.

Chapter One

What You Will Need

ESSENTIAL TOOLS

'Essential' items are only those necessary for a particular model, nothing more: they are described here simply to offer some suggestions as to how they might be used. Certainly the French prisoners-of-war sent to Dartmoor Prison, in Devon, during the Napoleonic wars, who produced some stunning museum-quality models of their own sailing men-o-war, made out of cattle bones from the kitchens, did not have much in the way of essential tools!

Whatever tools you use, do learn how to use them properly: read any instructions, and protect yourself, especially when using power tools, or anything with teeth or a sharp blade. After all, they are designed to cut things – be this pieces of wood, or by default, fingers. There are plenty of 'How To' videos on the internet, so there is no excuse.

Drills and Drilling Holes

To start with, 0.5mm, 1.0mm and 1.5mm diameter drill bits should cover most of the really fine

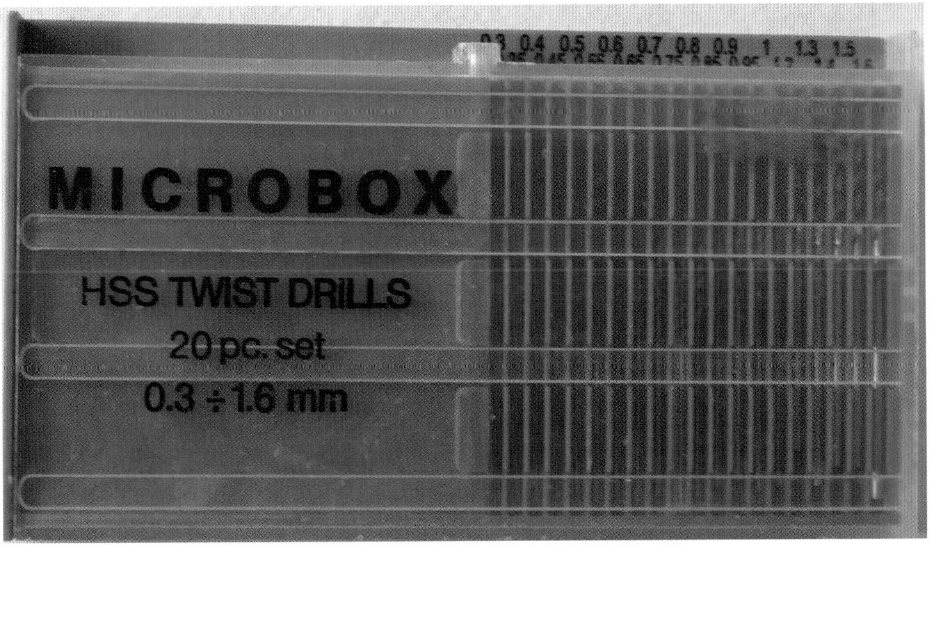

A good quality box of high-speed steel twist drills. Some in this set are more use than others – anything less than 0.5mm will probably get lost before it is worn out. Be careful, as they are sharp.

For simple drilling, this small hand-drill is useful – anything larger will throw a strain on the drill itself. Suitable for anything up to 2mm diameter drills.

A small power hand-drill. This one is battery operated and rechargeable, which means you don't have to turn the drill with one hand whilst holding the hand-drill with the other; also the speed is adjustable. It will have many other uses, as will be seen later.

work. These usually need a specific small holder, as normal hand-drill holders are far too heavy and cumbersome, and the drill itself will bend or break if attempts are made to use them.

Tools for Marking Out

When working with wood or plastic, a sharp nail or a scriber can be used to mark where the hole should be. On metal or curved surfaces it is essential to centre-punch the position, otherwise small

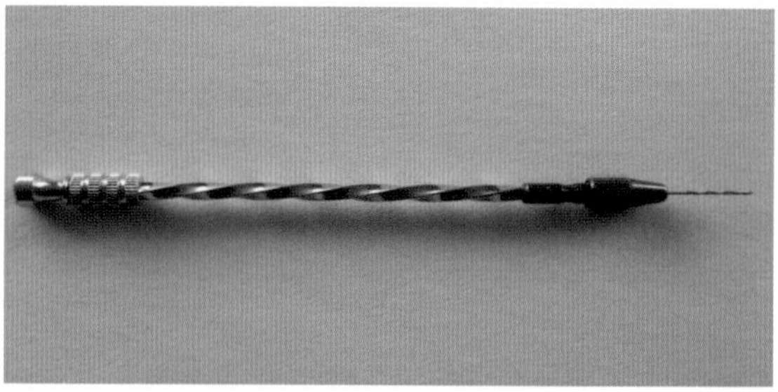

Known as an Archimedes drill and used for anything below 1.00mm, this is an invaluable little drill for the really small holes. It twists by moving the slider up and down, thus rotating the bit in both directions. Pressure is applied by placing a finger on the separately rotating top.

drills will bend or snap and skid away from where the hole should be, with the result that the hole will be off-centre at best, or at worst the work will have to be scrapped.

Tools for Cutting and Trimming

For cutting or trimming plastic sheet, plywood or laser-cut parts, *sharp* knives are essential. More people are injured by using blunt knives when trying to cut something, which then slip, than probably by anything else, so get a set of knife handles that have replaceable blades. Your average pocket knife does not come under the category of a craft knife!

To start with, a set of three will be more than enough. Something thin and pointed for fine, delicate work – an 8mm-diameter handle; a heavier holder with a rounded blade for more robust work – an 11mm-diameter handle; and finally a heavy handle where a strong grip is needed. Swann-Morton's non-surgical packs of five blades are usually the most economical to purchase. By their very nature they have to be ultra-sharp, and thus are made from hardened steel, which makes them tend to be brittle, especially the pointed ones – so don't be surprised if the point snaps off. However, they may still be usable as a secondary blade for initial rough work. Do not use too much force, but allow the blade to actually cut, even if

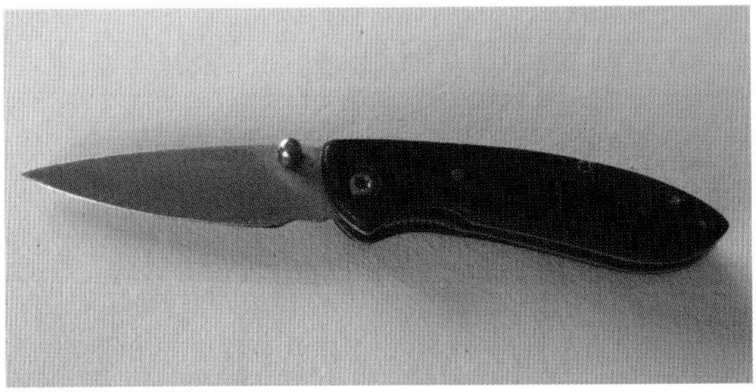

Definitely not a craft knife. It might be useful for whittling a stick, but not for modelling. It is likely to be too blunt and the blade far too thick.

A basic set of three knives: with these to start, it will be possible to do virtually any cutting task necessary. Craft knives often come in sets, with numerous chisels and routers that are unlikely to be used.

this means using repeated strokes to get through the material being cut.

The scalpel handles made by Swann-Morton are actually for surgical work, and their blades are for a 'one-handed quick release' by the operating surgeon when necessary; however, they are still easy to use, and are ideal for modelling. The law states that you must be over eighteen to purchase knife blades.

Cutting Mat

A cutting mat is essential. Some commercially available cutting mats are self-healing and will to some extent 'fill in' any cut marks caused by

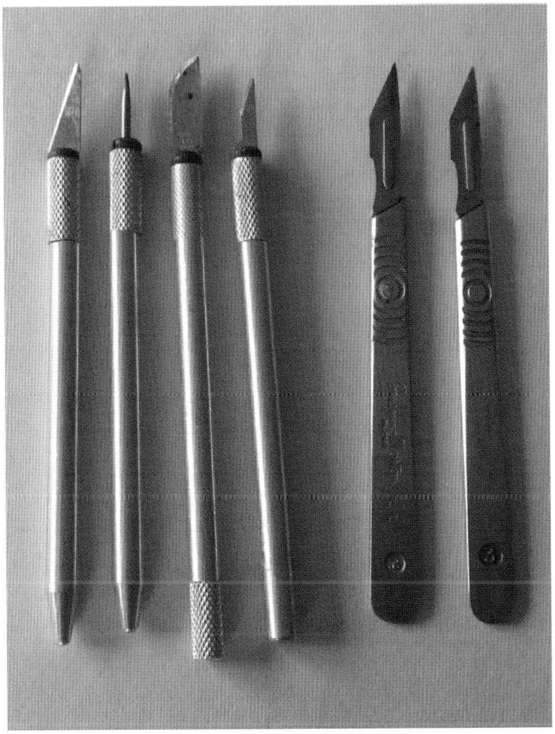

Over time you will accumulate other knives/handles, each with a different blade for a specific purpose; this can save time if changing blades is necessary.

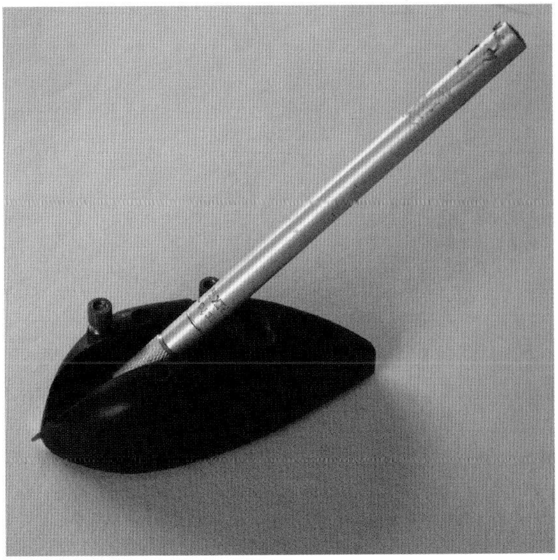

This accessory is best avoided: it's a plank splitter, which at this point is unnecessary. However, after making a few models it can prove economical to make your own planks in the future.

These cutting mats are available in different sizes. The most common is 18 × 12in (450 × 300mm), which will cover mostly anything. An alternative or addition is an old offcut of oak or other flat hardwood.

a knife blade. They also have a very convenient printed grid on both sides for marking out a part prior to cutting it, in order to keep it square, which can be very useful.

A rough cutting board can be home-made, and this piece of flat, smooth oak has been used for many years as a cutting and hand-drilling board. A thicker, rather than thinner board such as this, which gives more stability, is a better choice. A thick plywood offcut is fine but generally the wood is softer and will not allow a smooth cut. What is more essential is that the wood does not warp, and is totally flat.

Tools for Measuring

Most people will have a ruler in the house. As a guide to cutting material with a craft knife it is perhaps not ideal, especially if it is made out of wood or plastic, as the knife can easily ride up over the guiding edge and cut a finger. It is suggested that you purchase a metal straight-edge rule especially designed for this task. Also, never forget the old woodworkers' saying: 'Measure twice, and cut once.'

It is almost guaranteed that you will make the mistake of taking the wrong measurement and destroying your workpiece early on – it's a mistake you never forget, and hopefully do not repeat.

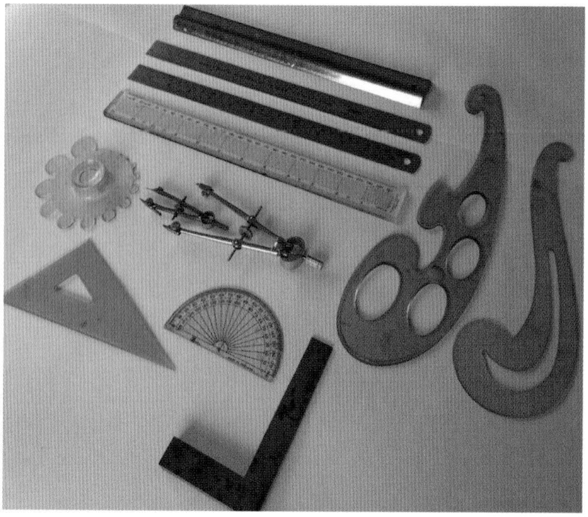

A special metal rule specifically designed to deflect the blade away from the fingers, at the top of the picture. Basically, it is a pressed-steel corrugated section. Ordinary plastic/wooden rules should not be used as the cutting blade can ride over the rule and cut fingers as pressure is exerted on the workpiece. The other drawing tools will be helpful at the design stage, in the future.

Draughtsman's tools, French curves, compasses, protractors, set squares and scale rules are the result of the author's apprenticeship as an engineering draughtsman, and really come under the category of desirable, rather than essential tools. They will likely be of more use when actually designing and drawing out a 'scratch-build' later down the road of model boating.

Tools for Holding Work

Clamps are essential, and there are literally hundreds of them. The simplest is some kind of weight holding down two pieces on a flat surface when you are trying to glue them together. The most readily available is the ordinary clothes-peg.

A small vice has jaws around 1in (25mm) wide, and clamps to the edge of the table for really fine work; sometimes it can help to tie knots with fine twine, when three hands are required. Most of them only need to be able to open the jaws to, say, $\frac{1}{2}$in (12mm) or so. For really large items the slide clamps shown could be used; or

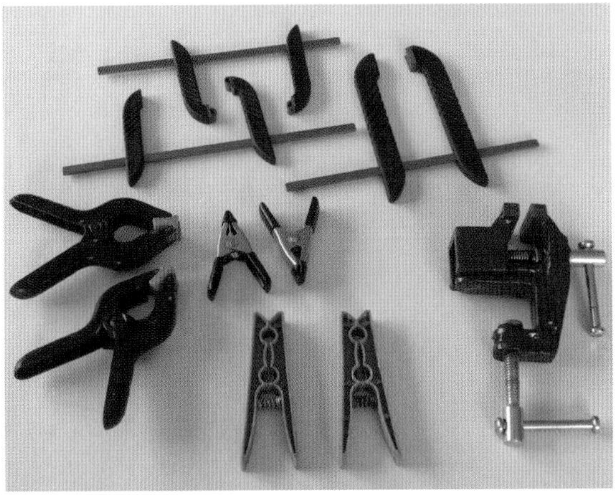

A small range of clamps designed to hold work, usually after you have glued pieces together; some are spring loaded, like clothes-pegs, to grip better. Make sure the spring is not too strong so that it damages your workpiece. It is not unusual to need fifteen to twenty of these during the initial phase of gluing the deck supports to the hull.

Simple is Best

Don't overlook a large rubber band: often this will do the trick more simply than anything else. Even a piece of string or a paper clip might just help for that 'hard to hold' component whilst the adhesive sets.

Avoid that well-known transparent self-adhesive tape used for sticking down torn paper or photographs. The adhesive might need a solvent to remove it, which in turn may damage the workpiece. If you must use a tape, use a low-tack one made for the purpose, and test it first overnight on something that doesn't matter, especially if it is already painted.

use 'G' clamps when you want to position larger items that perhaps are curved, or are awkward in shape.

Pliers

Where fingers are too cumbersome, or simply not strong enough, then pliers are more than essential. There are long-nosed pliers, a pair with serrated faces for grip, another for cutting out small pre-moulded parts, or sprues, another old standard type for wire cutting. Keep the two separate, and do not use the sharp ones for routine wire cutting.

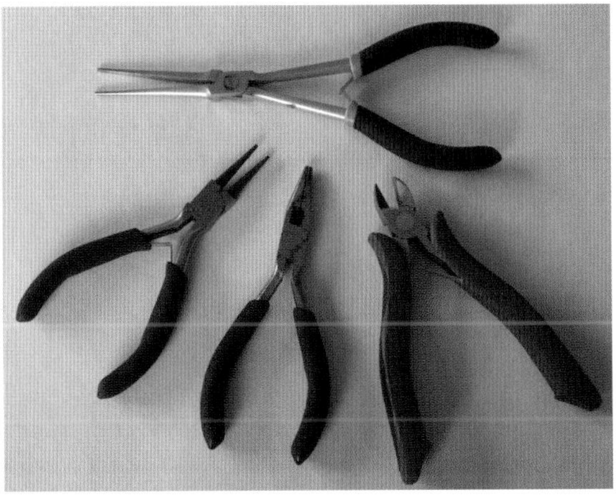

A small selection of pliers: these will include long-nosed, serrated and round-nosed, for different tasks. Always keep a pair such as the red-handled ones shown for cutting only soft parts: this will keep the edge sharp; use another pair for cutting brass wire and suchlike.

Tweezers

Tweezers are really an extension of long-nosed pliers, again, where fingers are simply too cumber-

Tweezers come in many sizes, usually as a set. They are an extension to your fingers for getting into the many tight spaces, both on and within a typical model.

some. They are really useful for threading wires or rigging twine through small holes with limited access space. Whilst they may not be regarded as essential, they take the frustration out of many tricky little jobs. It is worth paying a little more for a good set of tweezers, as cheap ones usually cross over at the ends after a time, resulting in them slipping and throwing a tiny item somewhere never to be found again.

Storage Containers

Jars and 'throw-away' plastic containers are invaluable for screws, wood, rubber bands and small components, all of which easily get lost. Any kit will have a number of small parts that need to be stored, but which also need to be accessed quickly. This is useful when dealing with very small parts, when they fall (or fly off) into a cluttered area, or on to the floor.

Recycle small bottles and plastic take-away containers to use for storage. They are invaluable for the multitude of small parts in any model construction, because once you start building a model, many parts have to be separated, and are easily lost.

Files

Files comprise probably the largest range of a single item that you will find, apart from drill bits. Avoid the temptation of taking a short-cut and using a large-toothed engineering or woodworking file: usually a strategy of the 'finer the better' is the most appropriate, even if it does take longer.

A vital and cheap way of keeping your 'toolbox' tidy, or for storing small parts.

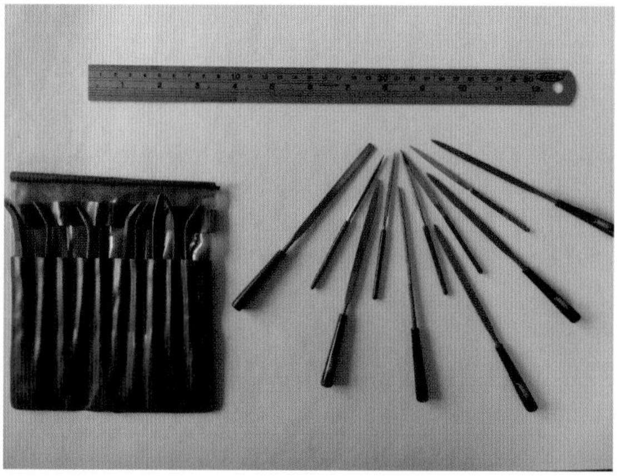

A selection of flat files – taper, rat-tail, half-round, fine, rough, square, triangular: try to acquire only a small selection at first, and only those you need.

Filing a flat surface is something that takes skill and practice, and perhaps even a little of a 'black art' on a curved surface. Always ensure that the sharp tang of a file is embedded in a comfortable handle that is not loose or likely to fall off. Place a finger on the far end to apply light pressure, and don't grip it too tightly as you 'push' the file across the surface: keep it flat, and release the pressure on the return stroke.

Helpful Tip

As you are using (hopefully) a very fine-toothed file, it will need clearing, or the teeth will clog up: use a fine wire brush, or even an old toothbrush to clean the teeth. Soft lead or white-metal clogs easily and debris may have to be removed with a sharp-pointed nail, a needle or a scriber.

DESIRABLE TOOLS

The following tools are really a selection for the dedicated tool-collector. They are items that you can easily do without, but which can make your model so much better, and make life less stressful in avoiding problems.

To put modelling into perspective, when something is going wrong, repeat the mantra 'Never forget that you are doing this for fun'. So if you don't have that particular tool at the time, or can't think how to achieve something – walk away and leave it for tomorrow, and a solution will probably come to you.

Metal-Etched Tools

Illustrated is a set of metal-etched tools for a scale model tool-box that was needed for a particular model – nothing to do with real tools, but included simply to illustrate what is available to make any model just that little bit more spectacular. Many of them are less than 5mm long.

A sample of commercial brass-etched sheets, showing a complete range of miniature model tools to enhance the detail of your boat.

Powered Drills

A hand-held power drill is so versatile, with dozens of accessories available for most jobs. Ensure that you have two batteries so that one can be in use whilst the other is on charge. There is nothing more irritating than a battery going flat half-way through a particular task, and no spare.

Apart from the drill function, you will also find that a sanding-disc attachment is invaluable. There are a number, with varying grades of grit from coarse down to very fine. Over a period of time it is likely that the hand-drill will be used far more with a sanding-disc attachment than for actually drilling holes.

Probably the most useful accessory is a drill stand, into which the hand-drill fits. Now you will have two hands free to hold and make the necessary holes in your workpiece, and the holes will be perpendicular to the piece – unless you wish to drill them at a slant, in which case the unit can be easily swivelled to the appropriate angle.

Always use a square piece of softwood underneath your workpiece, which helps to support the

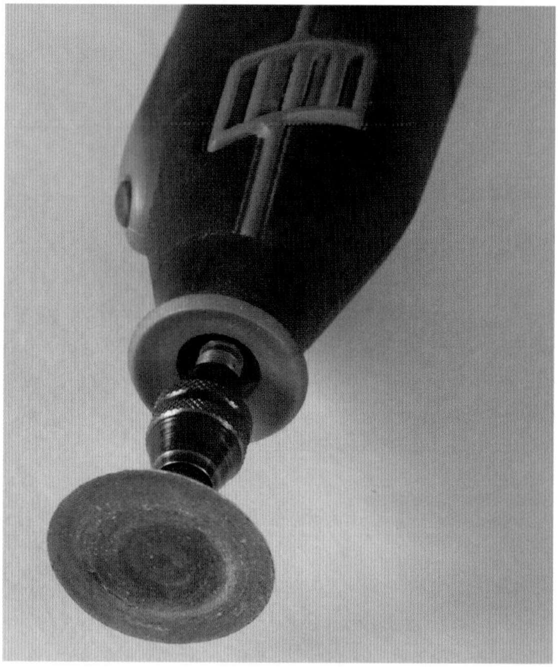

A quick-release sanding-disc attachment. It uses the same drill head that holds the drills, and is a simple 'press and twist to release' so as to change to another grade of disc, or to replace a worn-out disc.

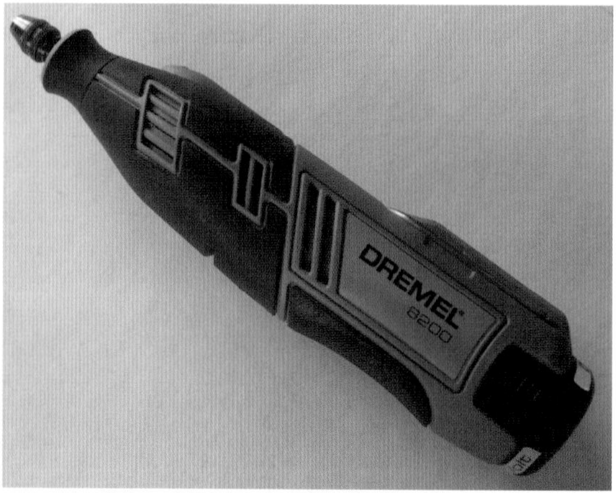

This hand power drill is essential to many modellers, equating almost to a third hand, and with its accessories is an absolute bonus for so many different jobs, from drilling, routing, grinding and smoothing, to polishing and finishing. It can speed up repetitious jobs to save a great deal of time.

Sanding discs come in many finishes or grades; get two grades, 60 and 240, to start with. The other disc is a carborundum cutting disc; saw discs are also available, and are useful for cutting out larger plastic parts and awkward shapes.

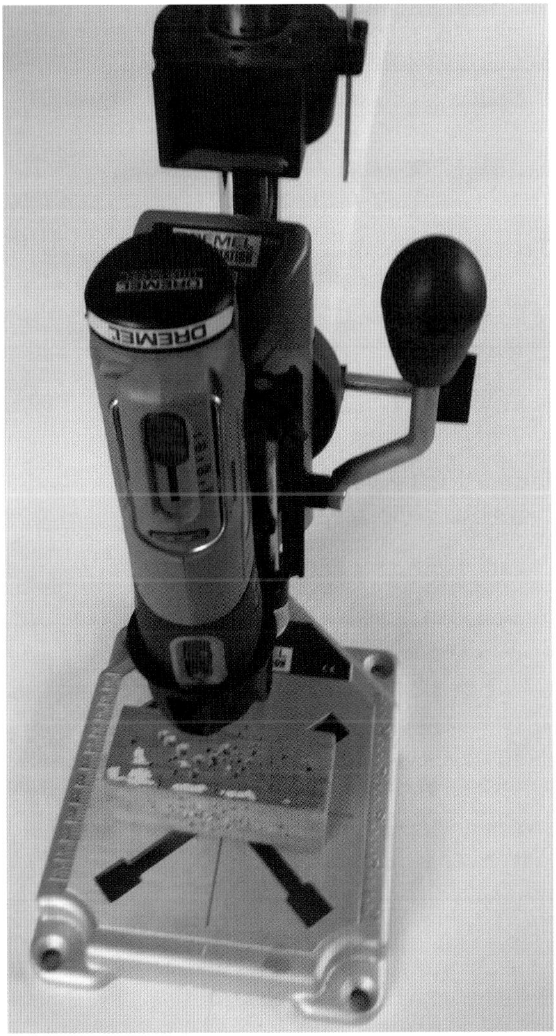

A more sophisticated drill stand to hold the hand-drill, for a hands-free option for what is quite a heavy robust hand-drill.

work and will also help to stop the drill-bit tearing the back face as the drill head pierces your material – softwoods being the worst for this.

A full-sized pillar drill is used for a multitude of purposes, from the typical DIY projects down to 1.5/2mm jobs. It is maybe not for the average model enthusiast, but it comes in handy for drilling thicker material. Note the guard over the drill chuck to protect your eyes from spinning swarf, and also to stop your hair or clothing becoming

A simple wooden block to save breakout underneath the workpiece as the drill goes through. It is always a good idea to control the drill penetration speed, rather than just ramming it through as quickly as possible: allow the drill time to do what it was designed for. Complete with a drill vice to hold the work, rather than vulnerable fingers.

entangled in the rotating chuck, with potentially disastrous results.

Even when using the hand-held drill, use some eye protection – your eyes are far too precious to damage whilst making a model. Also, use a drill vice or a pair of pliers when holding thin metal sheet, which could spin out of control and cut your fingers, or wreck the work.

Bending Planks

A plank bender is very useful when making a wooden-hulled boat where the planks need to be curved to the shape of the hull. Basically it has a blunt knife edge that will groove or bruise one side of the plank as you squeeze. This is repeated down the plank to help form a curve. It does not circumvent having to soak the planks before bending, it just makes them take on a tighter curve.

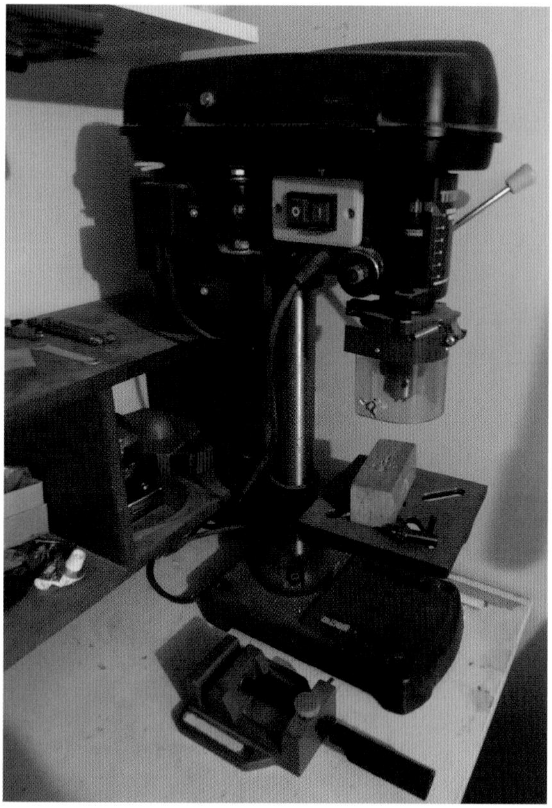

A full-sized pillar drill is used mainly for household DIY work, but is often useful for drilling boat stands and making trolleys, test tanks and the like.

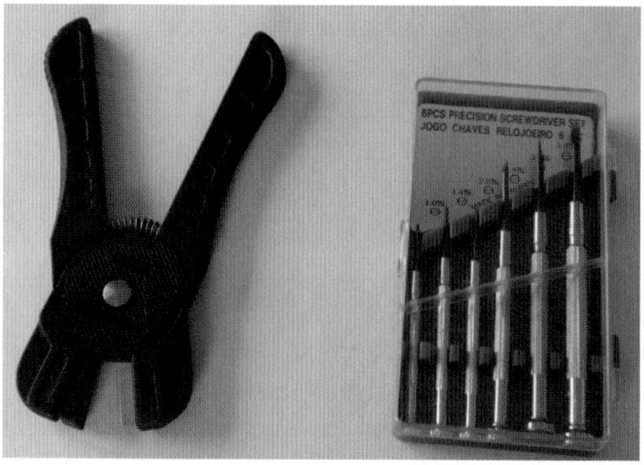

A simple hand-held bending tool, to get the required shape down the length of a boat hull for the planking, after the raw planks have been soaked in water to make them more flexible. Next to them is a set of watchmaker's screwdrivers, for all those tiny screws used in miniature electrics.

Whilst a plank bender is quicker, the same effect can be achieved by simply scoring the back face of the plank by pressing a chisel into it.

Small Screwdrivers

There are likely to be small screws somewhere on the model, and these watchmaker's sets of screwdrivers can come in very useful at times. There is always the temptation to use the end of a penknife or an oversize screwdriver, but these will simply destroy a screw slot and may prevent the screw being removed at all.

Digital Callipers

Digital callipers are very helpful when you buy a kit as there are likely to be various brass rods or tubes that come with the kit, for handrails, rigging eyes and suchlike. They may or may not be labelled with their size or diameter, and you will be dealing in parts of a millimetre or fractions of an inch, where a simple ruler and eye measurement may not be good enough to tell which size is which. The scale is calibrated in both imperial and metric measurements, and these callipers are normally battery operated.

Tool to Hold Odd-Shaped Parts

Pictured is another little tool to assist with holding very small parts. It is adjustable, and might be the only solution to gripping an odd-shaped workpiece whilst you work on it.

Taps and Dies

Taps and dies for cutting screw threads may occasionally be needed. However, often it might be better to buy a length of screwed rod, or to use a long bolt and cut it to size.

As an apprentice, many years ago, the author was taught how to cut threads, and it can take more skill than would initially be apparent. But if you keep everything square and perpendicular, and take it carefully, then there is no reason why you cannot do it, where there is no alternative. Brass will be self-lubricating, but if it is steel, especially stainless steel, which is harder, then oil

Digital callipers are especially useful for measuring small dimensions and fractions of a millimetre, where a ruler and judgement by eye is not accurate enough.

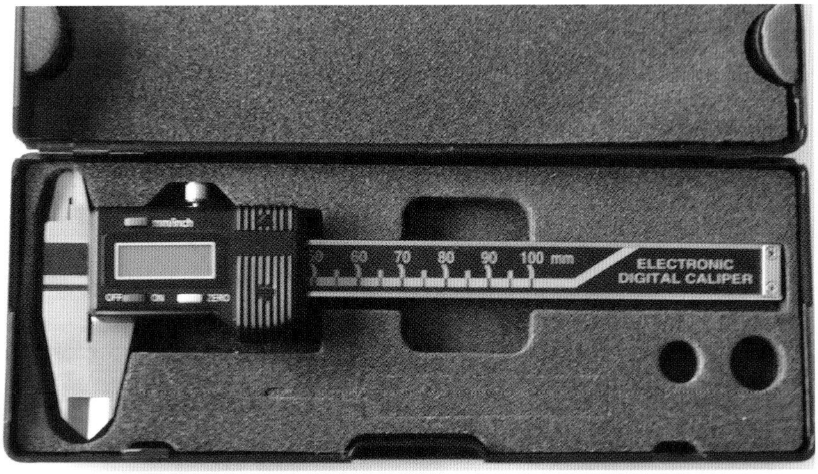

A very useful tool for holding small circular or odd-shaped objects that can be easily crushed in a vice, when working on them.

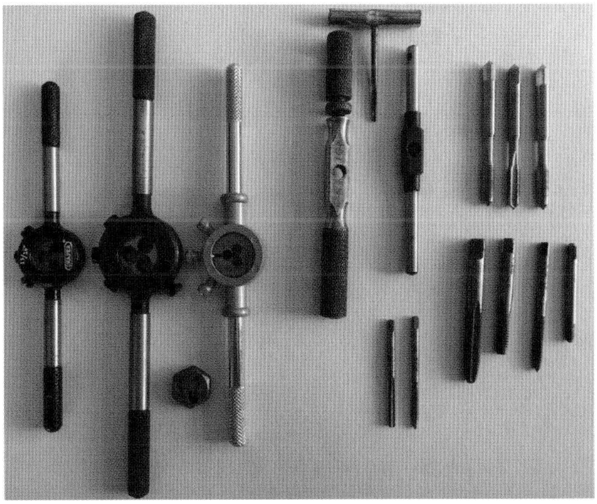

An assortment of taps and dies for cutting threads on metal bar, or for tapping holes. The taper tap is used first, and then the plug tap to finish the thread in the hole. The die has a taper underneath to start the thread, so ensure it is started the correct way up.

it to stop the tool binding as you work. Always turn the tool half a turn at a time, then back a quarter, to break the partially cut metal out of the cutting area.

Remember to insert the rod to be threaded into the tapered side of the die. There are two or three taps for threading a hole – a tapered one to start the thread, and a plug tap to finish. The initial guide hole that is drilled should only be the diameter of the bottom of the thread, so ensure it is not too large or too small.

When working with brass or any polished metal then it is a very good idea to clamp the work in a vice with a soft material, thereby protecting it from the serrations in the jaws of the vice. A 'clip-on' soft jaw is available for this; alternatively wrap the material in thin card, but be careful not to tighten the jaws too tightly, which could mark or crush the workpiece.

Punches

Punches are crude, in that they are placed over the sheet to be cut, and hit with a hammer. It is better to drill a smaller hole and file it out with a rat-tail circular file, to avoid damaging the workpiece. Sometimes, however, when a large number of small discs are required, or when punching soft material such as leather, they do provide a solution, providing they are sharp.

Pipe Benders

These are miniature versions of the pipe benders in common use, and are ideal for small handrails or anywhere where a neat, curved pipe is needed. However, one word of advice: be careful how far you bend the tube as you might not be able to extract it once it is bent to the shape you require inside the pipe bender, due to the amount of friction generated.

Mitre Block

A small version of a woodworking mitre block is useful, to be used in conjunction with a fine tenon or razor saw for cutting 45- or 90-degree angles with a reasonable level of accuracy. Alternatively these guides can be made with a few pieces of accurately planed timber; just make sure everything, including the saw slot, is perpendicular.

Bending Brass-Etched Sheet

Many model kits either come with brass-etched small thin parts, or you can buy them as an 'add-on' extra. They will be part-etched through where it is necessary to bend them, so they should already have a 'crease' to ensure a clean bend. A pair of smooth-faced, long-nosed pliers will enable you to grip and fold the item at the crease if it's a simple fold. For greater accuracy and control this tool is invaluable and well worth

A set of small punches. It is better to drill out and use a file to enlarge a hole, rather than use a punch, which could easily damage the workpiece.

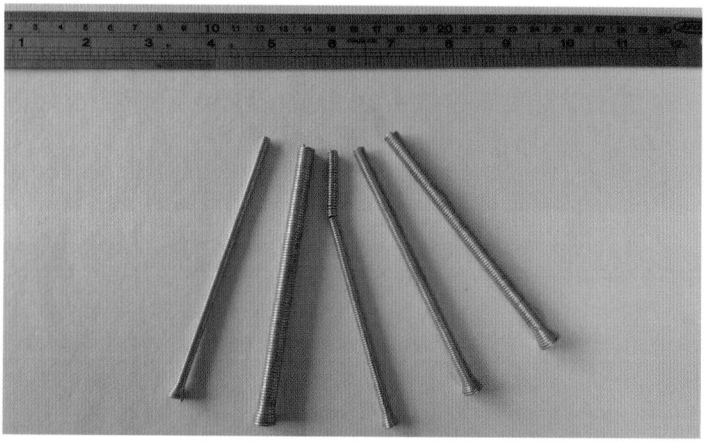

A miniature pipe bender is very useful for small tube and rod in the order of 2mm to 4mm diameter. Trying to bend a tube without these usually ends up making a kink in the tube.

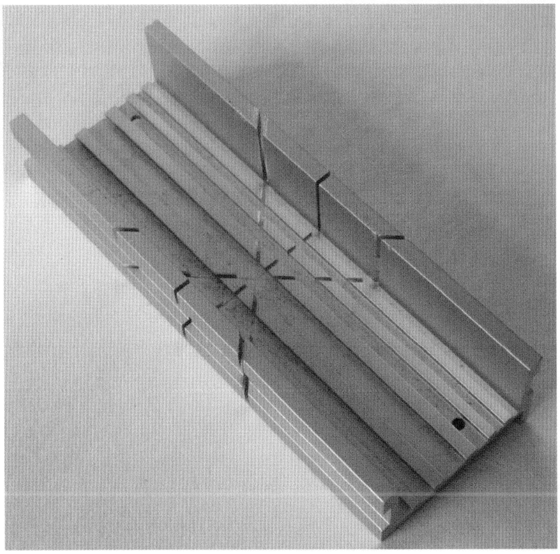

The mitre block is used for cutting wooden or plastic parts to form a right-angle between the two parts – say, the corners of a picture frame or mounting blocks.

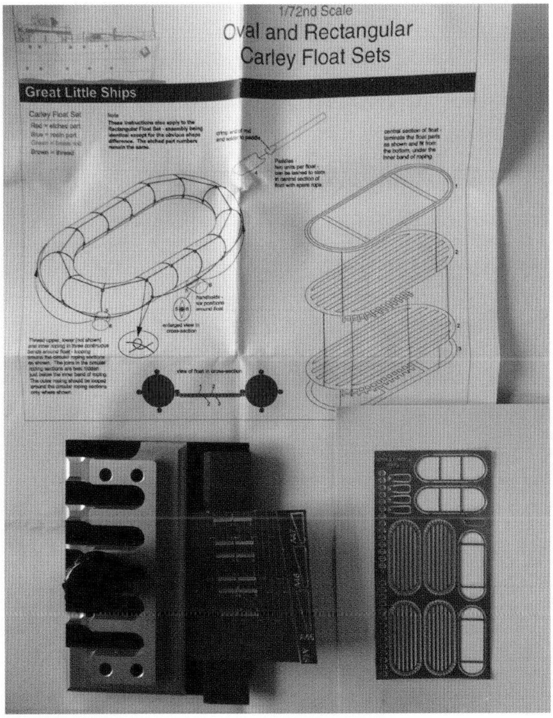

When you get into the very fine detail that is possible with brass-etched parts, usually such as for masting, ship's boats, radar and winches, then this tool enables easy, accurate folding of the material.

the outlay, because if you crease thin brass sheet incorrectly it is almost impossible to smooth out your mistakes.

Guillotine

When you have to make a large number of cuts in wooden planking at a specific angle, then a small guillotine can avoid a lot of sore, tired fingers, especially if you are using a hardwood, so that you get exactly the same square or angled cut each time. The blade and handle can be swivelled to any angle you need. It will also cut thin plastic strips in the same way.

Accessory Kits

There are so many sets of tools available, all with an endless and bewildering function, but be aware that many of the small grinding wheels and discs will never be used, likewise felt polishing wheels, augers and so on. Only purchase what is needed to complete the model in hand, because anything beyond that is likely to be a complete waste of money at this stage.

Jigs

Jigs can be home-made with a few nails and a flat plank of wood. But the jig pictured can come in

A guillotine speeds up plank/decking construction where numerous pieces have to be chopped up. The blade does need regular sharpening to keep a keen edge, and to ensure accurate cuts. It can easily be adjusted to cut at any angle.

Avoid kits such as these accessory packs, as usually they contain many items that will hardly ever be used.

A commercial rigging jig. This is a complicated jig for sailing-ship models; however, often you can easily make your own by laying out a simple grid on a piece of wood and nailing in panel pins to guide the twine and tie it off to.

very useful if you embark on a period-style ship or anything with shrouds and rigging. Over time you will probably make many jigs, specifically for a particular model, say for soldering a brass handrail, the upper levels of naval topworks, radar, davits – in fact anything that is repetitious, but requires a level of accuracy.

And Finally…

A number of other things could be regarded as essential or simply desirable – typically electrical items, and preparation and painting items – and these will be covered in the sections specifically dealing with that element at the appropriate stage later on.

YOUR WORKSPACE

This can be as simple as the kitchen table, a corner of the garage, a garden shed, or a spare room/space in the attic. What is important is that it is safe from young children or pets so they cannot access sharp knives or adhesives/solvents that could harm them.

Ideally it must have a large ventilated window to allow plenty of light and fresh air into the workspace; a large, white-surfaced workbench with plenty of power sockets underneath the window; a dry storage space/shelves for all the models, tools and materials; comfortable seating and heating (especially in Britain in winter); and a smooth floor covering, preferably of a pale colour that will show up small dropped parts.

A Clean Area

A massive working area is not necessary; more space would always be nice, but in the last few years all the models illustrated have been made on the table shown.

Clamped to the corner of the table is a flexible lamp with a large magnifying glass, another accessory that some may find helpful when natural light is not good enough.

Always try to use a corner of the room that is well lit and facing the window. Aim to do all the heavy or dusty work somewhere else so that this area is kept clean.

The other side of the room is used for design and reference work, and to store some of the models.

A Design Area

The design side of the room, showing some of the models; on top of the glass display case are a few of the awards the author has been lucky enough to win.

One of the biggest disadvantages of model boating is that some of the boats can be quite large, and storage where they do not get damaged, or too dusty or are exposed to damp, is often at a premium. This observation may surprise you, considering they are designed to sail on water! However, the terminals and contacts of the electrics and batteries and suchlike will tend to corrode, especially if they are not dried and cleaned after being outdoors on the lake and are left in a damp place.

Dirty Work Area

The rear of my garage is where all the dustier and heavier work is completed. Note the white worktop as mentioned earlier. Behind is a normal wood-working bench for the more usual DIY jobs, but also where spray paint can be used without causing overspray on what is beyond the workpiece.

The rear of the garage, used for heavy or dusty work. Note the power points and white-topped working area, so that small items stand out when dropped.

Chapter Two

Choice of Model

So a choice has been made to build a model boat, and all that is necessary now is to decide what kind. Sailing craft have already been ruled out, as mentioned earlier, which narrows down the choice to perhaps a few thousand!

From the environmental standpoint, an electrically powered model is the most popular choice. Models with an internal combustion engine need extensive silencers and produce fumes and oil residues. Steam engines do much the same, and in addition require legislative pressure testing and periodic certification of some pressure parts before their use is allowed; furthermore many lakes ban them anyway.

This is not to say that these models do not have a dedicated following: where they can be used, they are most certainly another fascinating avenue for modelling – offshore racing boats and dedicated steam craft are both exhilarating and a lot of fun.

DESIGN OF CRAFT

Let us look first at naval ships, or 'the grey boats' as they are sometimes called: starting with the largest there are aircraft carriers, then battleships, cruisers, destroyers, minelayers, frigates, tugs, submarines, MTBs, corvettes, fleet auxiliaries and tenders.

Then there are merchant ships, and pleasure craft, liners, cargo ships, tankers, bulk freighters, puffers, container ships, more tugs, paddle steamers, coasters, fishing trawlers, canal barges, and so on and so forth. These can be any colour chosen – but now perhaps you are beginning to see that it is not such a simple choice after all. Lastly there are novelty models, which just about cover anything that will float!

All these craft can be obtained as a kit, which is probably the best to begin with because all the components will be included, except glue and paint usually. Finding a supplier for 1mm square strip, say, can be frustrating if you are not familiar with providers. It has been said that a kit is really nothing more than an 'assembly task' – but as you will discover it is far, far more absorbing and challenging than that.

Apart from kits there is the ARTR: 'almost-ready-to-run'. Here the model only needs final assembly out of the box, and is supplied virtually finished; consequently there is no gluing or painting. Should a modeller want to experience the end result of actually controlling a model on the water, without the construction time element, then this is another possibility.

Some of these can be taken straight out of the box and put on the water with no assembly at all: these are termed RTR, or 'ready-to-run', and probably also include a radio transmitter.

An example of an ARTR sailing yacht. All that was necessary was to bolt on the keel and rudder, assemble the simple internal electrics and rigging, and stick on the decals. Everything else was already completed out of the box.

Internals screwed in, battery connected, and the model is now ready to go. The red bar is on top of a servo to control the rudder. The long white lever is part of the sail winch servo.

Check Out Before You Buy

Before going to the expense of buying a model, check out the lake area where you intend to sail it. Are there any restrictions to use on specific days, or to types of craft that the lake authorities, owners or club will allow on the water? Many ban electric high-speed racing boats, or those with internal combustion engines as a danger to wildlife and the environment, and only allow sailing yachts perhaps. Maybe there are specific areas for different classes of boat. There may be explicit days for different craft. Is the lake deep enough for something with a very deep keel? The simpler the model, the more likely it is that you will not be limited as to its use.

Hull Shape

Taking the Oxford and Cambridge Boat Race as an example, the craft that are used are as narrow as they can be made, and as long as is practical. Now, apart from the fact that this makes them very difficult to turn, it also makes them as fast as possible given the amount of power available – in this case the rowers.

Back in the 1800s William Froude came up with something we now call 'the Froude number', which basically says that the Froude number or speed/length ratio of a ship is equal to the speed divided by the square root of the waterline length. In other words, the narrower and longer the boat is, the more speed and less power you will need to push it through the water, within practical limits.

High-speed ships are narrow across their beam relative to their length, such as naval destroyers

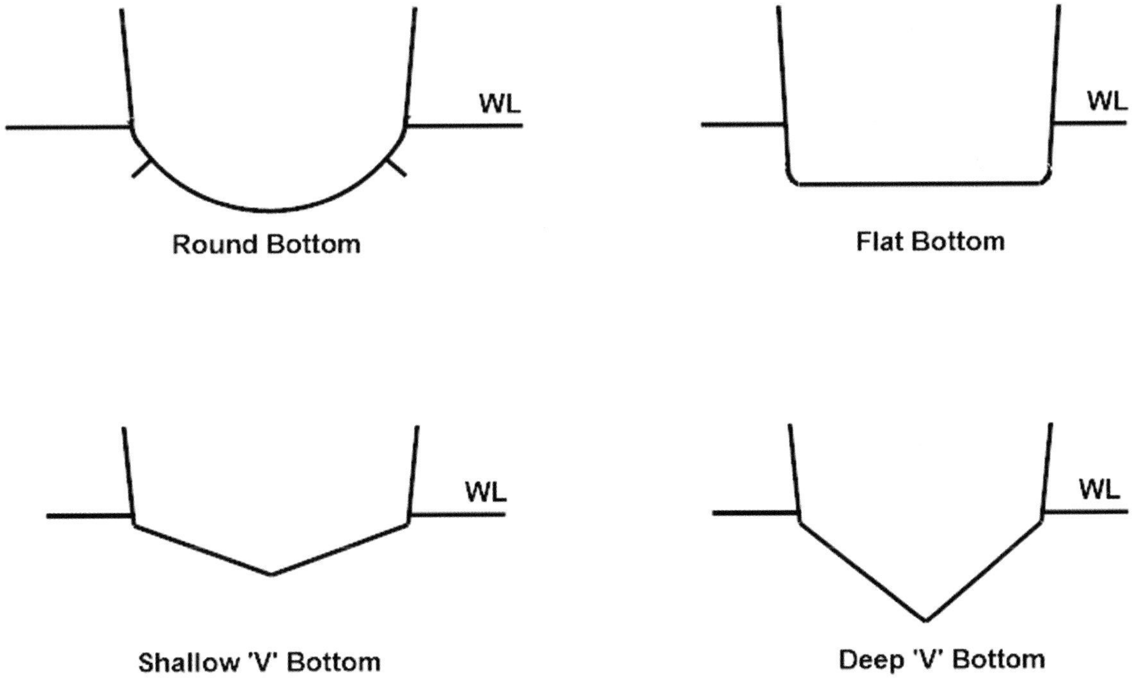

A simplified cross-section of the main model hull profiles most often used. The 'WL' refers to the 'waterline' – that is, the point at which the model should float when fully loaded. As rounded-bottom hulls tend to roll, notice the stub 'bilge' keels on each side, a common feature.

and frigates, whilst something like a trawler is very fat and short – it is only ever designed to go slowly, and plenty of working/storage space within the hull is needed, near to where the nets are handled.

Most craft are termed 'displacement' boats in that they sit on the water and 'displace' their own weight in it (the Archimedes principle), and push water, or a bow wave, in front of them as they move. High-speed 'planing' craft need more power to climb up on to that bow wave, such that under maximum speed only the last 10 per cent or so of the hull bottom, at the stern, is actually in the water together with the propeller.

Then again there are hulls with a square cross-section – such as freighters – or a 'U' shape; faster, smaller planing boats may have what is called a deep 'V' profile, which cuts into the water and doesn't slam down on each wave as would happen with a flat-bottom surface. RHIBs (rigid-hulled inflatable boats) are of this type. Faster still are catamarans, or trimarans, twin and triple hulls, and hydrofoils on stilts. The fastest of all was a strange ship with short stubby wings and eight engines built by the Russians in the 1960s, which actually used a cushion of air under it and travelled just above the water at around 400km/h, called an Ekranoplan.

Another variation, often seen in harbours that dry out at low tide, is termed a cathedral hull, which basically has an arch on each side of the keel; in effect it therefore has three keels

A typical model trawler; note the very wide beam relative to the length. It is a good choice as it gives plenty of internal space for batteries, electronics, speakers and so on. It is an example of a 'displacement' hull.

An example of a 'V' or 'deep V' hull, offering high speed and comfort to the occupants. Also an example of a 'planing' hull used on small, light craft.

A rounded-bottom 'displacement' craft: long and narrow to give good speed, with multiple rudders to ensure manoeuvrability, yet with good internal space for plenty of accessories.

so it can stand upright on a flat surface, unlike most monohulled single-keel craft, which would topple over. Your model is likely to do this unless you make a stand for it: this will be covered in Chapter 9.

Lastly, there are second-hand completed models. Like buying a second-hand car, if you are intending to purchase, it is always advisable to have somebody with a knowledge of what to look for. All the electrics must work, also ask how old is/are the batteries, does it leak, is there corrosion, is there a radio transmitter with it that works? It is always a wise move to try to see the model running on the water before purchasing it, or at the very least ask to see it all wired up and running on the bench.

Unusual Models

A real challenge is finally to make a model from something that was never designed to be used in this way, and here the possibilities are endless, from Loch Ness monsters to mechanized rowers in rowing boats. The only thing that must be considered is that the item can be waterproofed and perhaps cut open and reassembled later after fitting the controls.

This model provided a platform for a camera on the water in order to approach wildlife. Any unusual subject such as this will provide a real challenge to your ingenuity.

Any non-boat subject can be used, provided it does not contaminate the water or do harm to the wildlife. You will be amazed how curious waterfowl are when they do not feel threatened, and how close you can get to them. This model of the Loch Ness monster is carved from wall insulation blocks.

STARTER CHOICE

Whatever type of model is chosen, try not to take on too much to start with – a simple two-channel radio system, controlling rudder and engine, or sail, is a good starting point. Aim for something with a robust, simple hull (you will also have to learn to drive it, and will likely hit things), and also with easy access to the internal workings. A model around 3–3.5ft (1m) long, which should weigh about 12lb (6kg) plus, will give plenty of scope.

Don't take on a highly detailed model with lots of fiddly small parts that can easily be broken off as you launch or retrieve it. Lastly, check out the dimensions inside your car against the maximum size of the model, to ensure there is ample clearance all around it – many models are damaged in transit this way.

Always remember that the larger the model, the more ballast weight it will need to float correctly, and therefore the heavier it will be to carry about, and more importantly, the harder it will be to launch. It is worth bearing in mind the weight of a model if plans are scaled up to a larger size: if the size is doubled, then the weight will be eight times greater. Anyone with a weak back should consider this carefully.

Hull Material

The simplest hull is a blown or vacuum-moulded smooth styrene hull, which will have no external makings on it such as hull plating, portholes or hawse holes for anchors. ABS (acrylonitrile butadiene styrene) is often used, especially in kits from Germany: this is moulded or deep-drawn, giving a thicker wall and some external features; however, it is much harder to glue, and the glue itself is very expensive. (*See* 'Adhesives' in Chapter 3.)

Also popular is GRP, or glass-reinforced plastic – 'fibreglass': this is an epoxy resin mixed with chopped glass wool, and a catalyst hardener to set it. This enables a female master-mould to be made with plenty of hull detail. The end result is very strong, easy to work and paint, and to glue other components to.

Wooden plank-on-frame is the oldest way of boat building, and still very common for those who like working in wood. Literally the keel is the starting point, followed by ribs or bulkheads, and then a planked layer of softwood. It is essential that all the formers, or bulkheads, are sanded down on their edges to the shape of the hull, mostly at the bow and stern. The whole thing is then sanded smooth, and another layer of hardwood planks may be glued on, one at a time.

Nowadays all the bulkheads will be laser cut, when buying a kit, taking away much of the laborious labour of hand fret-sawing plywood.

PROPULSION SYSTEM

Another consideration before you choose a kit is how it is going to be powered. In full-sized boats there are 'outboards' for small craft, where the engine is separate and clamped to the stern, then 'inboards' where the engine is mounted in the boat with a shaft through the hull to an outside propeller in the water. This is the one normally used by modellers, with up to four separate engines or motors in a model boat.

Many craft now use something called a 'stern drive', where basically the engine is inboard with a vertical shaft (like an outboard engine) and with a right-angled drive to a propeller, such that the whole thing swivels and can drive the boat in any

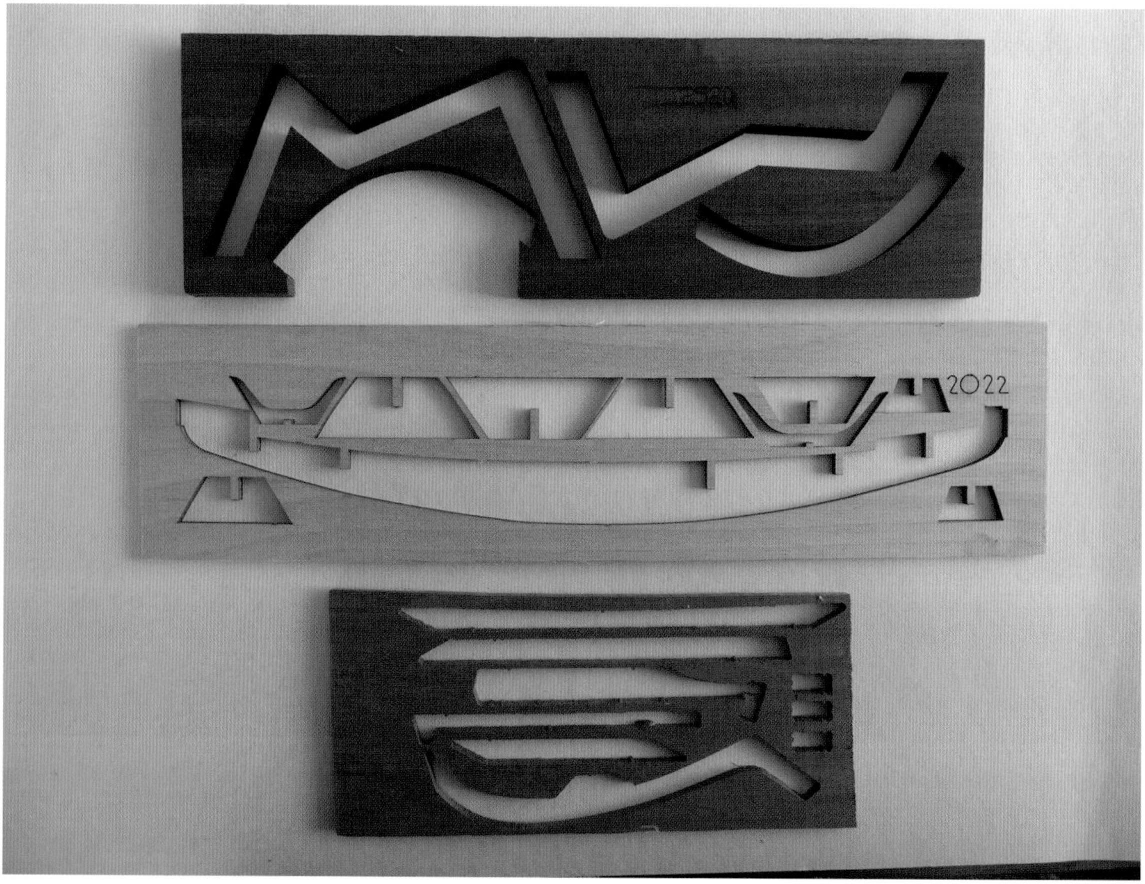

Examples of laser-cut sheet, commonly used in modern-day kits. They will often have burnt edges, which will need sanding off to prevent discoloration to painted edges.

direction; this does away with a rudder. Some craft also have a bow-thruster, which is another drive across the bow underwater, mounted in a tube, to move the bow sideways, giving greater manoeuvrability. Sometimes the propeller is shrouded with a protective short tube called a Kort nozzle, just larger than the blades, which can also increase efficiency and offer greater protection to the rotating blades.

Small craft may use a jet-drive: there is a water inlet to a powerful pump, which ejects the water at the stern, thus driving the boat forwards. Lastly there is an air propeller, used by hovercraft and Everglade craft.

Initially you should choose something with only one motor, or two at a maximum, connected to one or two propellers and steered by a normal rudder at the rear. Anything more than this will be over-complicated; it will also use more power and drain the batteries faster. Motors will be discussed in detail in Chapter 5.

Remember that a single propeller should be installed on the centre line (keel) of the model, whereas twin motors will be on each side of the keel, involving more work in cutting holes in the hull, longer propeller shafts and external supporting frames. Similar comments apply to the rudders, which are normally mounted behind the propellers to deflect the thrust from the propeller.

SCALE

The scale of a model is usually written down as 1:35, 1:250, or 1/35th, 1/250th. More often than not it is the former style, which means that if we take 1:35 as an example then 35ft on the real thing will be 1ft on the model, or 35m will equate to 1m. You can see from this that if the full-sized thing is a given length, then a model at 1:50 will be twice as big as one at 1:100. What is important is the actual length of the model, not the scale, or ratio.

Most model kits suitable for radio control are around 1:24 to 1:60. This should translate to a model that is, say, very approximately 3ft (900mm) long. Don't be tempted to go for a model of something like the *Titanic* at these scales because it will be far too large, will weigh far too much, and will be very difficult to launch, quite apart from being very expensive.

Choose instead something such as a small tug, a harbour launch, or perhaps a fishing boat, something with plenty of space inside with a wide beam, that you can get your hands into easily to fit everything. This will mean it is manoeuvrable on the water, and you will soon be able to learn how to use a radio control transmitter without having to worry too much about the boat itself.

When a model is 100m away it is often quite difficult to actually tell which way it is going if it is head-on, or stern-on, with the result that you turn it in the opposite direction to where you intended it to go. If two models are on a converging course at this distance, that could be annoying, or even embarrassing, until you can train your eyes and judgement to appreciate the potential problem.

Aim for the minimum of detail in the deck and superstructure initially, such that an understanding of construction, assembly, painting and so on can be mastered first. All the fine detail can come later. Look for a kit with a moulded, formed hull, rather than a plank-on-frame model, which will take much longer to construct.

Weight of Model and Marking the Waterline

Most model kits will say on the box what the total weight of the model should be: its displacement, or the weight of water it displaces. However, if the kit has a moulded hull there is a quick way to find this out, or to check it. Before starting to drill holes in the bare hull, follow the procedure in the photographs. This assumes that the household bath is not available or is not large enough. If there *is* a bath large enough, put tins of beans, or whatever else is in the kitchen cupboard, into the bare hull until it sinks to the waterline; then weigh all the tins on a scale, and that is the boat's displacement and the weight of 'electrical kit' that can be placed

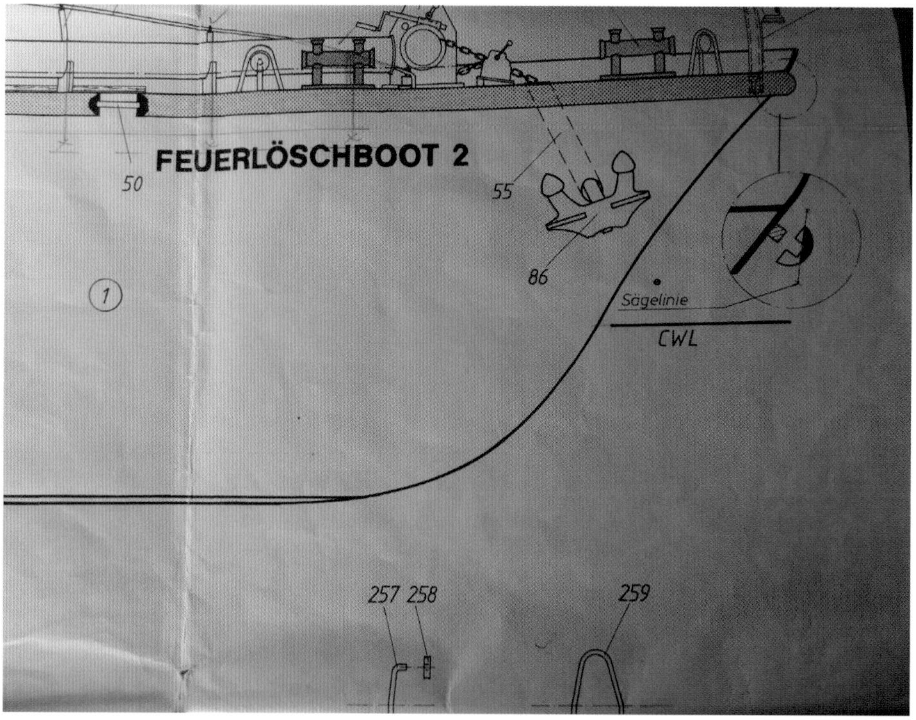

Take a look at the drawing in the kit and find the WL mark.

Transfer this mark on to the hull at the bow with a pencil. Do not use an indelible felt tip, as it will bleed through your finished paintwork, and then mark it.

Carry out the same procedure at the stern.

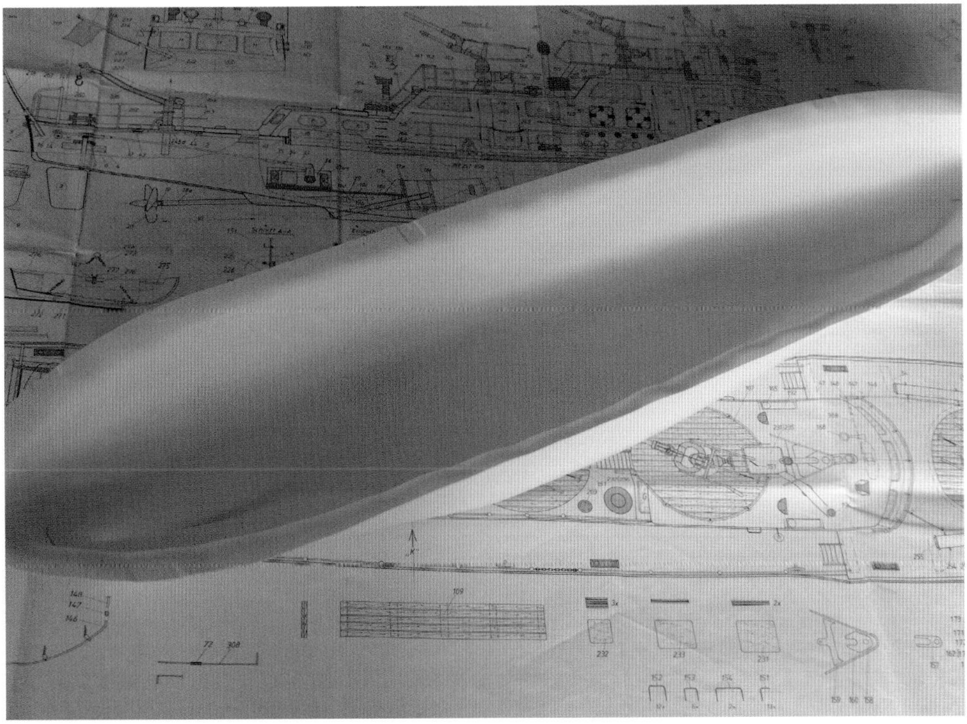

The hull may be semi-transparent, so transfer the marks on to the inside of the hull. Felt tip is fine here as it will be below the deck level and will not be seen.

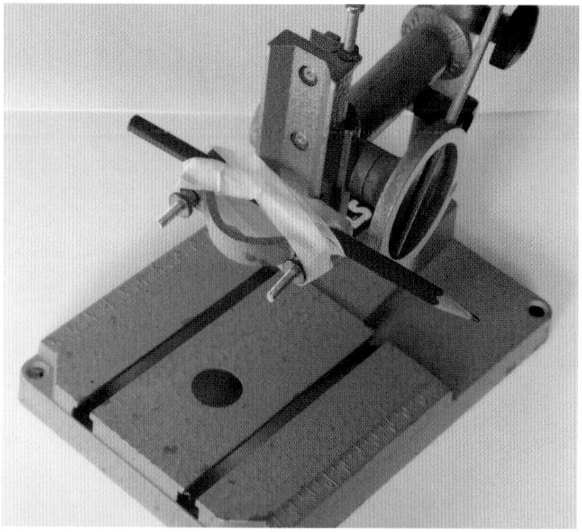

Make up a pencil holder/marker from an old jig or drill stand, or if necessary purchase a commercial one.

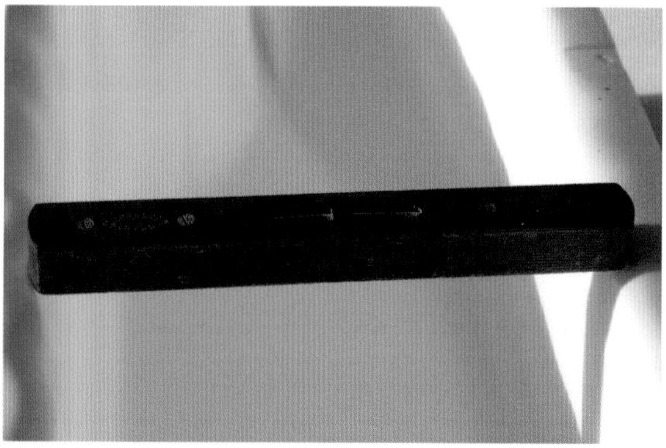

On a flat, level table ensure that the hull is level with a spirit-level.

Elevate the bow or stern with packing pieces until the bow and stern marks match with the pencil point in the jig.

Check out both ends again, and then draw a pencil line around the hull, which will give the WL level for later, when it is time to mask off and paint the hull.

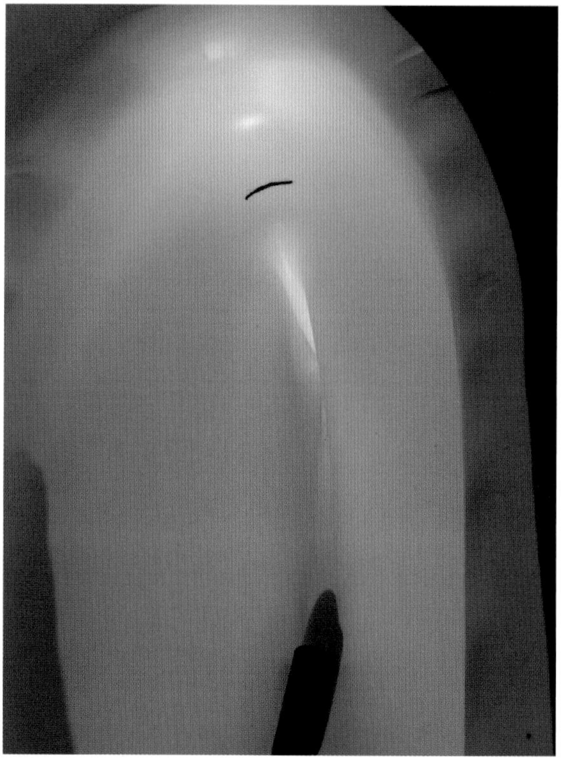

Now fill the levelled hull to the marks on the inside of the hull with water. If everything is still correct, the internal marks should both be level with the water surface.

Once filled, the water can be poured carefully into a measuring jug. Say there are 10ltr of water, then the boat should displace this amount of water when it is sailing – that is, 10ltr, which equals 10kg (22lb). Therefore the finished boat must weigh 10kg with all the batteries and other electronics fitted.

in it, minus the weight of any wiring, glue, paint, topworks and so on.

Superstructure

Whilst an open rowing boat is an example of a boat with no superstructure, a liner is totally the opposite, such that there is ample access for electronics, motors, batteries, speakers and so on. Generally the superstructure, or part of it, must be removable for servicing the batteries (and for their removal), and for any other internal maintenance necessary.

On/Off Switch

Most skilled modellers will aim to place an on/off switch, to isolate the battery circuits, somewhere on the deck that is easily accessible. More often than not it can be disguised under a hatch cover, winch, or other working component, so it is not 'on show'. Whatever cover is used, it must be a tight fit, or secured so it will not blow off on the lake when the boat is under way.

An interesting variation is to have a switch for a submarine, which must be waterproof. It could also be used in the hull of a surface model, if

An imitation winch casing hides a concealed on/off switch.

The on/off switch is an essential item to ensure the battery is not being drained unnecessarily when everything is connected up before sailing takes place.

necessary, where it is not possible or practical to disguise a visible switch.

Plasticard or Styrene Sheet

Apart from thin plywood, Plasticard or high-impact polystyrene sheet is the most common construction material, normally used in 1.0, 1.5, or 2.0mm thick sheets. It is not to be confused with expanded polystyrene foam used in packaging or ceiling tiles. It is easy to glue (*see* Chapter 3), and easy to cut by scoring with a sharp knife and then bending until it snaps off

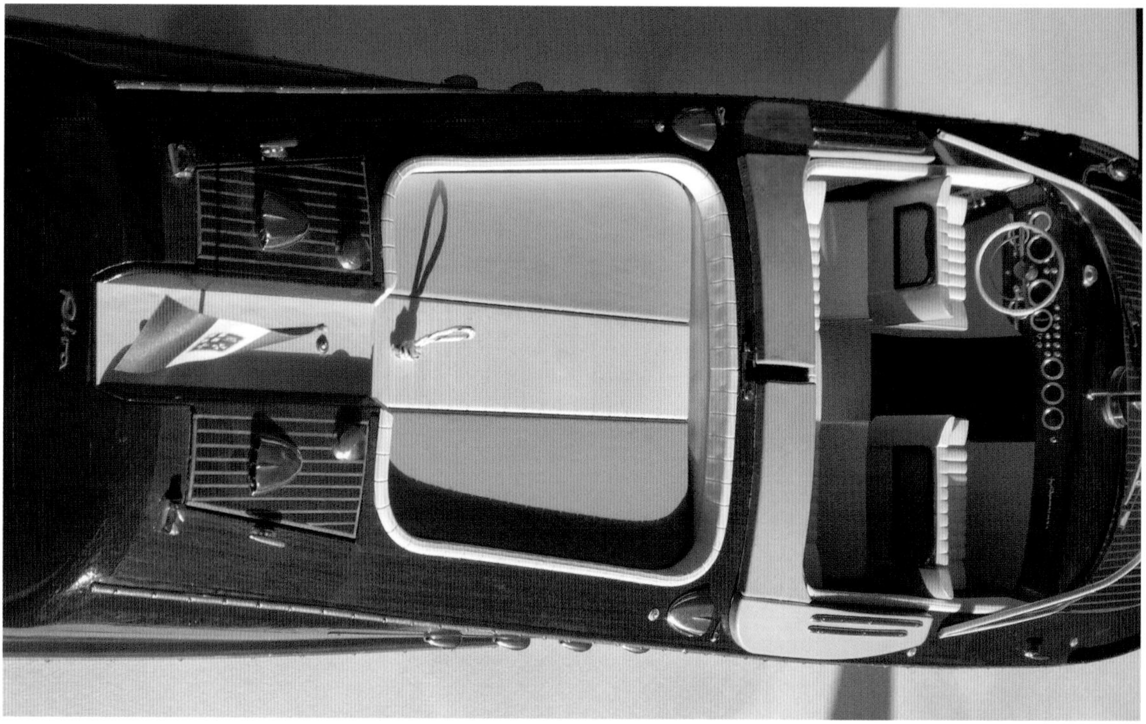

A removable cover on the Riva Aquarama, *which simply clips into place.*

With the cover removed, access is gained to switches and internals.

Readying a submarine for a sail. Here the on/off switch has to be waterproof, and is an internal magnetic type. A high-powered Neodymium magnet is passed across the internal switch, from outside, from stern to bow, activating the switch. To turn it off, the magnet is passed back in the opposite direction.

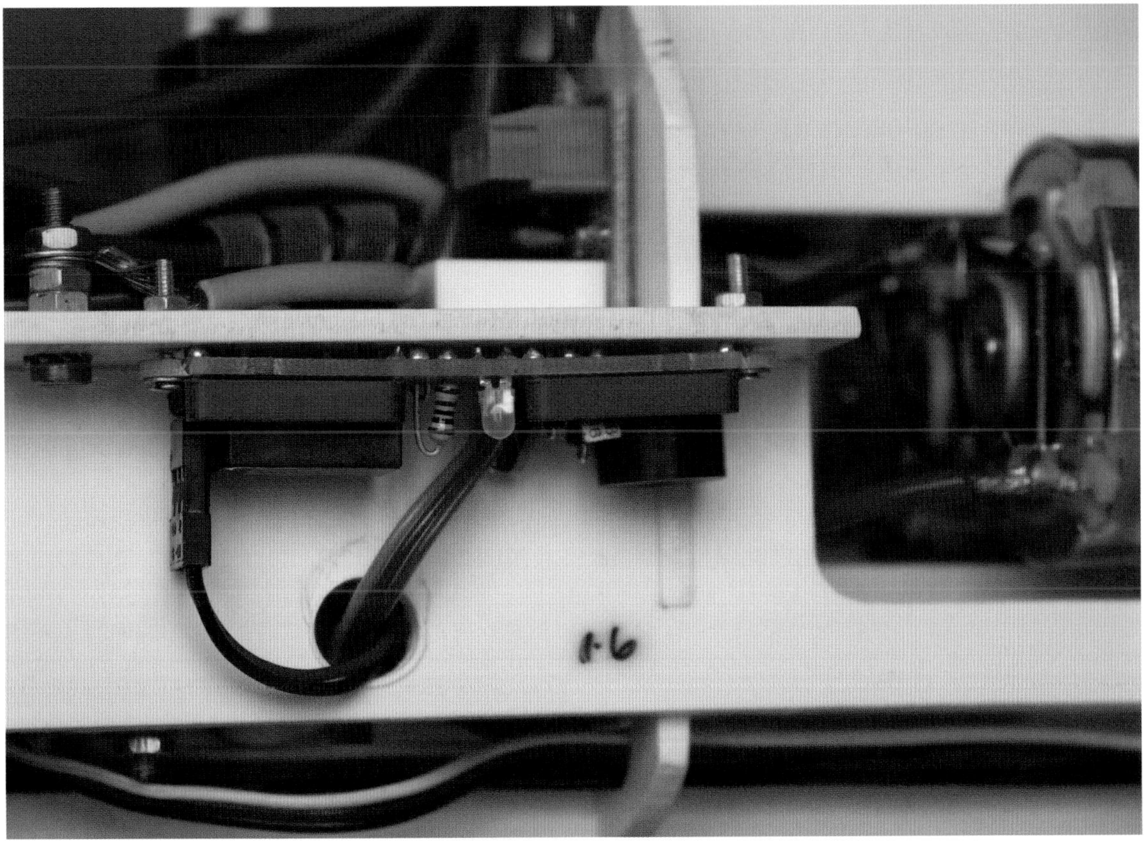

Here, the internal magnetic switch system is displayed, placed as close as possible to the outside shell of the submarine.

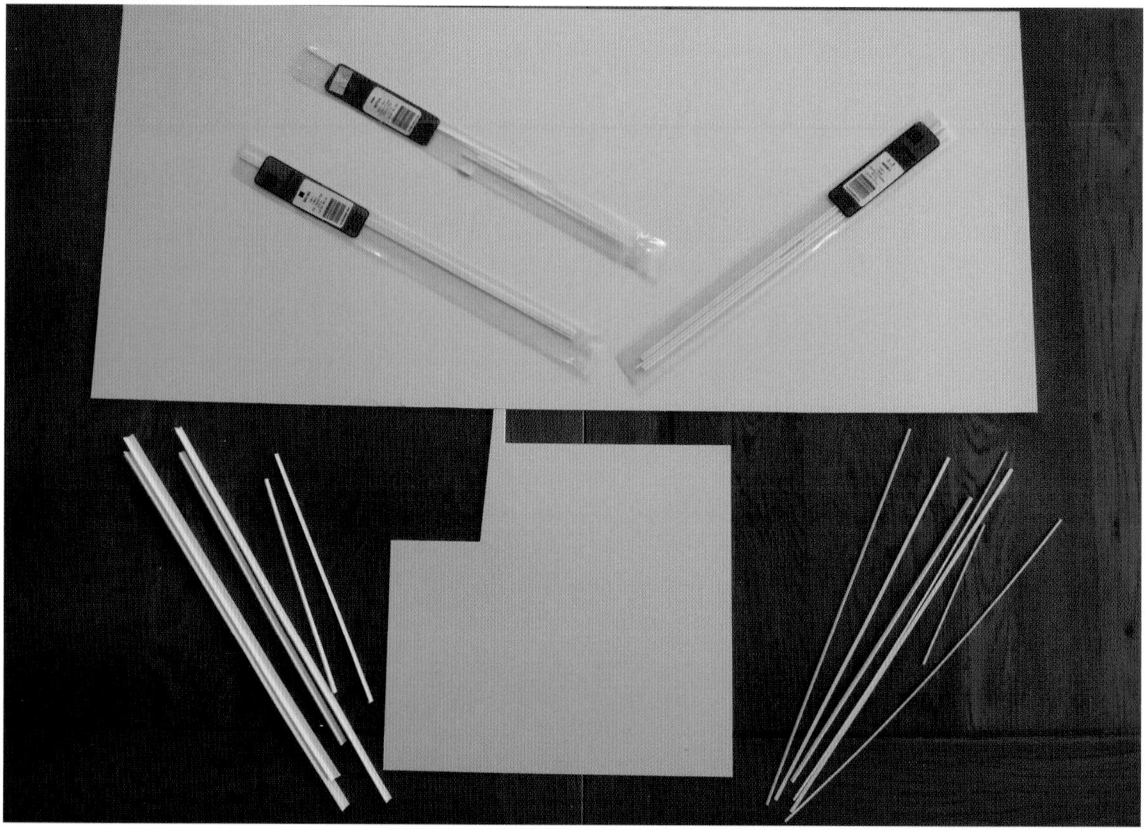

A selection of Plasticard styrene sheet and strip. Strip is usually purchased in small packs of the selected profile, often in 12in (30cm) lengths. Sheet comes in 12 × 24in (30 × 60cm) pieces, although some model shops do sell larger sizes, up to 39in (1m).

cleanly. It is also available in many different colours and strip profiles, although generally white sheet is the standard used.

Ballast

Ballast is used to stabilize any ship or model. In medieval times, sailing ships would have used stone ballast in the bilges to counter the thrust of the sails; later, when the grain clippers raced across the world, the actual cargo would have been the ballast, swopped for stone on the return journey. For the modeller the position of any ballast needed is important; either lead shot, or sheet lead is usually chosen.

If some ballast is required to make the model sit correctly on the waterline, it is essential that it is distributed evenly from bow to stern so that the model does not sit on the water bow or stern heavy, or worse still, tilts to one side. Once positioned, the ballast must stay there, so packing or some other means must often be employed to keep it in place.

Chapter Three

Adhesives, Fillers and Finishing

COMMON ADHESIVES AND THEIR APPLICATION

There are so many adhesives on the market these days for seemingly sticking anything to anything that it can be a minefield to the new modeller and very confusing at first. If the instructions with the kit are not specific, then either the model shop where the kit was purchased may be able to help, or alternatively any model boat club, or on-line forum could be consulted.

Some adhesives, whilst bonding the materials perfectly in a warm dry environment, may lose their strength when exposed to moisture, so always check before using for the first time. If necessary, contact the manufacturers, who usually have a technical section on-line that can offer assistance.

The most commonly used adhesives: superglue, acetate or styrene glue, and PVA wood glue, together with syringe applicators for PVA. Any sharpened dowel can be used for really small spot placing. Always try to use the minimum amount of any adhesive.

Plasticard Adhesive

Unless the superstructure is a preformed unit, the most common material will be Plasticard styrene sheet. It may be laser cut already and simply has to be eased out of the sheet, or could be printed only, in which case the parts have to be carefully cut out with a sharp knife by the modeller.

The best applicator for the adhesive is the Revell Contacta Professional. The glue is of a water-like consistency and will run into the crack between the pieces by capillary action – simply run it sparingly along the join.

Another way of sticking the material together is to use Plastic Weld, which is basically a solvent. Again, the idea is that it will melt the two surfaces, only this time a small brush is used to apply the solvent along the join.

The pictures show a small selection of components built up from a flat sheet of Plasticard. All

Gluing Plasticard relies on the action of the thin adhesive being drawn into the gap, melting the two surfaces and effectively welding the join. This precision applicator gives a really thin film of adhesive just where it is needed.

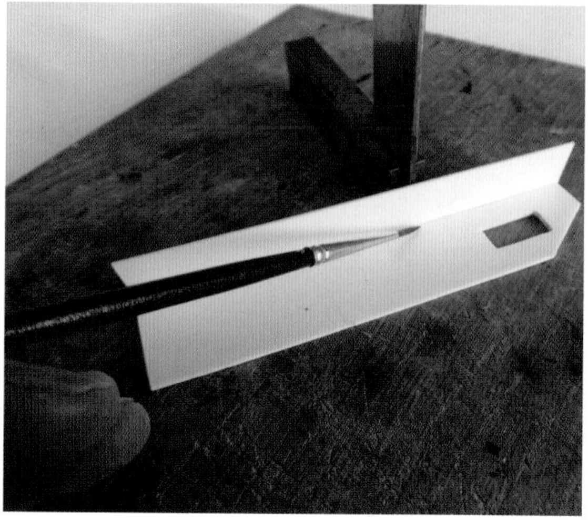

Using the same principle as before, a good join can be achieved. Notice the square to support the join whilst it sets. Setting time will depend to a great extent on the air temperature: if possible allow an hour or so before further work on the workpiece.

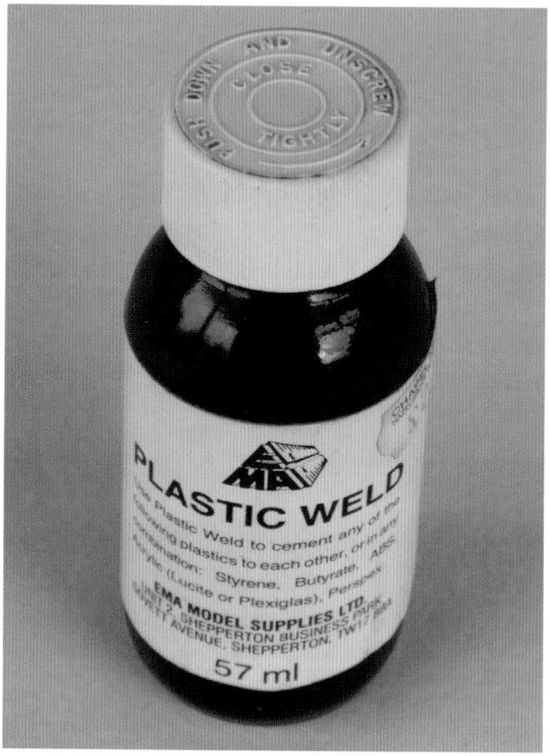

Use straight out of the bottle and apply with a fine brush. Sometimes a few Plasticard shavings can be mixed into the bottle to thicken the adhesive, if required.

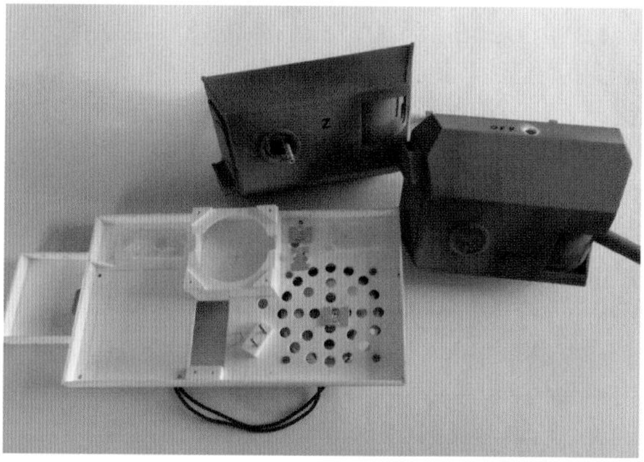

A small selection of some of the easily fabricated shapes that can be made. Always stick, sand down, fill if necessary, sand down again, and clean, before finally painting.

the ship's boats, funnels, and the main superstructure of the Komet build in Chapter 7 were made up from blown or vacuum-formed and flat styrene Plasticard sheet in this way.

Superglue

To give it the correct name, cyanoacrylate glue, or cna, was developed in World War II, and adapted

Cleaning Tip

Most model kits will now have laser-cut parts; however, should they be on a plastic sheet and are printed out and require cutting, then ensure that the marking ink is removed after cutting, and before it is painted later, or it may bleed through the paint. Usually the easiest way to do this is with methylated spirit on a rag. Do *not* use styrene or cellulose solvent, as it will melt and mark the surface of the material.

later for closing wounds in the Vietnam war. It can be purchased in various thicknesses and with different setting times, but normally is almost instant. It reacts with moisture in the air (or in your fingers) to set it, and even if stored, will set over time purely in reaction with air moisture. It will also degrade if in contact with water continually, so will have a shelf life accordingly.

It will stick most plastics, white-metal, brass parts and so on to each other quite well, and tends to be the first adhesive that modellers will turn to, and is used extensively for small components. It may be a skin irritant to some people, and it is advised to use it in a well ventilated space.

The little 'Loctite' dispensers are ideal with a small nozzle for fine application, although many others are available. Apply it sparingly – not much is required.

Superglue Debonder

It is almost a guarantee that some superglue will attach itself to fingers or exposed surfaces at some point. Usually it is possible to separate them quickly before the glue sets, but very occasionally perhaps not, which could result in a visit to A & E to separate them. As a safety measure, keep a bottle of Debonder close to where the work takes place. Never, *ever* touch the eyes when using superglue, in case there is any on fingers, which could be transferred into the eyes.

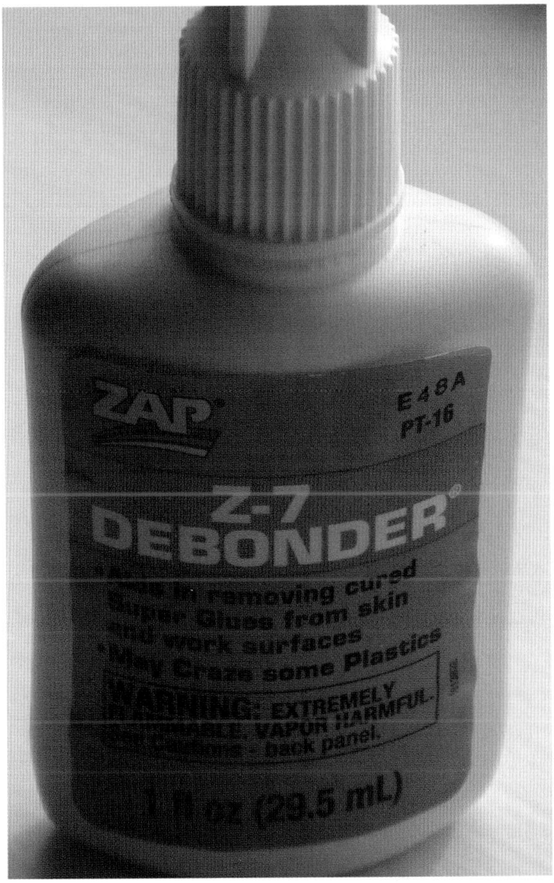

Debonder, an essential safety measure for when superglue sticks your fingers together.

Epoxy Bonding Material

This is usually a two-part bonding agent, consisting of an epoxy resin and a hardener. Equal parts are mixed to form a thick, treacly material that will bond most things together strongly. Various setting times are available, from a few minutes to twenty-four hours – probably the best known is Araldite.

General Purpose Glue

There are many types of these adhesives, probably more commonly used on wooden or repair applications. These are often already in the household for general DIY purposes, so check before using them on the model that they will actually do the job – rather than relying on the fact that they happen to be at hand.

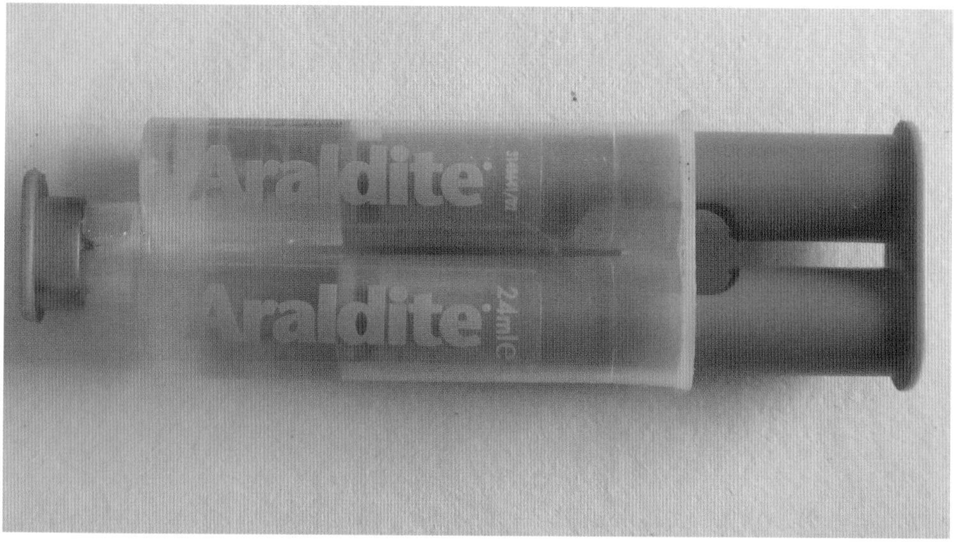

Araldite can also come in dispensers to ensure the correct amounts are mixed each time.

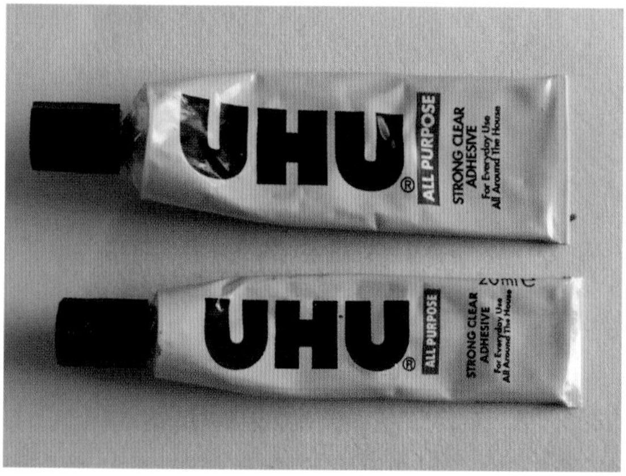

General purpose glues, probably not used very often in most instances, but still a good standby when a clear adhesive is needed.

Glazing Adhesive

This is a very useful material for holding clear plastic windows in place, as it sets with a clear film, such that the windows are not stained or smeared with unsightly glue residue.

Ultra-Strong Bonding Adhesives

If the ordinary two-part epoxy bonding adhesives have been tried, but have not given a strong joint, then the problem can get technical, and expensive. As mentioned earlier, some German manufacturers

Glue 'n' Glaze, for sticking transparent plastic windows, when the actual glue would be unsightly. It is milky in colour when applied, but dries clear.

use an ABS plastic, which is not easy to bond parts to. Stabilit Express is a two-part glue that can be used, but is not suitable for polyethylene (PE) – or, as it is more commonly called in the kitchen, polythene. Nor is it suitable for polypropylene (PP), or PTFE, soft PVC or nylon, according to the manufacturers. Typically, if purchased direct, it will cost around 26 euros plus 10 euros postage, and more than one pack could be required per model.

Another two-part bonder, methyl methacrylate, is made by Infinity Bond in the USA, labelled MMA-500: this claims to bond the 'non'-bondable materials above at approximately the same cost.

Another alternative similar material available in the UK is Fusion glue from DeLuxe Materials,

One of the expensive solutions where nothing else will do, from Germany. It is very strong when set, and adheres to those hard-to-stick plastics.

Another version of the same thing, available in the UK, but still very expensive. Good ventilation is essential for these glues.

at around £20 per pack, and claims to be suitable for nearly all plastics such as PVC, styrene, acetate, and acrylic. It also bonds polyester, epoxy and carbon fibre GRP. It is likely, although not stated, to have the same limitations as Stabilit Express. The author has used both with great effect on ABS plastics, GRP hulls and the like, where strength is required, although it is suggested where possible to also include some form of mechanical assistance such as wire, or thread, to back up the joint.

Warning! It is essential when using either of these materials to have good ventilation, as the fumes emanating from the glue as the chemical reaction takes place can be quite strong. Use disposable gloves to protect the hands to avoid irritation to the skin, and follow the instructions closely at all times.

Gluing the 'Swan'

For an unusual challenge, the decoy swan proved to be the hardest, due to it being made from flexible polythene, or polyethylene to give it the correct name, which had to be bonded to a wooden base. This material has a 'soapy' texture, similar to PTFE,

This was a last resort, discovered online, when nothing else would adhere to a polyethylene model swan. A preparatory chemical is used to prepare the surface, and then something similar to superglue to actually bond. The instructions were sadly not in English.

or silicon, which makes bonding other materials to it, hard, if not almost impossible.

A two-part pack from Poland produced quite a good bond where it was necessary to fasten the body of the swan to its wooden platform; this was necessary for all the internal components, after trying all the more commonly available choices of adhesive.

Disposable Applicators

These applicators offer a solution to those hard-to-get-to places. For most two-part bonding adhesives, they are a 'one-off' use as the needle cannot be cleaned before the glue cures. However, for PVA wood glue, use a small quantity and wash out after use in water, or alternatively stick a pin in the end to keep the air out.

PVA Wood Glue

The most common glues are those used with wood. Normally called white glue or PVA adhesive, these are water soluble when wet. The waterproof version is the best option for models, although most are painted anyway, and not left in the water for long periods, so a non-waterproof version is acceptable.

A selection of adhesives that were tried before the material in the last picture, without much success, illustrating the sometimes trial-and-error nature of modelling.

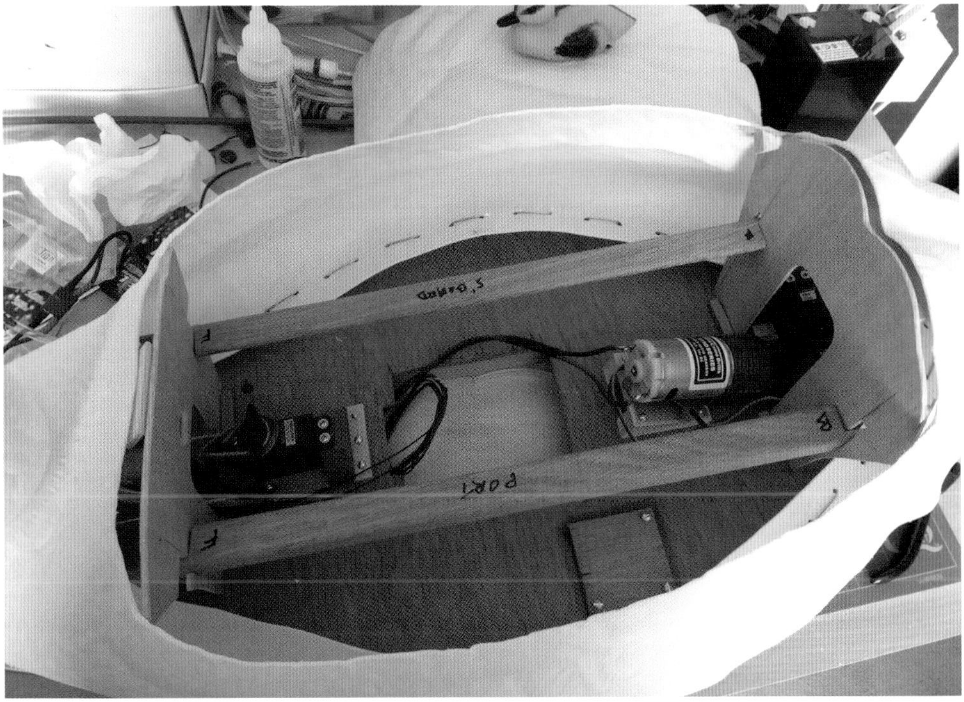

The model swan itself. The difficult area is between the wooden base and the white body. Notice the copper wire stitching to give extra strength. Any unevenness was filled in with chicken wire, Isopon and a two-part resin.

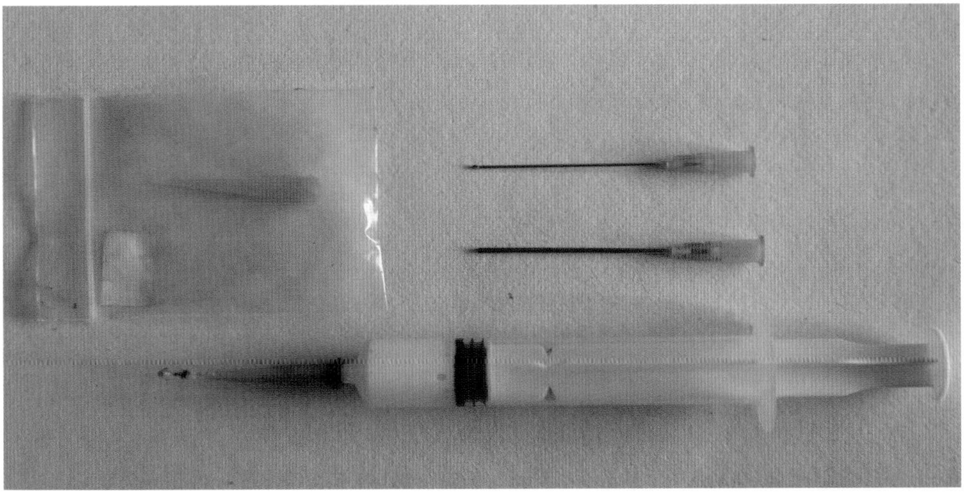

A useful selection of syringes and hollow needles, particularly for small wooden components and PVA glue. Always wash out the needle to avoid the glue setting after use.

FILLERS

A number of commercial products can be used to fill, say, air holes in glass-fibre hulls, or edges of components that are not matched perfectly. The choice is almost entirely dependent upon the size of the crack, gap or hole that needs to be filled. Milliput putty is a popular choice, which, as its name implies, is a putty-like material that can be shaped and cut, or sanded down when cured.

Always aim to test-fit parts before actually gluing them, especially if using 'instant' adhesives such as superglue, where there is no 'second try'. Also choose a filler that will be compatible with the material of the model, so that there is a chemical bond between the surfaces, rather than a simple mechanical one, which could crack over

Isopon P38 and P40. P38 is ideal for filling small and larger gaps and then sanding smooth. P40 is used where structural strength is needed, or for very large gaps, before a final top finishing with P38. It is available from car-body repair shops.

time. This can be important if there is any flexibility, and consequent movement between the parts.

Often when adding the decking to larger models there is a small gap all around, especially with pre-formed hulls, which must be sealed. Many of the proprietary fillers are supplied in small tubes, so to use these can therefore prove expensive, and it is suggested that Isopon P38 filler is used. Designed primarily to repair car bodies, it is easy to sand and shape, it is readily available, is waterproof when cured, and has a long shelf life; also it adheres to GRP, wood, metal and styrene well. Once the initial purchase has been made, it can be used for a long time, even in small quantities.

Again, use rubber gloves to protect the skin from the chemicals used in the material, and ensure there is plenty of ventilation when working near these products.

When even stronger bonds and strength are needed – such as rudder posts and propeller shaft housings through the hull, or where internal structural bulkheads need extra bonding to the hull, or even large holes – then Isopon P40 can be used. This has chopped glass-fibre mixed into it, and when mixed and cured is extremely strong. It can be shaped and cut easily. For final finishing P38 will probably be needed.

FINISHING

Sanding Down

Files were discussed in Chapter 1, so it is assumed that any really rough areas have already been smoothed down, prior to this stage.

Wet-and-dry sandpaper purchased in packs is the simplest solution, and can be torn into smaller

Wet-and-dry sandpaper in packs is very useful. Start with 400 grade and work even finer, depending on the finish required. Most glasspapers are not so durable and may be too coarse. Always wrap the sandpaper round a cork or plastic sanding block, which will give better control of the process.

pieces, as necessary. There will be some considerable time spent in sanding down large areas of the model. Ordinary glasspaper is usually cheaper, but mostly does not have the durability of wet-and-dry.

Sanding sticks can prove useful, or wrap a piece of wet-and-dry around a smooth rat-tail file, and use that. A cork sanding block will offer a good grip with wet-and-dry wrapped round it.

Tack Cloth

Sanding or rubbing down any styrene or GRP component will produce a great deal of static electricity on the surfaces. The resultant dust of sanding will happily stick to them, no matter how much care is taken. Wiping down with a moist cloth will only streak the surface, and will not remove all the dust. The finish on many models is spoiled by lack of attention to detail at this stage.

Sanding plastic produces dust and an electrostatic charge on the surface of the plastic. It is essential that this dust is removed prior to painting, so a 'tack-cloth' can make this much easier.

The tack cloth, as its name implies, has a sticky surface and is well worth the investment. It is sealed, and even when opened will retain its effectiveness for a long time.

Masking Tape

Ordinary masking tape from a stationery supplier is not good enough for a finished edge to a paint line on a model, in spite of its name. The paint will creep under its edge during drying and leave a ragged line, which is unsightly at best, or could ruin the finish, such that it has to be rubbed down and started again.

Thin Tamiya dispenser masking tape gives a sharp crisp line, and will bend around corners to some extent. In addition it is low tack, so is less likely to lift the base colour underneath, or leave adhesive residues. Ideally use this, plus ordinary masking tape and paper to cover any areas that need to be protected from overspray. Some spray paints can melt newsprint, which will mark the model, so use another kind of paper without print on it, or thin polythene sheet, if possible. Another alternative is to use kitchen

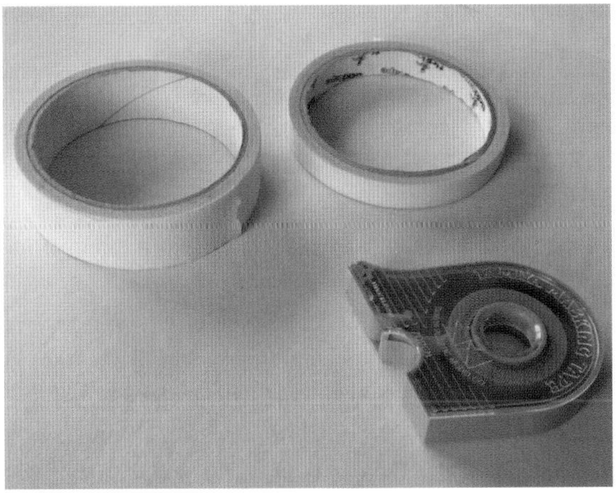

Try not to use ordinary masking tape, as used by car repair shops. Tamiya tape, or similar, and its dispenser offers a much cleaner and sharper edge, and will not 'bleed' under the edge as the paint dries. If a slight ridge is not acceptable where the paint meets the edge itself, sometimes it is better to remove the tape before the paint dries, allowing a softer edge – but take care.

Specially made to stick on over the proper masking tape, this commercial solution provides a polythene over-sheet, to prevent overspray spoiling another part of the model.

foil instead of paper, as this easily moulds to the model contours, does not blow away as the item is being sprayed, and will not mark the finish underneath.

Alternatively, where large areas need to be protected from overspray, a commercial solution with masking tape attached to a folded polythene sheet can be stuck on top of the Tamiya tape.

PAINT AND PAINTING

Throughout this book, paint finish is often mentioned because it is the single item that will potentially spoil the look of a model that may have taken many hours of painstaking effort to produce. There is a temptation to rush to get the model finished, but always remember that it is the detail and finish that is looked at first by any observer – not what is inside the model.

Acrylic paint has taken over from enamel in many areas, because it is quick-drying, and everything can be washed out with water; furthermore it doesn't 'skin' over in the tin like enamel paints, although there are special thinners that can work better to actually thin the paint when required. Using acrylic as a brush paint can be more difficult because of the quick drying time, so complete areas need to be finished, rather than left part finished for later completion, when a join will be visible.

Painting the Model

It is possible to purchase a spray gun and compressor suitable for modelling, starting at around £200. This is in the long term, and will prove a much cheaper option than buying spray cans for each model at £6 to £8 per can, where you may need three or four cans. Generally the paint must be thinned when using a spray gun, and all the parts cleaned after use, especially the nozzles when using quick-drying acrylics. It does require practice on something that does not matter in order to appreciate the control necessary to deposit the correct amount of paint.

A selection of spray cans. Halfords, the car spares outlet, carries many colours that are suitable for modelling. Smaller cans are available online from model retailers or from model shops. Satin finishes are the norm for models, as a 'gloss' finish to scale looks out of place.

However, when starting out, spray cans are likely to be more practical. Always ensure that the spray can does not blow away small workpieces during painting, by holding them down with tape or Blu Tack. Spray paints in aerosol cans have a ball bearing inside to stir up and mix the paint with the propellent, so ensure that the can is shaken for a couple of minutes, otherwise a dilute paint will be sprayed as a result.

If a choice is made to hand paint the model with a brush, then this will prove to be much more laborious, and the finish probably not as good, unless it is a very small model; nevertheless, most small fittings and deck items are normally hand painted.

It is worth considering the overall view of the model at this point. With a few rare exceptions – such as the wooden speedboat, the *Riva Aquarama*, shown before, or a lifeboat – then the scale view of the model will need some adjustment over the real thing.

In general terms, most models should never be gloss finished, to scale – it simply looks wrong, so go for satin or matt. The actual colour may also need toning down, because at a distance on the boating lake, a garish bright colour will not look as it should.

Another Cleaning Tip

Whenever a spray can is used, the nozzle should be cleaned of paint when finished, by inverting the can and spraying for a few seconds so the nozzle does not clog up with paint. By inverting the can and spraying it into a little scrap jar with a lid, the paint can be saved for touching up when necessary. Just add some solvent if it has set.

A typical 100ml model spray can from Revell, and a container to catch the excess for touch-up purposes; this avoids having to buy a separate touch-up tinlet. The can must be inverted after every use to clear the nozzle, so catch the paint in the jar.

If the paint solidifies, simply add a very small drop of cellulose thinners and reconstitute the paint to touch up a missed area. But don't use it on top of oil-based enamel paints.

Using a Turntable

During spraying, small workpieces may need to be turned to paint all the sides, and a simple revolving turntable can be helpful. Hold down small lightweight items with Blu Tack, or similar. An old cake-decorating stand can provide another solution.

Brush Painting

For painting small parts, or for retouching, tinlets are invaluable, generally from Humbrol or Revell. Originally these were all oil-based enamels, but latterly acrylics and water-based paints – which are more environmentally friendly – have taken over, although white spirit is still often needed to clean some of them.

To start with, a selection of five small brush sizes will be enough. Try not to cut corners on price here: the final finish of any model will depend on how paint is applied, and cheap brushes will produce a cheap finish – and after all the hard work invested earlier, it is simply not worth it.

Paint pens are often useful for small lettering or marking; also, most wooden decks can be improved by staining them a slightly darker colour, but do be careful of overdoing it: two thin applica-

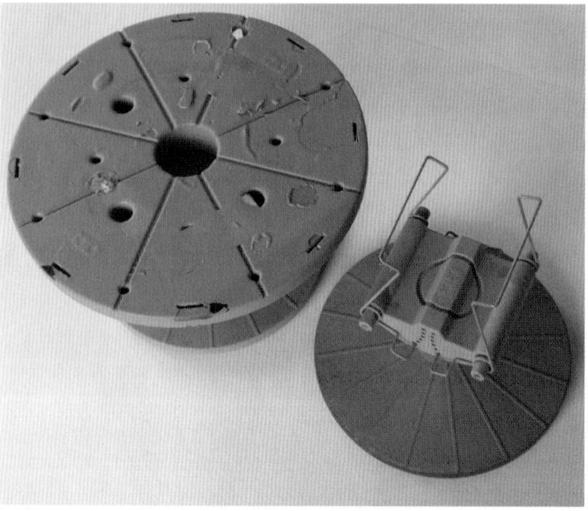

A turntable is invaluable when small components need different sides spraying at the same time. Always anchor them down to stop them being blown away by the spray.

A collection of acrylic and enamel tinlets. Over time these are accumulated for different models, and often used again, and again later on. Providing they have not gone solid, a suitable solvent will usually resurrect them.

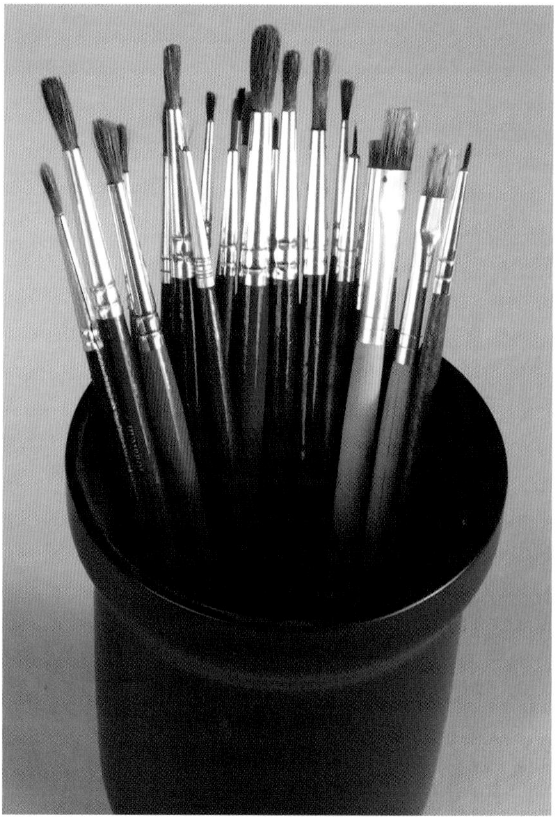

Take care of paint brushes – wash them each time, and they will last for years. The better the quality, the better the finish obtained, so an investment here will pay off many times over.

Paint pens and stain can help in those hard-to-reach places, but they quickly go off once opened. They are very useful for finishing off miniscule lettering in confined areas.

tions are better than one thick one that proves to be too dark.

Paint Thinner

Oil-based paints can be thinned, and brushes cleaned with white spirit or turpentine substitute – 'turps' as it is usually termed. Water-based paints can be thinned simply with water, and cellulose or acetate paints with cellulose thinners. Methylated spirit (denatured alcohol) is ideal for cleaning any grease prior to painting, or for removing felt-tip markings. Do not use acetate thinners for cleaning any surface, as they may mark it.

The three most used liquids by any modeller – always essential, and used for cleaning brushes, diluting paint and so on: turpentine substitute, or white spirit for enamel/oil paints and cellulose for acetate/cellulose paints; and third, methylated spirits, purely as a cleaner as it will not damage or melt other plastics.

Moisture Problems

Whenever a can of spray paint is used it is essential that a few precautions are taken. Let us consider how a spray can works. First, there is an aerosol propellent to force the paint out of the can. This is often propane or butane, which is highly inflammable. Second, the solvent, which is the paint carrier, may be a cellulose or similar, which again is inflammable, and can be a breathing irritant, so ensure very good ventilation.

Just as important is the temperature of the workroom. As the spray can is used, the can will suffer a drop in temperature (remember Charles's Law from school). As the paint hits the workpiece surface, the solvent will evaporate – reducing the temperature even further.

If there is moisture in the air, it is possible for it to condense on the painted surface, with the result that it can cause a paint 'bloom', or an orange-peel effect, or discoloration of the paint. This will not go away, such that the piece may have to be rubbed down again and repainted.

There are two solutions to this: either ensure the room is warm, and the paint cans are at room temperature, or heat everything with a hair dryer, and use it again immediately after spraying. Effectively this will stop the workpiece temperature dropping to the dewpoint of the moisture in the air, and the moisture condensing out. Do not forget to ensure that the work is fixed down, so the hair dryer cannot blow it away.

Moisture is the biggest problem when spraying the model, resulting in a crazed or orange-peel effect, or more commonly a dull milky sheen, which totally spoils the paintwork. Aim to spray outside on a dry windless day in summer, or use a hair dryer inside at other times, if it is damp.

Incompatible Paint

A similar impairment of the paint surface can occur when using an oil-based paint first and a cellulose spray paint later, where the solvent bubbles, or marks the paint surface. If there is ever any doubt, make up a test piece and paint that first, to ensure it will work.

Conversely, if the surface is spray painted first with a cellulose-based spray, then normally any of the other oil/acrylic paints can be used on top of it without any detrimental reaction – but again, test first if in doubt. However, always ensure that any paint is fully dry before attempting to apply a further coating, whatever type it is.

Preparing and Painting

The following is a sequence of steps to be taken when spray painting a model. In general it is advisable to start at the keel and work upwards to spray large areas. Small items should be sprayed separately, or brush painted and added to the model at a later stage. Each stage should be masked off separately, and the paint allowed to dry and cure before taking on the next stage, to avoid pulling off soft paint when the masking tape is removed.

Always try to hold the spray can or spray gun about 10in (25cm) away from the model. Use a smooth backwards and forwards motion, and carry on past the model before stopping the spray. Never stop halfway, and spray sparingly. It is always easier to go over the surface twice to avoid too much paint in any one area, when it may start to track down and produce 'runs' before it has had time to set.

Weathering

With more experience, many modellers want to aim at greater realism. Rarely do 'real' craft look new and in pristine condition. Visit any harbour

Step 1: *Rub down the surface with a fine wet-and-dry sandpaper after filling any obvious cracks/blemishes. This will also offer a better 'key' to the paint primer. Some plastics do not actually need a better 'key' and paint will bond well, but imperfections will need sanding back anyway.*

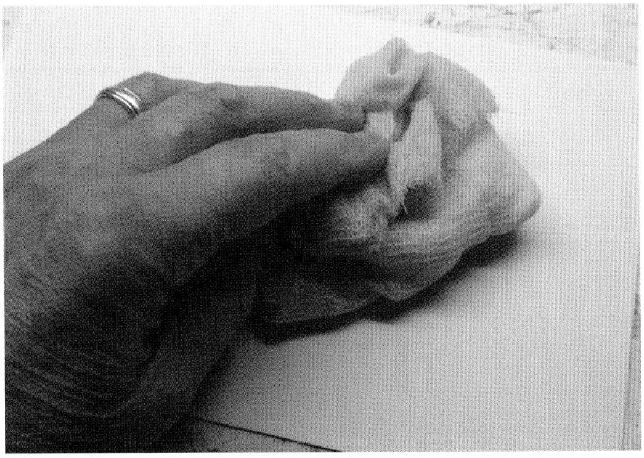

Step 2: *Remove all dust from the surface about to be painted using a tack cloth.*

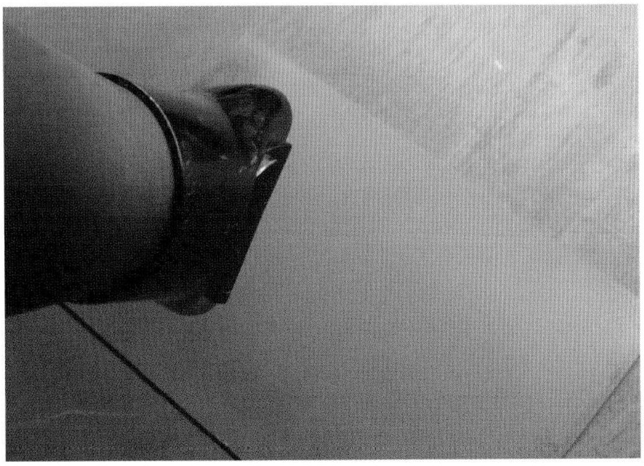

Step 3: *Spray with a suitable primer. Most topcoats will suggest a suitable colour for this, although as a guide use a darker primer for dark topcoats and lighter for lighter finishes. Leave to dry completely, and then repeat Step 1, if necessary, as further imperfections may now show up.*

Step 4: *Assuming that it is the hull being sprayed, mark a pencil line as a guide to the waterline of the model, as explained earlier. Do not use a felt-tip pen as permanent pens tend to bleed through the finished paint surface.*

Step 5: *Always aim to start spraying at the keel and work upwards, so place the masking tape above the pencil guideline, in order to spray below it.*

Step 6: *Protect the hull above the waterline from overspray with either newspaper or polythene, held in place with ordinary masking tape.*

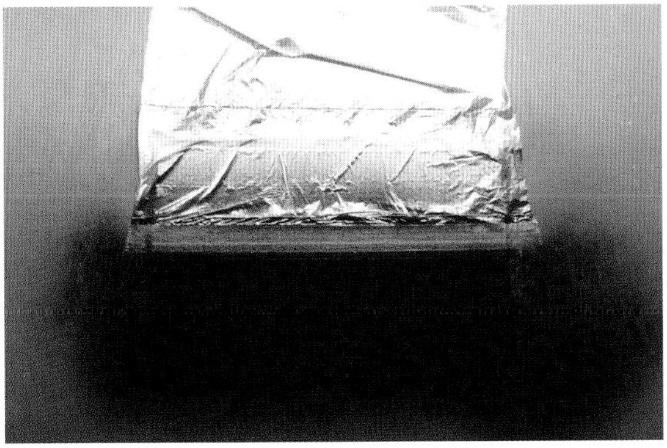

Step 7: *Before spraying the topcoat, ensure the surface is dust free. Carefully apply the topcoat, holding the spray about 10in (25cm) above the work; do not apply too much paint – another coat can always be applied later.*

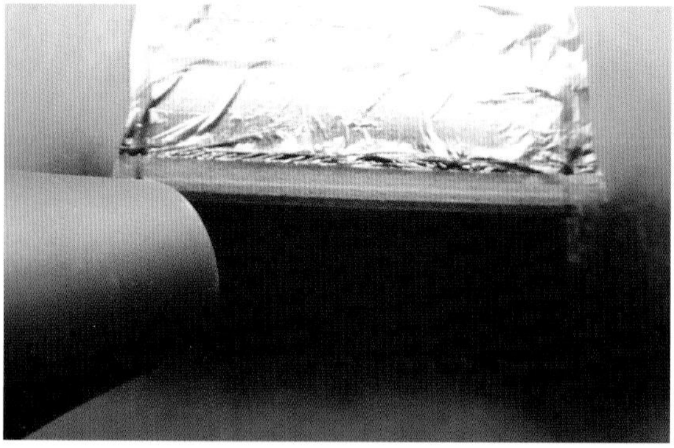

Step 7a: *Use a hair dryer if the air is cold and damp. Ensure that dust is not blown on to wet paint.*

Step 8: *Remove all the masking tape and inspect the line for imperfections, which may be touched up later.*

Step 9: *Repeat Steps 5 and 6, only the other way round, taking care to position the masking tape accurately.*

Step 10: *Repeat Steps 7, 7a and 8, as before.*

Step 11: *Finally apply a decal, boot topping or stripe, if necessary, or if dictated by the type of model. Not all full-sized craft have this extra, which is normally applied to give an extra layer of anti-fouling paint along the waterline, or simply used for decoration.*

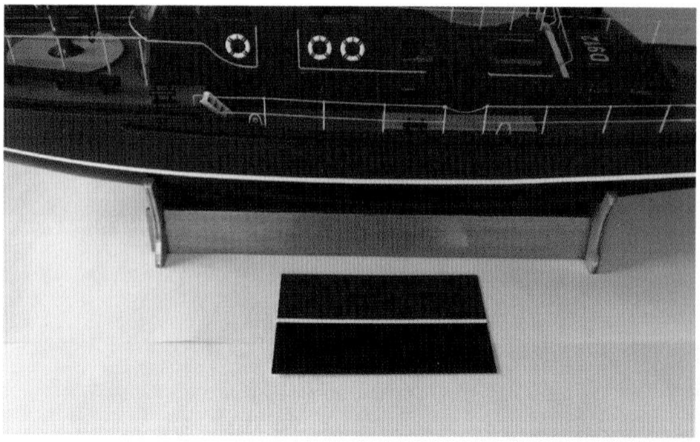

The earlier photographs were all taken in artificial light, which prevented a true colour rendition; however, the same sample shown against the real hull in natural light does illustrate how this model was painted.

A sample of touch-up paints, specifically designed as 'dirt' or 'rust', where the more experienced modeller can try a hand at weathering the model for greater realism.

A 'rust' kit: it is always a good idea to practise using materials such as this before applying them to the model, to get a feel for the amounts to use and to ensure that the desired effect can be created. Much of the 'weathering' effect is created by 'less', rather than 'more' application. It is easy to ruin the appearance of a model by overdoing the rust.

anywhere and look at the commercial or fishing boats moored up. They will be scuffed and rusty, with faded paint, blistered varnish, ropes and other deck material lying around, and in general, very untidy – totally unlike the model.

Careful weathering can impart a practicality and life to any model, and is not that difficult to do. Imagine where dirt or rust will collect, where contact might be made with a harbour wall, where rust is likely to run down a join and mark paintwork.

Various commercial touch-up paints are available, mixed to give numerous imitation dirt or rust colours. Model shops and on-line retailers dealing with railway enthusiasts have a similar range to choose from.

Examples of Weathering

Whilst not a floating, working model boat, this example of a static display, or diorama, as it is called, illustrates the dramatic effect of telling a visual story. Here displayed are scenes from the famous World War II film *The Cruel Sea* of the fictional corvette HMS *Compass Rose* in action, picking up survivors from the North Atlantic. The model has been brush weathered, to show the harshness of convoy patrol. There are a number of images/articles on-line, should you wish to research the subject further and discover

Much of this static display on first examination looks 'over the top' with the weathering effect; however, the real wartime craft were much worse.

Close up view of HMS Compass Rose *in action, again aiming to show the 'wear and tear' of actual wartime action on a display model. To gain an idea of scale, the figures are about 1in (2.5cm) tall.*

The Lady Lesley, *named after the author's wife, and spray weathered, rather than brushed. It was modelled on the real BM-77, which was far more battered and weathered in real life.*

more about the real corvette that stood in for HMS *Compass Rose* in the film.

The trawler *Lady Lesley,* modelled on the Brixham stern trawler BM-77 *Jacoba*, has been spray-gun weathered lightly to make it look more effective, as a working trawler. Other features included crew figures and working floodlights, backed by self-adhesive chrome strip to give more realistic reflectors, plus boxes of different types of fish, deck rope, fishing nets and so on. The inside of the wheelhouse was also fitted out completely; this is discussed elsewhere in this book.

Sizing

Decorator's varnish, or size, is a sealant and can be used on fabric or material to 'stiffen' it, when it can be moulded into a shape: for example a flag looks much better if it is curved as if being blown in the wind, as opposed to being lifeless and flat, so size it and wait until it is nearly dry, and then wrap one end round a pencil, and the other end in the opposite way around another pencil. Once dry the flag should form an 'S' shape. If loose rope requires a natural 'drape' then it can be stiffened in the same way and moulded to shape.

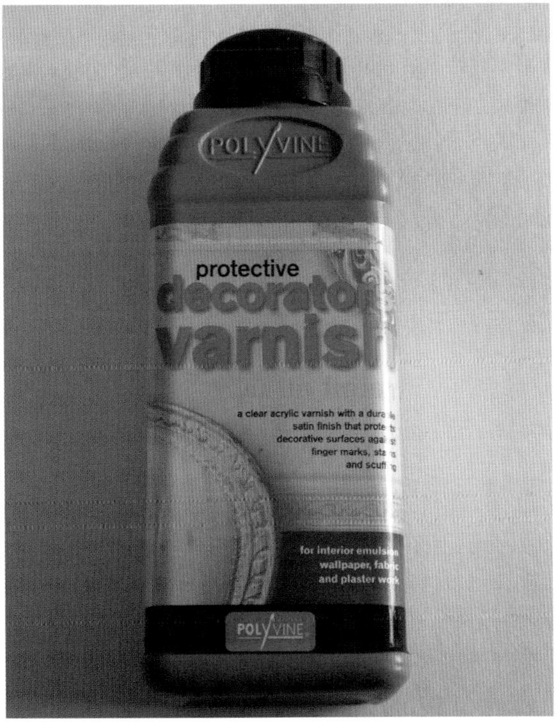

This varnish can be used to stiffen fabric, such as sails or flags, to make them appear to be flapping in the wind. Fold a flag around a pencil, and then fold it back to give a corrugated effect.

Decals

Many kits are supplied with decals specifically to finish off a model, but can be purchased separately when required. They come in two forms: one has to be soaked in water and the transfer is then slid off to be positioned on the work surface; the other is a self-adhesive thin printed plastic – this is a better, more permanent solution. These can be obtained as lettering sets in any colour – BECC is a good source. Once applied and the adhesive has cured, this type of decal is hard to remove, although it comes off easily if heated with a hair-dryer. It can also be 'stretched' a little to go round corners with a little application of heat.

Should the water-based transfer be used, then it will probably need to have a protective clear lacquer over it, to seal it and prevent it flaking or being washed off at some point. If a computer and printer is available, then special paper can be purchased and printed off to give any design required. (*See* the list of suppliers at the end of the book.)

Decals for a model usually come with a kit, but can be purchased as a pack from most suppliers, made by BECC Ltd, for virtually any military or civilian topic. Alternatively, using a computer and a special transfer paper from Lazertran Ltd, anything can be printed off directly with an ink-jet printer.

Chapter Four

Radio Control Systems

SUITABILITY

Number of Channels

Any investigation into the most suitable radio-control system to purchase for a model will most likely produce confusion if the reader has little or no knowledge of the subject. A good analogy here is to consider a car engine, be it a modern electric car or one with a more traditional internal combustion engine.

It is not necessary to understand the propulsion system of a car to actually drive it. The driver merely has to understand the steering principle, and a means of starting and stopping it. In other words, how to control it. Transferring this concept to a model electrically powered boat is exactly the same, because at a minimum the model must be steerable and capable of movement, and this involves two separate control functions, which the skipper must learn to use. But he does not necessarily have to know how the transmitter and receiver actually work.

It is necessary to have a radio transmitter (normally called a Tx) with two channels, which is able to 'talk' to a receiver (normally called an Rx), which can send a separate command to a rudder for steering, and to a motor for propulsion.

Many models only use a two-channel system, so anything over and above this is an unnecessary expense at this point. Sailing yachts often only have a rudder and a sail winch control, as an example. However, spare channels may come in useful for later when more complicated models are built, which have more features.

Frequency 40MHz

Without going into great detail, in the UK there are many simple toys that are radio controlled. Typically they use a radio frequency of around 27MHz (Megahertz). Until recently most surface models, as opposed to model aircraft, drones and suchlike, used around 40MHz, and this involved a pair of matched crystals, one in the Tx and one in the Rx. There was a slight variation on this frequency – that is, 40.665 to 40.995MHz – and this enabled a range of paired crystals to be used in the transmitter and receiver.

Do not get confused by wavelength and frequency. Wavelength is the distance between each wave. Frequency is the number of times the wave occurs – that is, one is a measure of distance, the other is a measure of time.

The main drawback with the old system was that anyone within range who was also operating on the same frequency would interfere with, or make it impossible to control the model. Therefore, at club meetings a 'Frequency Board Tag' would be displayed on a board showing who was operating on which frequency, meaning that a different set of crystals had to be chosen in the Tx and Rx if someone was already displaying a given frequency, or alternatively, wait until they

A wooden Riva Aquarama *model with two-channel radio control.*

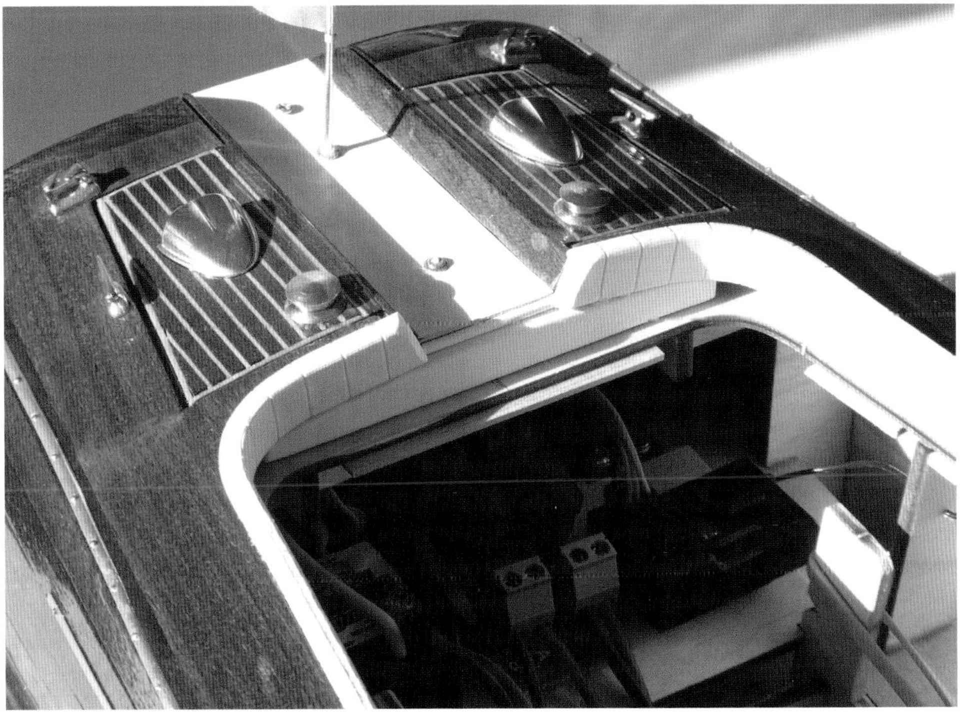

The black-cased instrument at centre right of the picture, the Rx, has a number of channels, only two of which are used, showing a number of coloured wires. Another grey wire on the right-hand side is the aerial wire. The centre of the picture shows two red plug-in fuses to protect the two motors.

The real thing being readied for a sail on Lake Garda, Italy. The Riva Aquarama *is regarded as the Ferrari of speed boats, a super-luxury but beautiful plaything of the rich and famous. For those who like wooden models this is one of the best to try.*

Essentials for the old 40MHz systems: a box for sets of crystals, one of a set of frequency flags to attach to the aerial, and a frequency board tag.

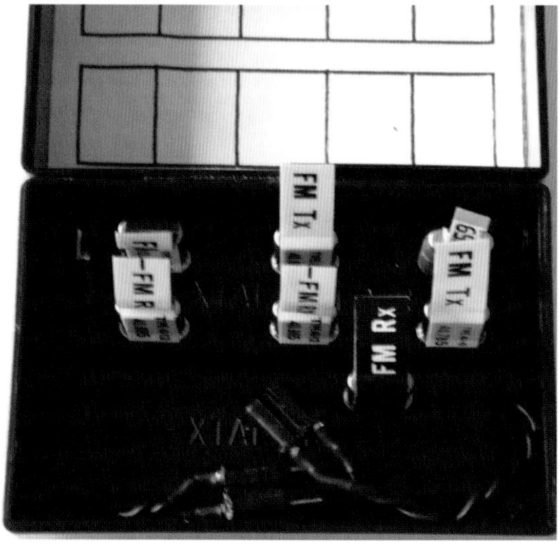

Various crystal pairs for the 40MHz range. Note the extension wire for use in models where the Rx is hard to get to, in order to swop the Rx crystal.

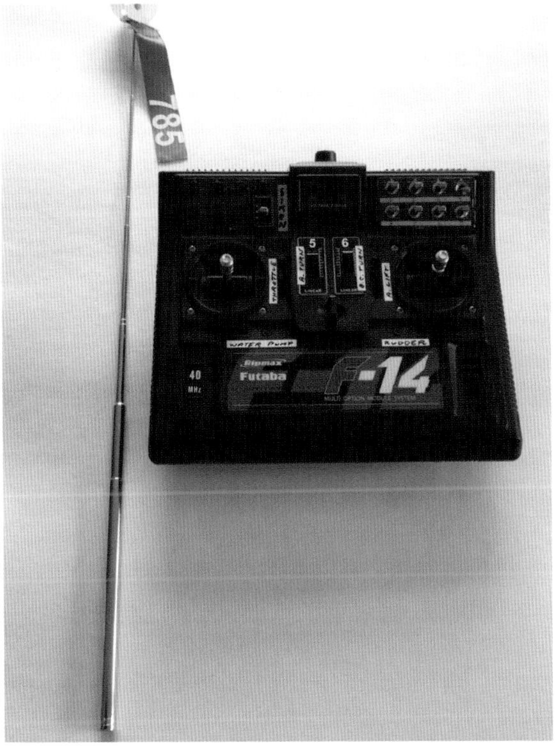

The Futaba F-14 40MHz transmitter, well known for its versatility and its ability to be modified with 'add-ons'. At the time of writing it is no longer manufactured, although there are numerous attempts to convert it to 2.4GHz. The aerial has been removed for the photograph – it normally screws into the top connection.

had stopped sailing. Also, as a back-up a flag would be attached to the extended aerial of the Tx to show which frequency was already being used.

Frequency 2.4GHz

The latest system uses 2.4GHz (Gigahertz). There are no crystals, and the equipment has the ability to swop frequencies automatically, so the 'frequency board' is obsolete for these systems, although there are many 40MHz units still out there in use that do require it. The aerial is a short, stubby extension on 2.4GHz transmitters, unlike the long retractable type used before, so it is easy to tell them apart.

Modern radio-control systems are termed 'plug and play' in that in general terms they are set up to use straight out of the box. However, it is still likely that they will require some basic configuring to use as the modeller desires. For example, is the signal to a specific function direct or reverse? And which channel is used for which function? And so on – so it is necessary to study the instructions that come with the system, before taking things any further.

A point worth considering before purchasing a transmitter is to buy one with more than one receiver included, as this saves extracting the

The unit in use at the lake. The aerial has to be extended to its full length for good communication, and it is obvious that the end needs to be protected with a practice golf ball to avoid hurting other lake users. The frequency flag must also be visible. It is easy to see why the 2.4GHz systems have taken over.

Typical 2.4GHz transmitters: apart from the short stubby aerials, the layout is much the same as older systems.

receiver for use in another model. Also, check how many servos are included, if any. It is possible to get an eight-channel system (even if they are not all needed at this stage) with two receivers for around £60.

Range

There is much discussion about the range of Txs: typically it is over 300ft (90m), and up to half a mile. However, it is 'line-of-sight' – that is, if anything is in the way it will degrade the signal/control. For submarines a lower frequency will penetrate further underwater, so 40MHz could seem better than 2.4GHz, and freshwater is better at the transmission of signals than sea water. But how far is a model submarine going to descend? Probably only just below the surface when it disappears from view, unless the water is really clear.

More importantly, if a model is 300ft away, it is almost impossible even to tell which direction it is travelling in, so this range is more than adequate. Most modellers will sail their boats well within, say, 100ft (30m) most of the time.

CHOICE OF RADIO CONTROL

2.4GHz Txs will come with a paired, coded Rx. This means that the Rx will only respond to the particular Tx to which it is bonded. There are about 130 million combinations of this code, so it is highly unlikely that you will ever come across a similarly bonded system.

Sets start at around £30/£40 for the most basic two-channel system, and rocket to around £3,000 for the most sophisticated. Always go for the best that you can afford, although at this stage avoid something that has multiple channels and is designed to fly a helicopter or fixed-wing aircraft. Many of the multi-channel sets have digital displays and can be programmed for each particular model, but are usually configured for flaps, ailerons, elevons and so on, for complex aircraft control, involving some relabelling for the model boating fraternity.

It may be noted that some Rxs have two short aerials rather than one, for better reception, and these must be placed at right-angles (90 degrees) to each other. Older 40MHz Rxs had a much longer aerial and the signal was capable of better penetration through hulls, decking, and so on.

There are different types of technology from each manufacturer, and the difference is usually reflected in the price. One of the latest is FASST, from Futaba ('Futaba advanced spread spectrum technology'). Then there is DSSS ('direct sequence spread spectrum'), FHSS ('frequency hopping spread spectrum') and DSS ('distributed spread spectrum').

The important parts are the 'spread spectrum' words. These systems allow the unit to hop to another, less congested part of the frequency spectrum. Going back to the car analogy, a car on a motorway can move to a less congested lane if it is busy, or even find a toll road for a different road altogether.

IMPORTANT START-UP TIP

Whichever system is used, always do a dry test of functionality and control of every channel and switch operation on land before launching a model.

The sequence of operation (assuming that everything is already switched off and connected up) is to check that all controls and switches on the Tx are in the neutral or 'off' position, and then switch on the Tx. Next check the central neutral position of the rudder (adjustments should have been made at home) and switch on the Rx, and/or battery isolator switch.

If the above sequence is not adhered to, it is easy to switch on and the motor (and propeller) will start up, possibly causing injury or damage, or other functions may move, and perhaps jam.

FITTING AND OPERATION

It is always worth connecting up the basic components on a workbench before they are fitted into the model, even to the extent that 'Velcro' tabs or double-sided tape is finally used for permanent fixture in the model. Always keep in your mind that any component may have to be removed at some future point.

Whilst a detailed knowledge of radio-control theory is not necessary, an elementary understanding of the 'hook-up' of each item, and the

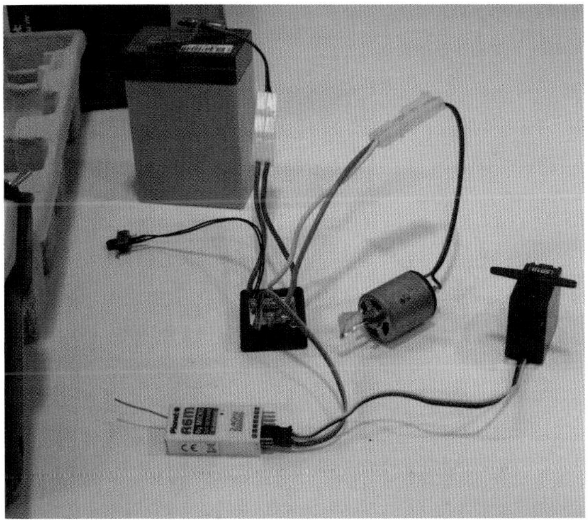

A simple 'hook-up' on the bench, using two of the six channels available with this particular Rx (the white unit in the foreground). The ESC in the centre also has its own on/off switch for isolation of power to the motor. The other channel goes to a servo to control the rudder.

opportunity to tune any programmable components, can certainly make it more enjoyable. All components will come with some instructions: some are simple, some are highly detailed, and it is recommended that these are closely studied before going any further.

At the centre of this simple hook-up is a small black square unit with numerous wires coming out of it. This is the electronic speed controller, or ESC as it is more commonly known. Its prime function is to regulate the power being transmitted from the battery to the motor, via a signal from the Rx, and it is important that an ESC electrical rating is compatible with both the type of battery being used and the power requirements of the motor. Various sizes and ratings of electrical power are available from the various manufacturers, normally measured in maximum current (amps) capability.

The larger the motor (and usually, therefore, the propeller), the more power will be required to drive it, and thus the larger will be the ESC. It often has what is called a 'heat sink' to absorb some of the heat generated, so ensure that there is adequate air space around it for cooling, necessary when using the larger brushless units.

Typical battery sizes are from 6 volts to 12 volts, although modern lithium-polymer batteries sometimes use a higher voltage. (There is more about this in Chapter 5.)

Try and install the ESC as far away as possible from the Rx and its aerials, and do not use any part of the model as an additional aerial: it is a designed, fixed length and should not be cut or shortened unless a connector is added so that the Rx can be removed separately, leaving the aerial in place. This comment only applies to the longer aerials used in old sets. Also, aim to keep power wires clear of the aerial where possible.

All the other components will also require some electrical power to drive them, usually

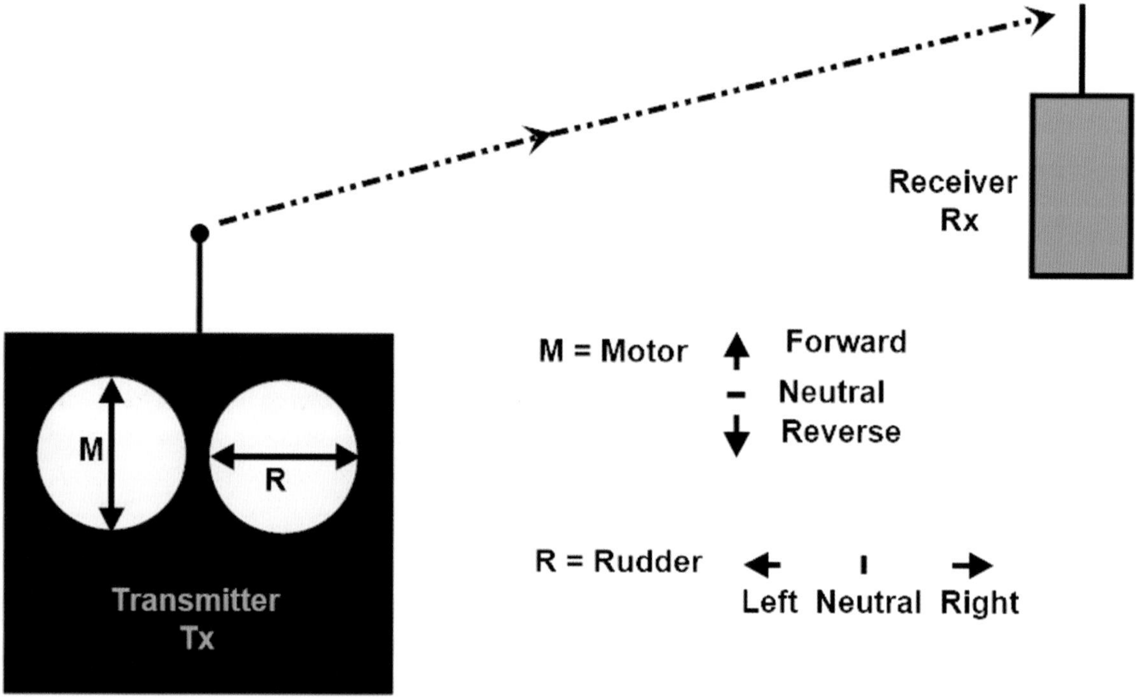

The two channels being used to send a signal to the Rx in the boat. Pushing the left stick forwards or upwards from the central position increases the speed, or the other way to reverse the propeller, for stopping. The right stick controls left and right turn of the rudder.

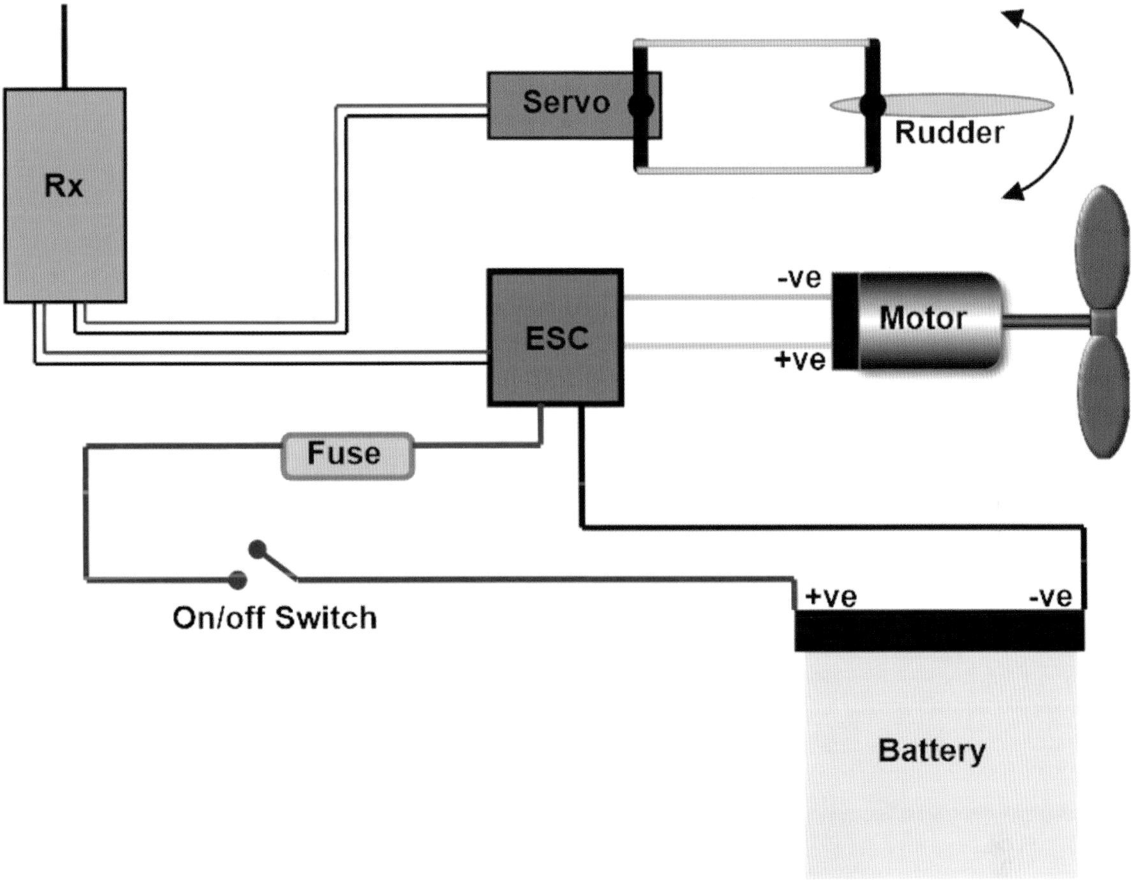

The same 'hook-up' as shown earlier in diagrammatic form. Note the on/off switch in the red (live) wire from the battery, and the in-line fuse to protect the system from overload in the event that the propeller becomes trapped.

around 4.8 volts, but nowhere near as much as the drive motor. This is usually resolved by having either a small battery to power other components via the Rx, or a 'battery eliminator circuit', or BEC, sometimes included via a power distribution board. Always refer to the manufacturer's instructions to ensure that the wiring is correctly connected (or disabled) so that only one 4.8 volt supply is connected.

Diagrammatically, the complete control system is now clear. By moving the motor stick on the Tx, a signal is sent to the Rx on the boat. As the stick is pushed forwards, the motor speed is increased via the ESC supplying more power to the motor. The ESC shown has a built-in BEC, which in turn supplies enough power to turn the servo connected to the rudder. Note the on/off switch and in-line fuse to protect the system in the event of something such as weed or rope stopping the propeller whilst the motor goes to full power to try to turn the propeller shaft.

Additional Tx Adjustments

The signal for each channel can be either direct, that is 0–100 per cent, or reverse, that is 100 per cent–0. In older systems this could entail taking the back off the Tx and actually changing contacts around, but now it is simply a little slider, or switch on the front of the Tx.

A sub-panel for each of the channels, where the signal can be reversed, if necessary. Sometimes it is easier to reverse a signal, rather than re-wire one of the functions, although care must be taken to ensure that the polarity is correct for whatever unit is reversed. Normally this would only be a reversal of the actual signal itself.

Below and to the right of the main stick control are trim tabs for fine trimming of the zero position of the main stick. Here there are two channels available, one vertical, the other horizontal.

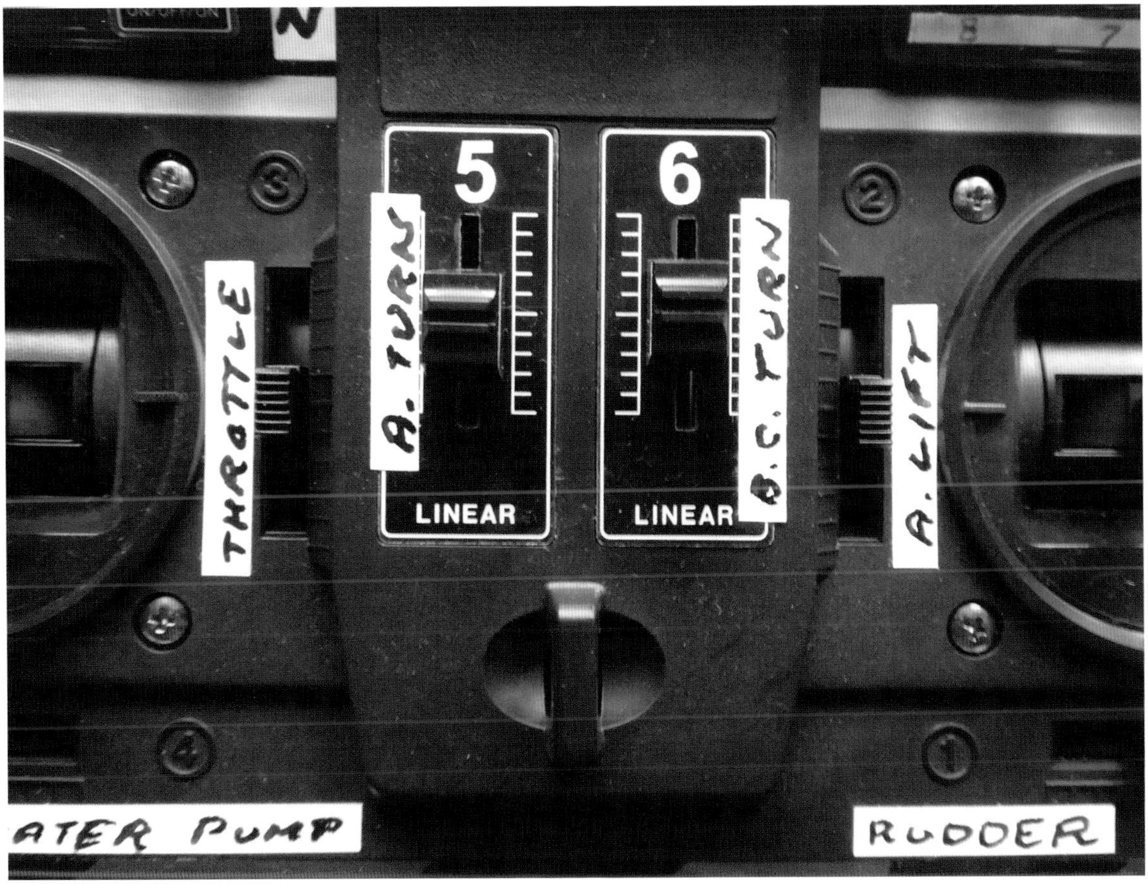

Two central linear sliders, offering full proportional control, in this case of fire-hose turntables on the model. These are not essential controls, but are necessary for this particular model. They are labelled to ensure there is no confusion during operation.

Whilst earlier it was suggested that everything be 'neutralized' before switching on the Tx, there are also 'trim' tabs next to the main channel sticks, enabling fine adjustments to be made to the neutral position once everything is switched on. Sometimes the propeller may turn slowly in neutral, or the rudder is slightly offset, and this can easily be adjusted with the trim tabs.

Another form of channel control is a slider that stays where it is placed, rather than using a spring-return to a neutral position, like the main sticks. Just like the main stick controls, it is fully proportional, and controls from 0–100 per cent (or 100 per cent–0, if reversed), where additional functions need to be controlled.

Later on, more features such as lights, bells, hooters and anchor winches can be activated by switches. Some will be 'latching' and some 'non-latching', depending on whether a continuous sound or light is required, or simply a horn that only stays on as long as the switch is pressed. As an example, a house room light is 'latching' (stays on) until you deactivate it, or, say, a door bell is 'non-latching' and only rings for as long as it is pressed.

The various sticks, switches, aerials and so on on the Tx are exposed and tend to be vulnerable, so always aim to protect them where possible, both from accidental damage and the weather: they may be splashproof, but they are not waterproof.

A panel of ancillary on/off switches to control navigation lights, emergency lights, searchlights, and radar or other features; some are latching, and some non-latching switches.

Some of the actual lights on the model.

The main horn, or siren, is on a separate switch, in the event that it is needed for a genuine emergency situation – as perhaps a car horn would be used when driving – to alert another boat user of a potential problem. It is much easier to activate a single switch, than a number all clustered together.

Many modellers will have a padded case for protection and storage when they are not in use, especially for the more expensive units.

It is not uncommon to have the same make of transmitter on the lakeside as another modeller, so label it to avoid confusion. Operating a Tx in winter with gloves on can prove challenging, so a full cover 'muff' may be the solution – these are available with a transparent front window for the really dedicated sailor who needs a nautical 'fix' in any weather.

Chapter Five

Essential Boat Fittings

DRIVE MOTORS

Brushed and Brushless Motors

Brushed motors have been used for many years in model boats, from the days when cars first had electric windows, and used the same, or similar, small motors. Typically they run on either a 6-volt or a 12-volt system. In general terms, at 6 volts the motor will run at half the speed of a 12-volt supply. An average motor at 12 volts could be running at over 13,000rpm, so will usually have a reduction gearbox attached to the shaft. The ratio necessary will be governed by the size of the propeller, and the speed at which the boat is designed to run – thus a tug is designed to go much more slowly with a large propeller, than, say, a speedboat, and so the 'scale' speed is important.

Brushless motors are a recent innovation, being smaller, lighter and more powerful, although more energy hungry (they use more battery power). They are very common in today's drone technology, using lightweight motors and batteries. However, unlike the brushed motor, which runs on DC (direct current) from a battery, such that it alternates between the coils, via the brushes, to generate an electromagnetic field to attract or repel as the shaft rotates, the brushless motor may use a system of electronics that alternates the current to the coils. There are also two different types of brushless motor, 'inrunners' and 'outrunners', which will be explained in detail later in this section.

In general terms, this makes brushless motors slightly more expensive, as they will also need a dedicated ESC to operate them. They may be able to use any battery type, but normally use 3.7- or 7.4-volt lithium Li-Po batteries, and again, the ESC must be designed to be compatible for this battery type, if used. They can use higher voltages where higher speeds are required, if necessary.

Brushed motors generate electrical 'noise' as they rotate (they 'spark' internally), and suppressors (or capacitors/condensers as they are usually called) have to be attached to the casing of the motor to avoid interference with the radio-control signal. Brushless motors do not suffer from this, although they can get hotter in use and may use a water-cooling jacket, heat sink or fan. Unless you need a lot of power and are planning on a high-speed, lightweight boat, brushed motors are more than adequate at this stage, although looking to the future, it is doubtful if brushed motors will be developed any further.

The range of motors is enormous, and it is worth some research, and/or advice from the local stockist or model shop, to ensure that the motor, or motors to be considered are suitable for the planned kit – often the instructions within the kit will supply suggestions. For a first kit a brushed motor/gearbox using either a 6-volt or 12-volt system will likely suffice, in order to avoid extra expense initially.

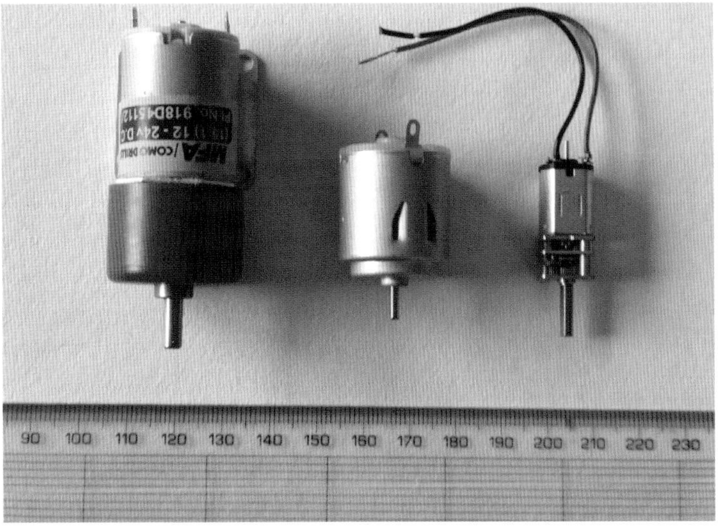

A selection of motors, including a main drive motor with attached gearbox; this is the smallest of that particular range. The others are for use to drive accessories such as radar reflectors, gun mounts, fire-hoses' mounts, to raise and lower anchor chains, small boats, and so on. Often these tiny motors run on 2 or 3-volt supplies, so should not be run directly off the main drive batteries, but via a separate voltage regulator.

Twin motors installed in the hull: note that they rotate in opposite directions, and as they are brushed motors, have a capacitor soldered across the terminals.

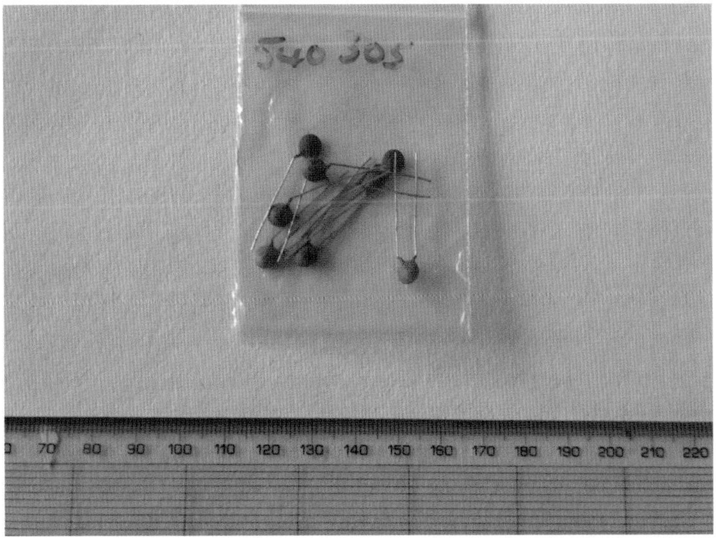

A pack of capacitors, for general use if not already supplied with a new motor.

DC Brushed Motors

Size	Voltage	Size (L x dia)	Voltage	Current	Revs	Torque	Weight	Motor only	With Bracket
0408	1 ~ 6V	8 x 4mm	3V	12mA	10000	0.4g/cm	1.4g	£1.50	~
0610	1 ~ 3V	10 x 6mm	3V	15mA	7500	0.6g/cm	1.4g	£1.50	~
K30	1.5~6V	20 x 8mm	6V	300mA	8000	4.2g/cm	3.75g	£1.75	~
N20	1 ~ 5V	15 x 12mm	3V	45mA	12100	2.1g/cm	10g	£1.50	£2.30
130	1.5~4.5V	25 x 20mm	3V	1.5A	12400	11.9g/cm	19g	£0.75	£1.85
140	3 ~ 9V	21 x 20mm	6V	0.22A	7070	35.1g/cm	20g	£1.60	£2.99
170	1.5 ~ 3V	32 x 19mm	3V	1.03A	10400	27g/cm	29g	£2.50	£3.99
260	3.0 ~ 6V	26.6 x 24mm	4.5V	0.3A	6587	13.6g/cm	29g	£1.99	£2.50
260L	1.5~4.5V	26.9 x 24mm	3V	0.4A	5100	11.6g/cm	28g	£1.25	£3.50
280/1	12 ~ 24V	30 x 24mm	12V	0.3A	8400	25.0g/cm	40g	£2.50	£3.70
280/5	3.0 ~ 6V	30 x 24mm	6V	0.51A	7664	25.0g/cm	40g	£2.50	£3.70
360	6 ~ 15V	32.5x27.5mm	12V	0.77A	9220	58.8g/cm	56g	£4.25	£5.50
380	3 ~ 7.2V	38 x 27.5mm	7.2V	4.4A	19000	375g/cm	70g	£4.50	£5.99
385	4.5~15V	38 x 27.5mm	12V	0.4A	9280	78g/cm	70g	£4.75	£5.99
385LN	4.5~15V	38 x 27.5mm	12V	0.4A	9280	78g/cm	70g	£6.95	£8.20
540	4.5~15V	50 x 35.7mm	12V	2.85A	13360	154g/cm	146g	£6.60	£8.10
540LN	4.5~15V	50 x 35.7mm	12V	2.85A	13360	154g/cm	146g	£7.80	£9.30
540H	6 ~ 12V	50 x 35.7mm	12V	9.6A	17500	262g/cm	155g	£5.00	£7.50
555	9 ~ 24V	58 x 35.7mm	12V	1.49A	5300	229g/cm	229g	£9.00	£11.50
775-5	12V	66 x 42mm	12V	1.8A	5500	400g/cm	364g	£15.00	£21.50
775-12	12V	66 x 42mm	12V	1.8A	12000	350g/cm	364g	£15.00	£21.50
800	12V	69 x 52mm	12V	5.3A	4280	837g/cm	502g	£21.00	£23.00
850	12V	69 x 52mm	12V	10.8A	8310	940g/cm	504g	£22.00	£24.00
M5	1.5 ~ 9V	19.5 x 32mm	6V	75mA	2300	10g/cm	45g	£3.00	~
M7	1 ~ 3V	13 x 24mm	2V	52mA	1760	5.4g/cm	20g	£3.50	~

Motor Accessories - Mounting brackets & RFI kits.		Price each
	Mounting bracket & screws for N20 size motors NEW	£0.95
724	Mounting bracket & screws for 130 / 140 / 260 / 280 size motors	£2.25
725	Mounting bracket & screws for 360 / 380 / 385 size motors	£2.50
726	Mounting bracket & screws for 540 / 555 / 700 size motors	£2.75
775BKT	Mounting bracket & screws for 775 size motors	£6.95
1114	Mounting bracket & screws for 800 / 850 size motors	£3.75
RFI1	RFI suppression Kit for small motors - up to 600 size	£1.00
RFI2	RFI suppression Kit for larger size motors - 600 size & above	£1.00

Selection of brushed motors.

Brushless Motors

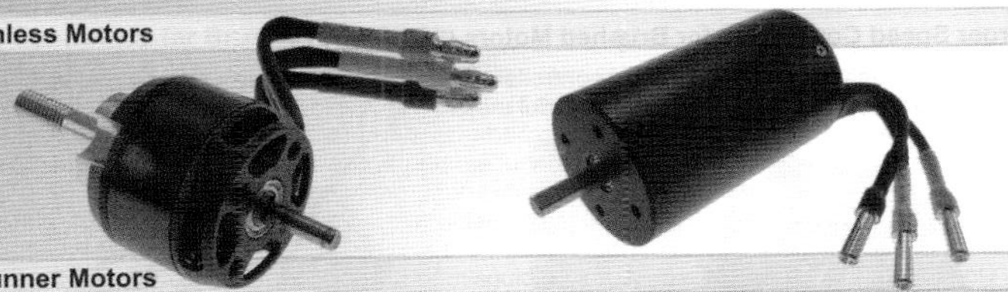

Outrunner Motors

Size	Turns	KV (rpm/V)	Lipo cells	Max Current	Power	Shaft dia	Max Pull	Weight(g)	Price
0603	NEW	17000	1	4.2A	15.5W	0.8mm	42g	1.7	£10.00
0703	NEW	17000	1	4.5A	16.6W	1.0mm	45g	2.2	£11.00
2212/14	14	800	2-4S	15A	220W	4.0mm	1.15kg	55	£16.50
2212/9	9	1250	2-4S	21A	300W	4.0mm	1.45kg	55	£16.50
2826/17	17	1050	2-3S	13A	155W	3.175mm	0.92kg	45	£15.95
2826/15	15	1150	2-3S	15A	171W	3.175mm	0.88kg	45	£15.95
2826/12	12	1380	2-3S	16A	178W	3.175mm	0.84kg	45	£15.95
2826/9	9	1820	2-3S	22A	230W	3.175mm	1.05kg	45	£15.95
2830/16	16	730	2-3S	14A	168W	3.175mm	1.0kg	56	£17.95
2830/12	12	980	2-3S	17A	204W	3.175mm	1.15kg	56	£17.95
2830/9	9	1290	2-3S	22A	244W	3.175mm	1.26kg	56	£17.95
2835/9	9	900	2-4S	24A	352W	4.0mm	1.8kg	68	£19.95
2835/8	8	1038	2-3S	24A	315W	4.0mm	1.62kg	68	£19.95
2835/6	6	1350	2-3S	29A	322W	4.0mm	1.4kg	68	£19.95
2835/5	5	1600	2-3S	26A	328W	4.0mm	1.3kg	68	£19.95
3536/14	14	560	3-5S	21.5A	441W	4.0mm	2.50kg	95	£23.50
3536/8	8	960	2-3S	35A	315W	4.0mm	2.45kg	95	£23.50
3536/7	7	1100	2-4S	36A	538W	4.0mm	2.45kg	95	£23.50
3536/5	5	1520	2-3S	55A	328W	4.0mm	1.82kg	95	£23.50
3542/14	14 NEW	380	4-6S	28A	377W	5.0mm	2.4kg	135	£27.95
3542/9	9 NEW	600	3-5S	28A	487W	5.0mm	2.8kg	135	£27.95
3542/5	5	1080	2-4S	55A	680W	5.0mm	3.05kg	135	£27.95
4250/9	9	480	3-6S	38A	706W	5.0mm	3.8kg	195	£39.95
4250/9	9	550	3-6S	42A	740W	5.0mm	3.1kg	195	£39.95
4250/5	5	960	3-5S	75A	820W	5.0mm	2.72kg	195	£39.95
5055/9	9	430	3-6S	55A	1390W	6.0mm	5.0kg	270	£49.95
5055/6	6	650	3-6S	68A	1400W	6.0mm	5.2kg	270	£49.95

Inrunner Motors (2 pole)

Size	Turns	KV (rpm/V)	Lipo cells	Max Current	Power	Shaft dia	Weight(g)	Price
1625/48	48	6000	2S	5A	37W	2.0mm	23	£10.00
2030/18	18	5160	2-3S	12A	135W	2.3mm	50	£13.95
2040/22	22	2600	2-4S	11A	230W	2.3mm	65	£17.95
2435/18	18	4500	2-3S	18A	230W	2.3mm	73	£22.95
2848/15	15	2630	2-5S	27A	510W	3.175mm	135	£27.95
3650/32	32	1185	4-9S	12A	500W	3.175mm	171	£28.95
3650/9	9	4370	2-3S	46A	550W	3.175mm	171	£28.95
3660/10	10	2450	2-4S	61A	1100W	5.0mm	280	£42.95

Inrunner Motors (4 pole)

Size	Turns	KV (rpm/V)	Lipo cells	Max Current	Power	Shaft dia	Weight(g)	Price
2845/5	5	1780	2-9S	24A	800W	4.0mm	125	£31.95
2850/3.5	3.5	2060	2-8S	32A	1000W	4.0mm	145	£32.95
4092/3 NEW	3	930	2-10S	80A	4200W	5.0mm	492	£82.95

Brushless Motor Speed Controllers (ESCs)

For boats - Waterproof with full forwards & reverse (with water cooling - 4mm coupling)

Rating	Peak current	Input Voltage	BEC output	Size	Price
30A	180A	Up to 3S lipo	6V @ 1A	54.5 x 28.3 x 18.7mm	£31.95
60A	360A	Up to 3S lipo	6V @ 2A	60.5 x 38.5 x 25.6mm	£59.95
120A	720A	Up to 6S lipo	6V @ 5A	68.5 x 39.4 x 32.0mm	£77.50

For Cars - Full forwards & reverse.

Rating	Peak current	Input Voltage	BEC output	Size	Price
18A	50A	Up to 3S lipo	6V @ 1A	31.5 x 24 x 15mm	£19.95
30A (waterproof)	180A	Up to 3S lipo	6V @ 1A	36 x 28 x 16mm	£24.95
60A	380A	Up to 3S lipo	6V @ 1.5A	31.5 x 27.5 x 24mm	£38.95
80A (waterproof)	540A	Up to 3S lipo	6V @ 2A	46 x 34 x 35mm	£48.95
120A (waterproof)	760A	Up to 4S lipo	6V @ 3A	59 x 38 x 34mm	£68.95

For Planes - Forwards only.

Rating	Burst current	Input Voltage	BEC output	Size	Price
12A	15A	Up to 4S lipo	5V @ 2A	32 x 24 x 10mm	£11.95
18A	22A	Up to 4S lipo	5V @ 2A	45 x 24 x 11mm	£13.95
30A	40A	Up to 4S lipo	5V @ 2A	55 x 25 x 9mm	£16.95
60A	80A	Up to 6S lipo	5V @ 3A	70 x 31 x 13mm	£38.95
80A NEW	100A	Up to 10S lipo	N/A	78 x 55 x 18mm	£65.45
100A	120A	Up to 6S lipo	5V @ 3A	83 x 31 x 16mm	£47.95

Brushless ESC Programming Cards

Marine / car ESC programming card	Forward only / forward & reverse Number of cells Low voltage cut-off threshold Timing	£8.50
Flight ESC programming card	Battery type Brake on/off, Cutoff mode / threshold Start mode, timing	£7.50

Motor heatsinks

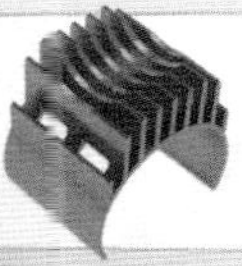

36mm clip-on finned heatsink Gold anodised aluminium. £3.60

36mm clip-on finned heatsink with fan (JST / BEC) lead red anodised aluminium. £6.75

Water cooling jackets

Size	Suits Motors	Copper connector size	Weight(g)	Price
28-30	2845	4.0mm (use 3mm i/d tube)	11	£5.75
28-40	2850, 2860	4.0mm (use 3mm i/d tube)	17	£5.75
36-40	3650, 3660	5.0mm (use 4mm i/d tube)	24	£6.50
40-68 NEW	4092	5.0mm (use 4mm i/d tube)	48	£8.95

Selection of brushless motors.

More often than not, ballast weight will be needed for the correct trim, so sealed lead-acid batteries (SLA) can serve two purposes, by providing the power and the additional weight necessary, which may dictate whether 6-volt or 12-volt systems are used – but more about batteries later.

Brushless motors, depending on the type, are, in very simplistic terms, a brushed motor turned inside out. Brushed motors have permanent stationary magnets attached to the inside of the casing, and the coils are attached to the shaft, which spins. A brushless motor has fixed coils, and magnets attached to the revolving shaft, or alternatively has them again next to the casing, so there is no directly moving electrical component making contact, as with the brushed motor brushes: hence they are quieter, and do not produce radio 'noise'.

Another reason for suggesting the use of brushed motors for the novice modeller to start with, is that at low speeds there is a little more control of the motor via the Tx, such that the model will be less 'jerky' as it sets off. Brushless motors tend not to throttle down to as low a speed as smoothly as a brushed motor. However, with more experience of actually controlling the model on the water, this will become less important.

Inrunner Brushless Motors and Outrunner Brushless Motors

When considering brushless motors, it is necessary to realize that there are two different construction versions, defined as 'inrunners' or 'outrunners'. The inrunner has the permanent magnets attached to the shaft rotating *inside* the coils. The outrunner typically has permanent magnets attached to a sleeve, or the casing, *outside* the coils. The casing is attached to the shaft and thus rotates, making it impractical to attach cooling jackets and so forth.

An inrunner motor is generally smaller in diameter, but longer in length than a comparable outrunner. It will have a higher Kv (defined as the number of revolutions per minute per volt).

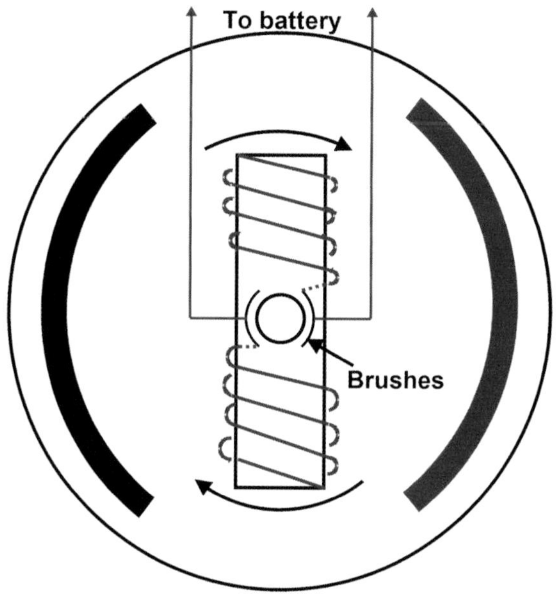

A very basic diagram of a brushed motor. The current is transferred to the coils via the carbon brushes alternately, which generate an electromagnetic force. Hence a spark is created at every revolution.

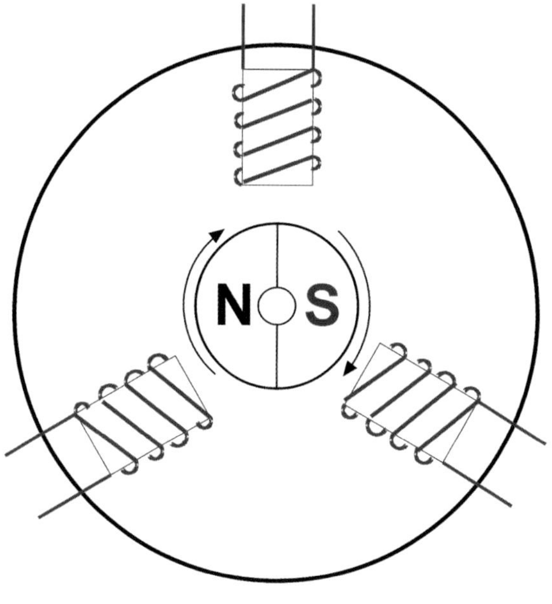

A brushless motor in simple form: in reality there would be many more coils. Current is applied to the three coils alternately, and they are switched in sequence from north pole to south: this attracts or repels the central magnets, turning the shaft. There is no direct contact with the shaft or central magnets, as in the brushed motor.

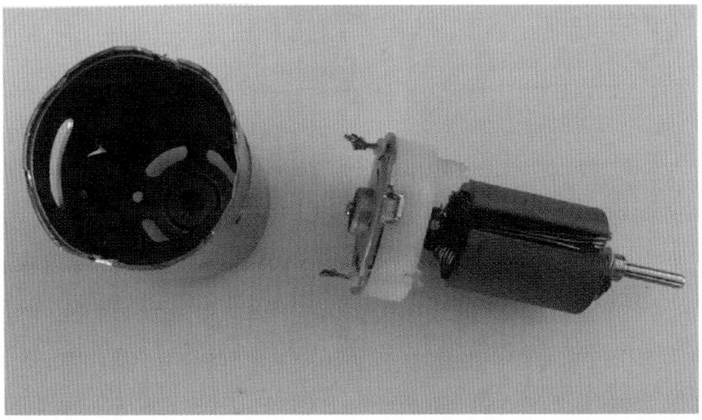

A typical brushed motor showing the casing containing the permanent magnets, the shaft and coils, with the brush carrier in the centre.

Close-up showing the carbon brushes on the left. These carry electrical current to the copper bearings on the shaft, shown to the right, which in turn carry the current to the coils.

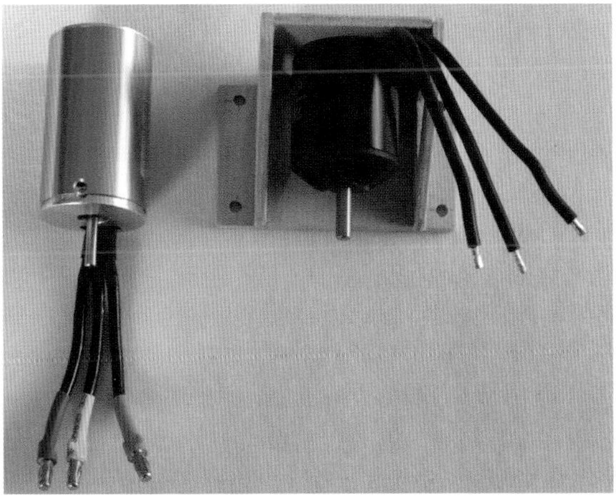

Two brushless motors: the left-hand motor is termed an 'inrunner', the right-hand motor is termed an 'outrunner'.

Close-up of the coils and shaft of the brushed motor; the brushes are at the rear.

Close-up of the two permanent magnets inside the casing of the motor.

Displayed here is an 'inrunner' brushless motor, with the permanent magnets attached to the shaft, rather than the casing, shown to the left. The coils are now inside the casing. For comparison purposes the brushed-motor central shaft is displayed on the right.

A typical 'outrunner' brushless motor, mounted in a wooden bracket. Here the casing rotates attached to the shaft; the back plate is stationary and allows mounting screws to be inserted at the rear. The ventilation holes can be clearly seen. This is almost a combination of a brushed and a brushless construction, with central coils and a number of permanent magnets on the inside of the casing.

Rear view of the motor, showing the small ventilation holes and brass mounting screws.

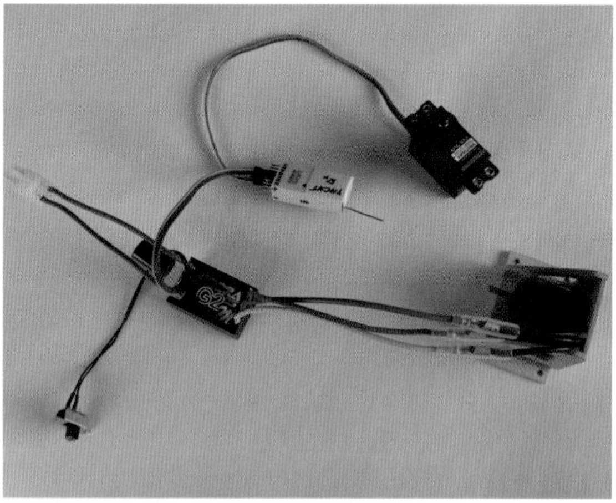

An ESC connected to the Rx with a two-channel system, one to the rudder servo and the other to the ESC. The three wires to the brushless motor may be extended in the real model situation, and are displayed here purely to demonstrate the hook-up procedure. Note there is no separate battery for the servo, as it uses a BEC. There is an on/off switch and the two leads for the main battery (not shown).

Because of its design, an inrunner can be cooled more easily and is more suited to high-speed boats. It has a lower torque (the force generated to twist the shaft), usually measured in Newton-metres (Nm) or pound-feet (lb ft), for its size than an outrunner.

In general, the outrunner is better suited to slower scale models, although it gets hotter and is harder to cool, as mentioned earlier. This is worthy of consideration in the confined space of a model boat hull.

There are three leads coming out of a brushless motor casing, and to change the direction of rotation, all that is necessary is to change any two of them at the ESC/motor connectors.

Brushless motors may be designated 'sensorless' or 'sensored'. For boating applications, a dedicated ESC is used in conjunction with a 'sensorless' motor, which is adequate for normal model boating. A 'sensored' motor (with its own built-in sensors) simply helps with low-speed operation, but adds weight, complication, cost and potential reliability.

Motor Cooling

In general terms, motors and electrical generators are very similar, in that a motor converts electrical energy into mechanical energy to turn a shaft, whilst a generator converts mechanical energy from an external source, into electrical energy.

They both have coils, and to some extent a motor will also generate some power as it turns. This is termed 'back emf' (electromotive force). This tries to oppose the movement of the coils and the self-generated emf that the motor is aiming to achieve.

This brings us to the aspect of mounting an outrunner brushless motor in the confines of a model boat where there is little cooling air flow (unless a cooling fan is included).

Because the shaft and casing revolve, it is not possible to attach a water-cooling jacket or heat sink, and thus an external fan may be required.

There is a train of thought that ferrous (steel) mounting brackets may potentially have a magnetic field induced in them as the motor turns, likewise with steel mounting screws. This could place an extra load on the motor, leading to more heating. The simple solution is to use a wooden or plastic mount with brass screws.

There are small ventilation holes at both ends of the motor casing; a fan placed close to the motor will help to dissipate heat. This one is taken from the CPU (central processing unit) of a computer, which conveniently runs at the same voltage as the model. Note the rubber air sealing strip around the edge of the frame to seal it to the deck.

Important Tip

The most important thing to remember is that air circulation and space around the motor should be carefully considered. Whatever mounting is used it is imperative that the mounting screws holding the non-rotating part of the casing to the mounting itself are not too long, such that they intrude into the internal windings of the coils or wiring. This could cause an electrical short and/or damage to the coils.

Propeller Rotation

Always ensure when using multiple motors that they rotate in opposite directions, the port side motor/motors (on the left looking towards the bow of the boat) rotating clockwise, and the starboard motor/motors anticlockwise. This is easily achieved by swopping the power supply leads from the ESC at the motor terminals. This will ensure that when the boat is under way and the rudder set to neutral, it will travel in a straight line; if both engines revolve the same way, there is a tendency for the boat to drift off sideways, making it harder to control.

Any discrepancy in straight-line travel with a centralized rudder/rudders can easily be neutralized by a small adjustment of the trim tab on the Tx rudder control.

If using multiple motors, the propellers will obviously rotate in opposite directions as well, so must be opposite handed – that is, to propel the boat forwards, one rotates clockwise, the other anticlockwise; this is normally termed right- or left-handed, such that the slope or angle of the blades will be the opposite way round.

Many ships today not only have a propulsion system at the stern, but also have side-thrusters, or bow-thrusters. The author's model, pictured elsewhere, of the *Lady Lesley* fishing trawler has a bow-thruster to offer greater manoeuvrability. This feature is a horizontal tube below the waterline at the bow, with a propeller inside and its own motor, supplied as a complete unit, although it also needed its own ESC to run. With the ability to turn the bow and also to use a mixer (more about these later) on the stern drives, this gives any model great turning and positioning ability. Most clubs run steering competitions, and these extra abilities then really come into their own.

A selection of propellers. The top row will run anticlockwise to drive the boat forwards, the bottom row clockwise. For normal use a nylon propeller is quite adequate; brass/bronze looks better, but will be more expensive. The white-metal units supplied with an old kit could be used, if filed and polished before painting, but really these are only satisfactory for display purposes. However, they do illustrate the left- and right-handed blade angles.

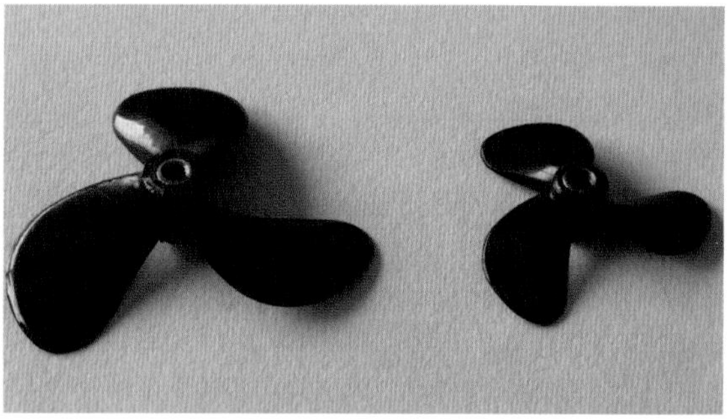

Here the threaded boss allows the propeller shaft to go right through so that the locknut is attached last. This may be useful should the propeller tend to unscrew when the model is running in reverse, although thread sealant will usually prevent this problem.

CHOICE OF PROPELLER

Propellers can be made from a range of materials – brass, bronze, white metal or nylon. Again, the choice is enormous – from two to seven blades all made right- and left-handed, usually measured by diameter to denote size. A model kit will generally offer some suggestions as to the most suitable size for the model, likely three- or four-bladed, the maximum diameter being governed by clearance with the bottom of the hull.

It is important to check that the thread type and size on the end of the propeller shaft is the same as the thread on the boss of the propeller: they can vary in size, depending on the diameter of the propeller shaft, and the manufacturer.

The most popular choices are either nylon, plastic, or brass. Plastic propellers are cheaper, but because they are softer, they will flex somewhat under load, and lose some power. This may be significant in high-speed racing boats, but for the newcomer who is not sure of which propeller to buy, it is probably a good first choice. It can always be changed to a brass one later on.

If the model is a scratch-build then try to look and compare similar types, sizes, weights and so on, of other craft to get a better idea of what will be most suitable. An old idea that is no longer really valid was to use the diameter of the motor as a guide and use the same diameter for the propeller. But motors are now much smaller and more powerful so this guide can no longer be used.

The angle of the blades will have a major effect on performance. High-speed racing boats will have multi-bladed propellers that can be expensive because they must also revolve at high speed, with relatively shallow angles, normally referred to as the 'pitch' of the propeller. This is also relative to the distance the propeller will move through the water for each revolution: the greater the pitch, the greater the distance, within the limitation of the power of the motor.

Imagine that the propeller is being screwed into a solid object. The pitch refers to the distance it will travel when screwed in one full revolution: the coarser the angle, or pitch, the further it will travel, and the more load that will be placed on the motor and transmission. In water, there will be some slippage and loss of efficiency, so it will not travel quite as far.

Because the motor/propeller shaft must be tilted and angled down to get the propeller below the waterline, the propeller will therefore not be at right-angles to the direction of travel, and will also be slightly tilted, which will reduce its effectiveness. To minimize this, the motor will be designed to sit as low as possible in the hull, and this will then achieve the greatest efficiency. Often the propeller shaft is extended to the maximum possible length to accommodate this need.

Many outboard motors on real craft suffer from poor positioning, because the motor is not correctly set at the right angle on the transom. Often, because they use lightweight, soft, aluminium-alloy propellers that revolve at high speed, a phenomenon called cavitation occurs: vacuum bubbles are created on the edge of the spinning propeller, and these will collapse and erode away tiny flecks of metal, giving the appearance of corrosion, exacerbated by actual corrosion in seawater. Cavitation can also occur on fast racing model boats, although more often than not it will more likely be air drawn into the propeller at high speed from above the water.

The Propeller Shaft

Propeller shafts and the housing are normally made from stainless-steel rod and tube, with a bronze bearing at each end. Each end is threaded and supplied with a brass lock-nut, also sometimes a brass thrust washer for positioning on the outboard end between the end of the shaft bearing and the lock-nut. This allows the thrust from the propeller to be transmitted directly to the housing and thus the boat hull, rather than pushing against the motor itself. Normally a longitudinal play of about 1mm should be aimed for in fore and aft movement of the propeller and shaft in the housing.

Universal Joint

The drive from the motor gearbox should be connected to a universal joint, so that any misalignment between the engine mounting and the propeller shaft housing can be absorbed. Normally the shaft will be threaded on both ends, one end for the propeller and the other for the universal joint. Take care to select the correct sized thread. Likewise check to ensure the diameter of the gearbox shaft fits the other end of the universal joint. The gearbox or motor shaft usually has a flat filed on to one side such that the universal joint is held secure by a grub-screw; if it doesn't, then a flat area needs to be carefully filed on the shaft. The propeller shaft should have a lock-nut on each end to secure the propeller and the universal joint.

Always aim to place the complete drive system in as straight a line as possible, rather than using the universal joint as a 'fall-back' to take up major misalignment. A poor initial set-up will generate more noise, vibration, wear and potential failure in the future.

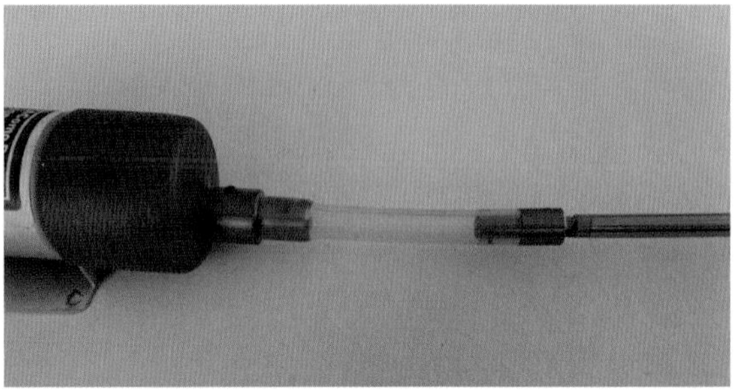

A different universal joint using a piece of flexible tube between the gearbox shaft and the propeller shaft.

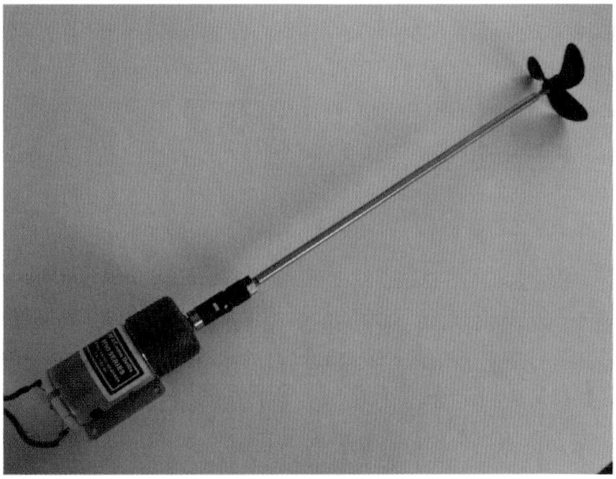

The complete drivetrain: motor, gearbox, universal joint, propeller shaft and housing, and finally propeller.

A very useful tool with all the different sizes of shaft and/or threads to ensure correct alignment between the motor and propeller-shaft housing. One piece fits on the gearbox shaft, the other screws on to the propeller shaft, and they fit tightly together.

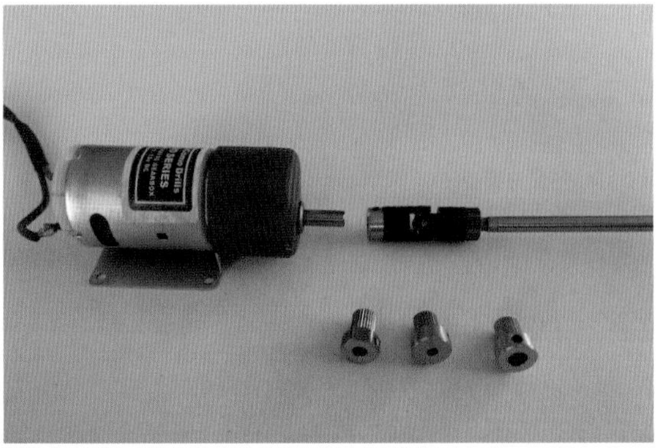

The universal joint: the end parts can be purchased separately to ensure they are compatible with the gearbox shaft diameter and the thread on the propeller shaft.

Some propeller-shaft housings have a vertical oiling tube attached, some not. Then again, the propeller shaft may be supplied with the kit. If not, check with the side-view drawing of the model to measure the correct length, before buying it. Propeller-shaft housings have bronze bearings at each end, with clearance for the shaft along the tube. To ensure water does not leak along the inside of the shaft/housing (the lower end will be underwater, remember), a thin marine grease or oil can be inserted with a syringe before use. Do not use thick grease as this will provide an unnecessary extra load on the motor, as it tries to turn the propeller shaft (and the grease) inside the housing.

Fixing the Propeller Shaft in Place

There will likely be only two points where a larger drill is needed on the bare hull of the model: where the propeller-shaft housing pierces the hull, and where the rudder pillar/housing is placed. Both of these holes (or sets of holes) are either below the waterline or very close to it. Great care is necessary here to ensure the holes line up with the respective shaft housings, without misalignment. To repeat the oft used phrase: 'Measure twice, cut once.'

The hole for the propeller shaft will likely be elliptical, due to the shallow angle of the shaft. Cut this slowly and carefully, measuring and trying it for a good fit as many times as necessary – do not rush this important step.

Particular attention must be paid to the actual strength of the surrounding support material to hold the shafts in place: fibreglass reinforcing may be useful at this point. Roughen the outer surface of the propeller-shaft housing with wet-and-dry sandpaper, to give it a better key to the fibreglass, before fitting it.

Helpful Tip

Remember that the propeller spins on to the shaft thread clockwise to tighten it, conversely, if the propeller is turned anticlockwise, it has a tendency to unthread itself. This is prevented by the locknut, which is screwed up against the back of the propeller. An additional precaution is the use of a thread sealant to hold the nut. But ensure that none reaches the propeller housing or bearing itself.

BATTERIES

Rechargeable Battery Types

Again there is a bewildering range of batteries, from sealed lead-acid (SLA, the heaviest and oldest) to lithium polymer (Li-Po), lithium ferrite (LiFe), and lithium iron. In between is the now largely obsolete nickel cadmium (Ni Cads), which has an annoying memory habit of diminishing lower power charge levels; there is also the damage cadmium does to the environment. It is now replaced by nickel metal hydride (Ni-MH), which is commonly used by modellers.

Lead-acid batteries, being heavier, tend to be a solution where the weight is also required as ballast for larger hulled models; typically they are either 6 volts or 12 volts, and supply at various ampère hours ratings.

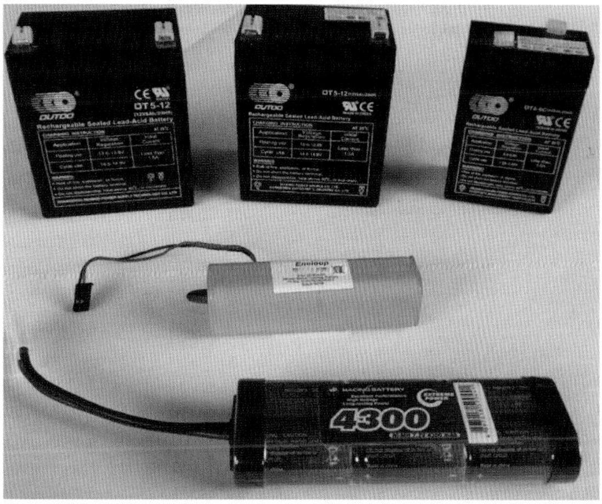

A typical range of sealed lead-acid batteries at the rear of the photograph, and nickel-metal-hydride in the foreground. If the final displacement of the model is known, then it is a good idea to get an approximate weight of all the main internal components, particularly the heavy battery, to ensure that it is less than the displacement weight, otherwise the model will not float to the correct level – that is, the waterline.

Ni-MH batteries are 4.8, 6.0, 7.2, 8.4, 9.6 or 12.0 volts. Li-Po batteries are 3.7, 7.4, 11.1, 14.8, 18.5, and 22.2 volts. If either of these battery types are chosen, the middle of the range will more than likely suffice to start with.

Large lead-acid batteries have been used in cars for many years, originally being a wet cell, rather than the sealed gel cells now in use. Basically they used a lead and lead-oxide anode and cathode (the terminals) immersed in a solution of weak sulphuric acid, termed an electrolyte. This is fine for cars, but not very practical in boats, which could rock about and spill a very corrosive acid solution.

Always keep batteries charged when in storage, and check they are full before sailing; take them out of the boat once sailing is over and you are back at home. SLA batteries in particular will degrade if left discharged. The reason for this is that a process called sulphating takes place in the battery cells during long periods of discharge, resulting in the battery resistance building up such that it will not recharge properly; to a great extent this process is irreversible, although modern battery chargers can help to some extent.

Non-Rechargeable Batteries

Lithium coin cells will probably not be used in a model, but alkaline batteries could be a quick solution for power to the Rx if nothing else is available. There were claims that devices could recharge old alkaline batteries, but the internal chemical change in this type of battery is irreversible, so the claims are highly questionable.

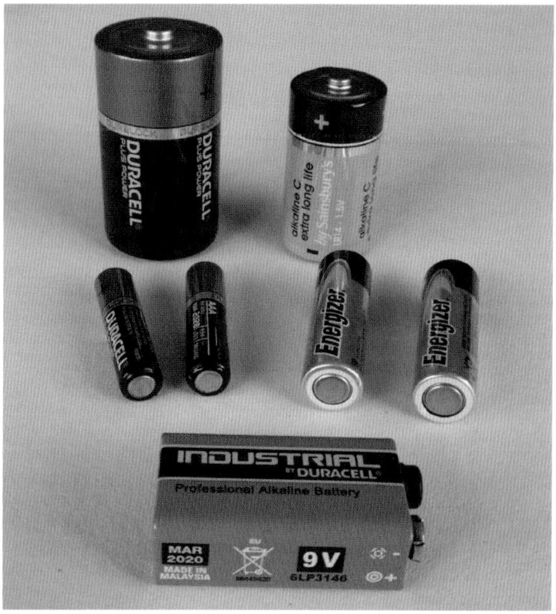

Alkaline batteries (or rechargeable alternatives) are often used for the power supply to the Rx, usually in multiples to get the correct total voltage inside a carrier, with a connecting wire and plug into the 'BAT' connection on the Rx. This assumes there is no BEC (battery eliminator circuit) via the ESC (electronic speed controller).

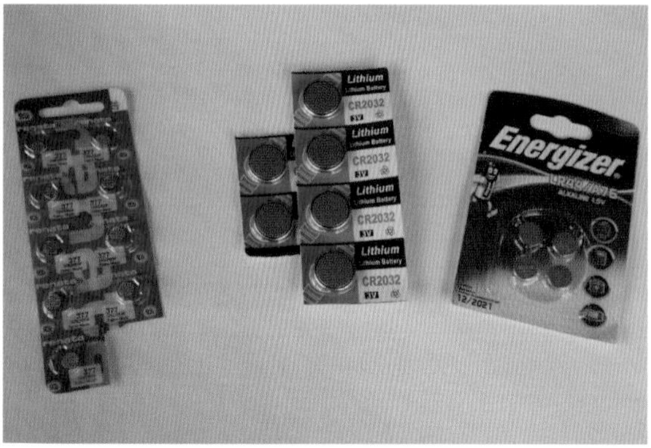

Coin batteries are unlikely to be used in a model, except for special instances where a larger battery is impractical, or where there is no other supply.

Battery Capacity

Any battery has a given capacity of how much power it can store, assuming that it is fully charged. Often at the lakeside a boat will run out of power because the owner has not fully charged the battery before setting out. However, this is a simple mistake to rectify.

All batteries will have a label denoting their type – SLA, Ni-MH, and so on – and the voltage – say 6V, 12V. Using a Ni-MH at 7.2V, and a capacity, say, of 4.3Ah as an example, or 4.3 ampère hours, it will have a voltage of around 7.2V, supplying 4.3A for one hour, or 2.15A for two hours, or

Basic Electrics

Voltage: (Volts, denoted by V): A measure of electrical pressure, which can be likened to water pressure in a pipe. The greater the 'pressure', the higher a motor will spin, or the brighter a light bulb will glow. Remember that polarity-sensitive components will burn out if connected the wrong way round, or if the voltage is too high.

Amperage: (Amps, denoted by I or A): A measure of the electrical flow or usage. The more a motor uses to turn it, the quicker the battery will discharge.

Wattage: (Watts, denoted by W): A measure of how much useful work is being done by the device. Normally found by wattage = voltage × amperage. Or amperage is wattage divided by voltage, to transpose the formula.

Resistance: (Ohms, denoted by R): A measure of the resistance to flow, again like water in a pipe, where the pipe is squashed to make the passage of water harder. Normally found by resistance in ohms = voltage divided by amperage.

Battery terminals are normally labelled positive (+) and coloured red, or have a red wire attached to them. The other terminal is negative (–) and is coloured black, or has a black wire. This used to be the convention for all wiring and is still largely used in modelling circles; however, for modern household wiring the convention is now brown for positive, blue for negative, and green/yellow bands for earth.

1.43A for three hours, and so on. It may show this as 4300mAh, or milli-ampère hours, depending on the battery manufacturer, which is the same thing.

Wiring Up Multiple Batteries

Seek advice before wiring up a model with multiple batteries. They can be wired in 'series', as it is known, but not in 'parallel'. 'Series' simply means 'daisy-chaining' them one after another, the positive of one to the negative of the next. Say the first is rated at 6V and the next at 3V, the total voltage across the end positive and negative terminals is 6 + 3 = 9 volts, which is fine if 9 volts are needed. However, doing the same thing with two 12-volt batteries could be disastrous as the overall terminal voltage will be 24 volts, and some electrical components may not be capable of handling this voltage.

Parallel wiring is likely to damage the batteries and/or the model electrics. This would be when all the positive terminals are wired together, and all the negative terminals are wired together. The effect of this is for one battery to try to discharge into the other, with potential injury to both. Here the batteries will be the same voltage anyway, as the total voltage is not additional. It is possible when using multiple batteries to include a 'battery parallel board' to increase capacity without damage to the batteries, for around £15.

It is not unusual for a model to have different circuits, using different battery voltages – say, 12V for power circuits and 6V for lights and other accessories. Some electrical accessories may only operate at a particular voltage, and require a power source all of their own on occasions, or a specific voltage regulator.

Battery Chargers

When using rechargeable batteries, a means of recharging them is obviously essential, because once flat they are unusable. A simple charger for, say, a lead-acid battery is fine, but in the modern world there are many different types of battery, as illustrated earlier, all of which need

On this model fireboat the main isolating switches are combined with voltage read-outs for the power circuits at 12 volts, and the ancillary circuits at 6 volts. The photograph was taken at the end of a day's sailing so the voltage has now dropped to 11.8 volts, although the ancillary circuit is still fine at 6.2 volts. Normally these items are hidden beneath the superstructure, which is shown raised on an exhibition cradle for clarity.

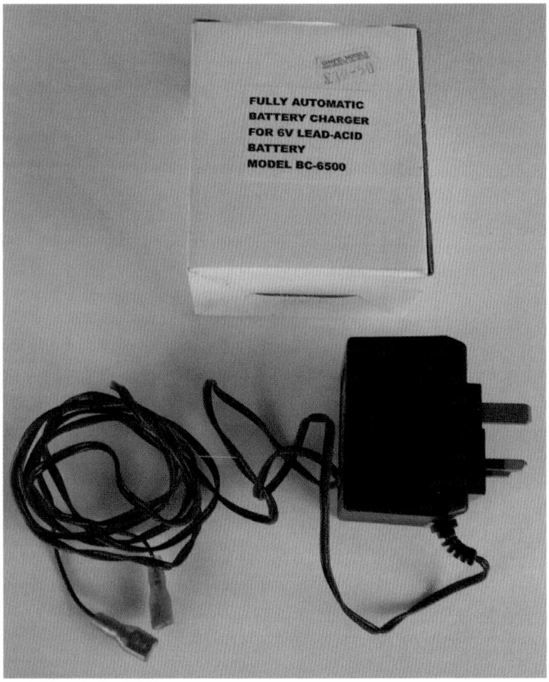

A simple, low-cost charger, only suitable for charging sealed lead-acid batteries.

their own particular way of being charged properly, for maximum charge or for safety reasons. All battery types are charged at different rates, so never try to charge a battery with an incompatible charger.

It is worth investing in the best charger that you can afford, which has the ability to charge any battery type currently available. Li-Po batteries, in particular, do need dedicated compatible chargers and a familiarity with their use, and it is essential that all instructions for proper use are followed.

In the past Li-Po batteries gained a bad reputation with regard to catching fire, but with a little care and awareness this can be circumvented. So do not over-charge Li-Po batteries – any good quality modern charger will ensure that this is avoided. Also, do not over-discharge them when they are in use. Some kind of on-board low-voltage alarm can resolve this potential problem. Lastly avoid accidental physical damage, for obvious reasons.

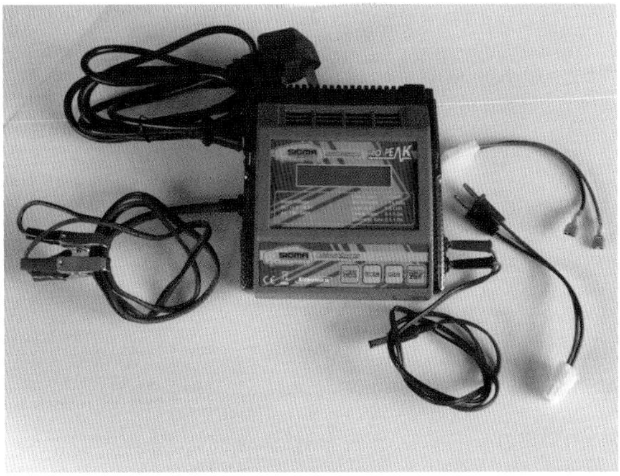

Modern chargers can charge all types of batteries safely, either from the mains or from a car battery. In addition they will have multiple connectors for the various types of plugs and sockets supplied with differing batteries. Always follow the manufacturer's charging instructions, especially when using Li-Po batteries.

RUDDER SYSTEM

Rudder Servo

A servo is simply a small, electric geared motor encased in a plastic case. It has mounting lugs at each end, and a three-wire connection and plug, typically about 6in (150mm) long, to plug into the Rx. If this is not sufficient then a simple extension lead is necessary. Power to it comes via the power source supplied to the Rx, so there is no additional power required. Often, one or more standard servos are supplied with a Tx/Rx package, so check before buying more initially.

Servos come with a set of mounting screws and rubber shock absorbers (really for use in model aircraft – their use in a boat is debatable). Always aim to make the servo removable for any potential repair or maintenance that may be required. They also come with a set of servo arms, and as only one is required, over time a large collection can be accumulated. Always saw off unnecessary arms that will not be used as they tend to get in the way, once the servo is installed.

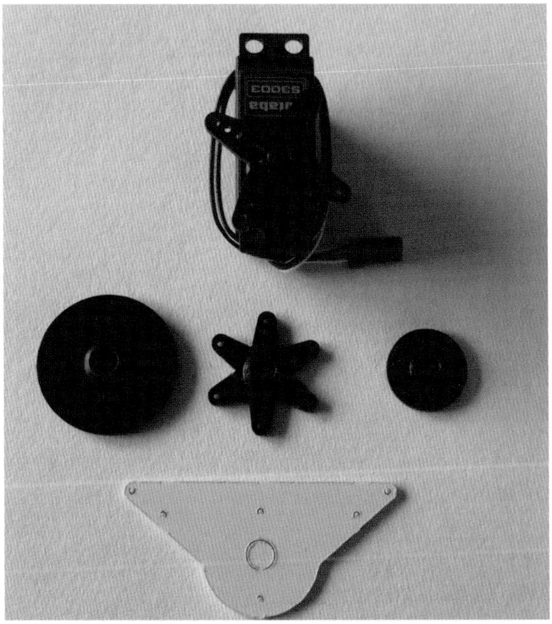

A standard rudder servo with connecting wire and plug to the Rx. They are usually supplied with a range of lever arms, rubber mounting shock absorbers and screws. They can be mounted in any position, and in general are very reliable, but always install them so they can be extracted or the linkages repaired, if necessary.

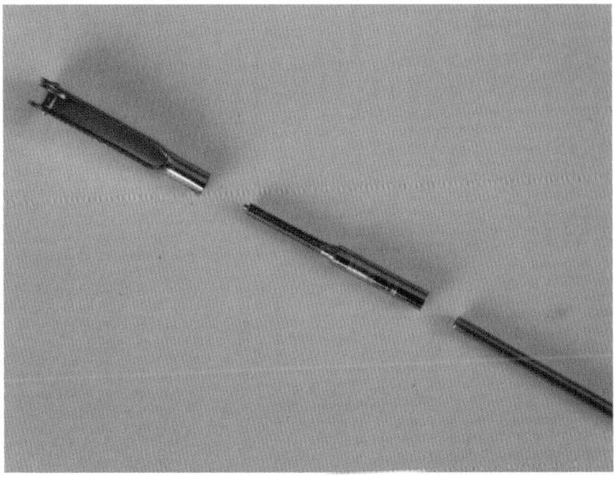

To make up an adjustable turnbuckle, simply epoxy the threaded adaptor on to the end of the pushrod, and then screw it into the turnbuckle to the depth required.

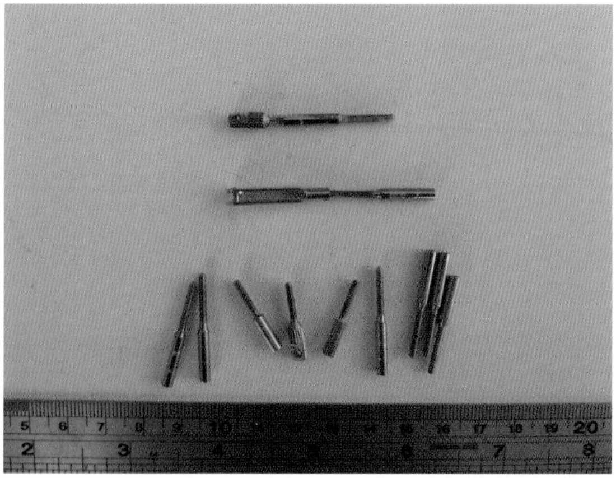

There are a number of adaptors, all of which serve the same purpose.

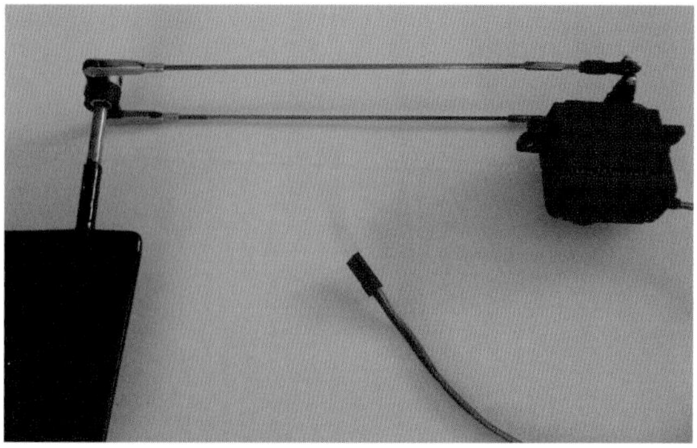

With the rudder post and servo mounted in the model, fit an arm to both, ensuring that everything is central and in a neutral position. Measure and cut the pushrods to the correct length: there is around $\frac{1}{2}$in (12mm) of adjustment on the thread into the turnbuckle for the final setting of each arm. Always ensure that each turnbuckle is fitted squarely and in the same pivot hole on each side.

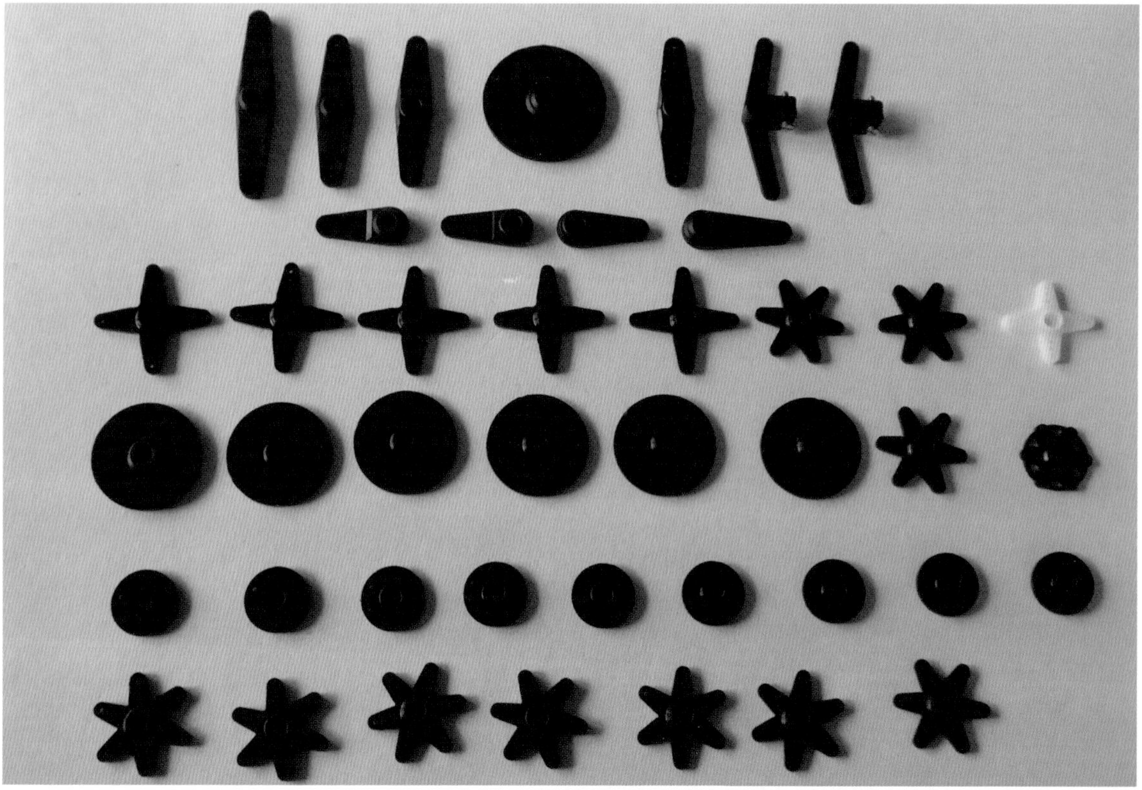

Some of the various standard lever arms available. The ones at the top of the picture are heavyweight arms for use with sail winch servos, and are not necessary for ordinary rudders. The two on the top right are for use to clamp to the top of the rudder shaft itself, and operated by pushrods.

Avoid using large sail-winch servos with large levers or drums as they are not necessary for simple rudder control, and are more expensive.

Attached to the servo lever will be a turnbuckle and push/pull wire to another lever attached to the top of the rudder shaft, to transmit the movement. Ideally two separate rods are better, one pulling, the other pushing, if space is available. This ensures that the pushrod does not bend when operating. Take care to ensure the pushrod/rods are the correct length – normally one end is threaded to go into the turnbuckle, allowing some adjustment. Should the pushrod be fairly short (say, under 3in [75mm]) and the servo mounted close to the rudder post, then one rod will probably be sufficient.

A very useful addition is a simple servo tester to check on movement. This ensures that the servo can be checked before it is fitted into a model, and also the finished installation can be checked without having to connect up batteries and switch on the Tx. It is essential that the rudder can swing under control, a full arc either way to ensure proper steerage. Around 30/40 degrees either way is usually enough.

Rudder Linkage

Many models will have more than one rudder, and it is important to ensure that they all move in the same way, at the same time. This is simply achieved by leaving a third leg on the servo arm in the form of a 'T', where initially it would have been supplied with four arms. Each subsequent rudder post has a single arm attached to the linkage, as shown in the diagram. If a turnbuckle adjustment is added at one end, then minor discrepancies in measurement can be rectified.

Long hulls with a narrow beam are typically harder to turn in the water, necessitating a large rudder – or, more practically, a number of smaller rudders are usually the best solution. The more rudders there are, the more work that will have to be done by the servo, so ensure that a good quality unit is used here to save potential problems later. As usual, cost is a good guide to safeguard this, as the better quality servos will have metal

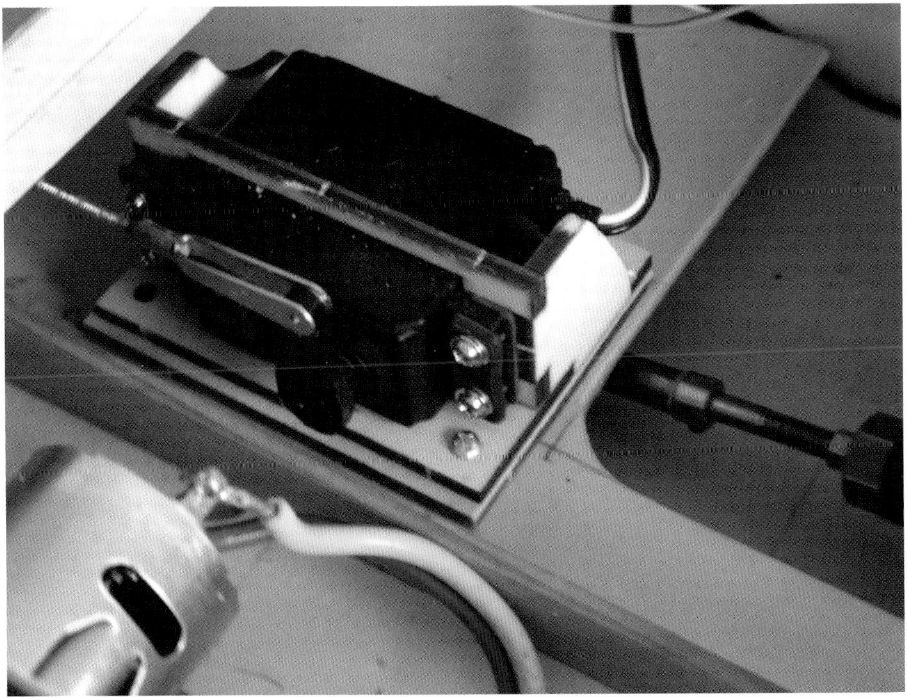

Here, the servo is mounted on its side. The lever has been cut down to remove all superfluous extra arms, and is connected to the rudder by an adjustable turnbuckle and pushrod.

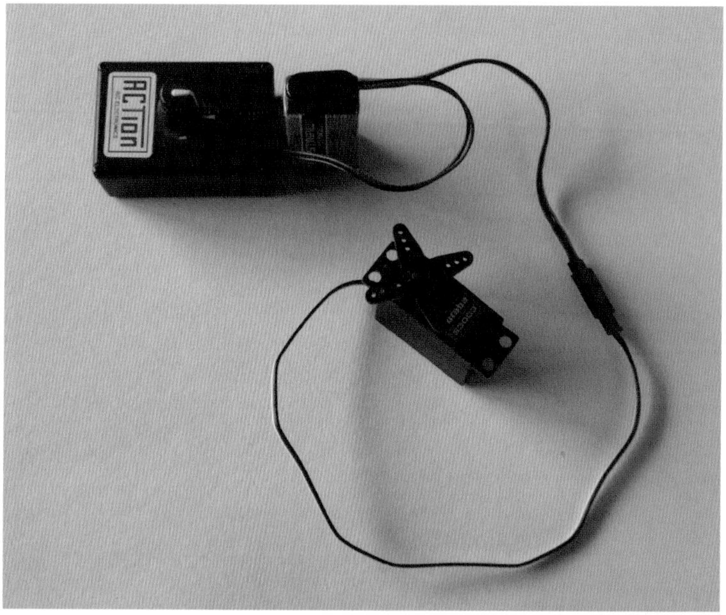

Investing in a servo operating device is a good idea. The servo can be tested out of the model, or after installation, without having to connect all the batteries, wires and so on; also the centre neutral position can be easily set up. There is a twist knob on top of the unit to fully stroke the servo in either direction, with an external battery for power.

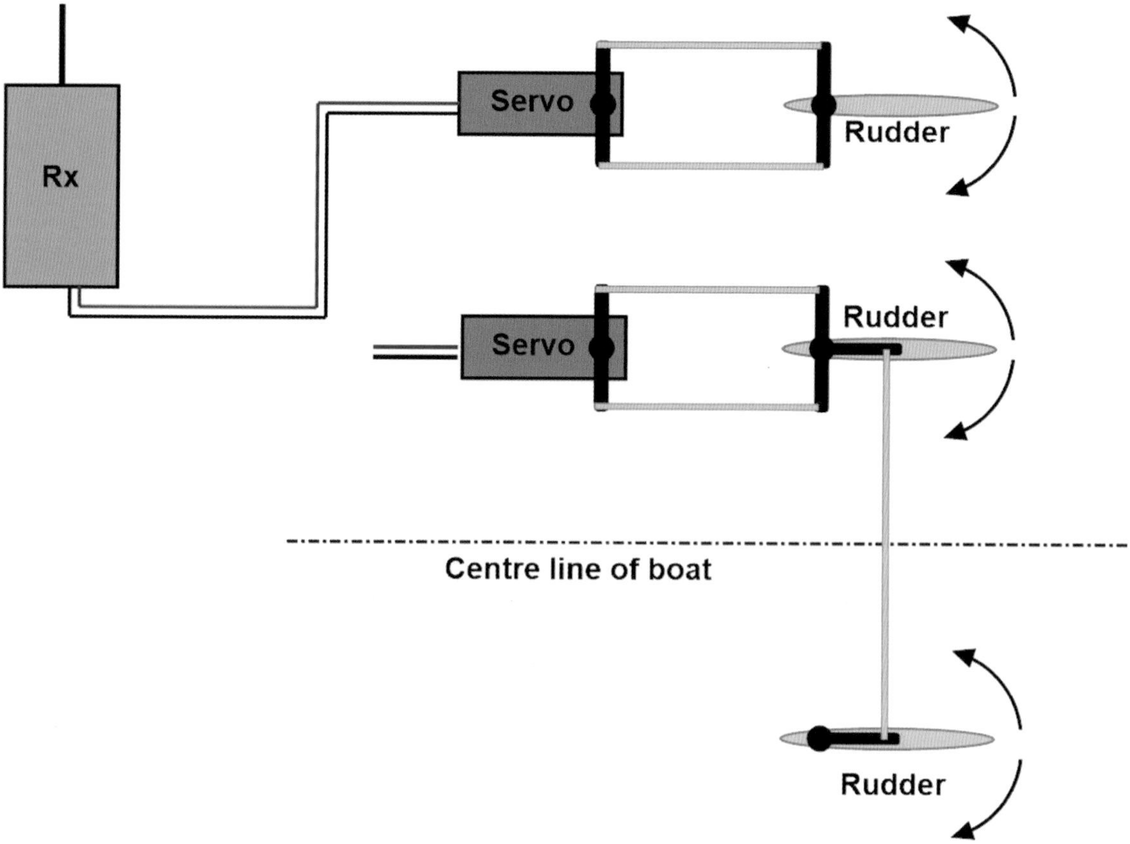

The top diagram shows the standard linkage for a single rudder with two push-/pullrods for better control. The lower diagram illustrates the procedure for two or more rudders.

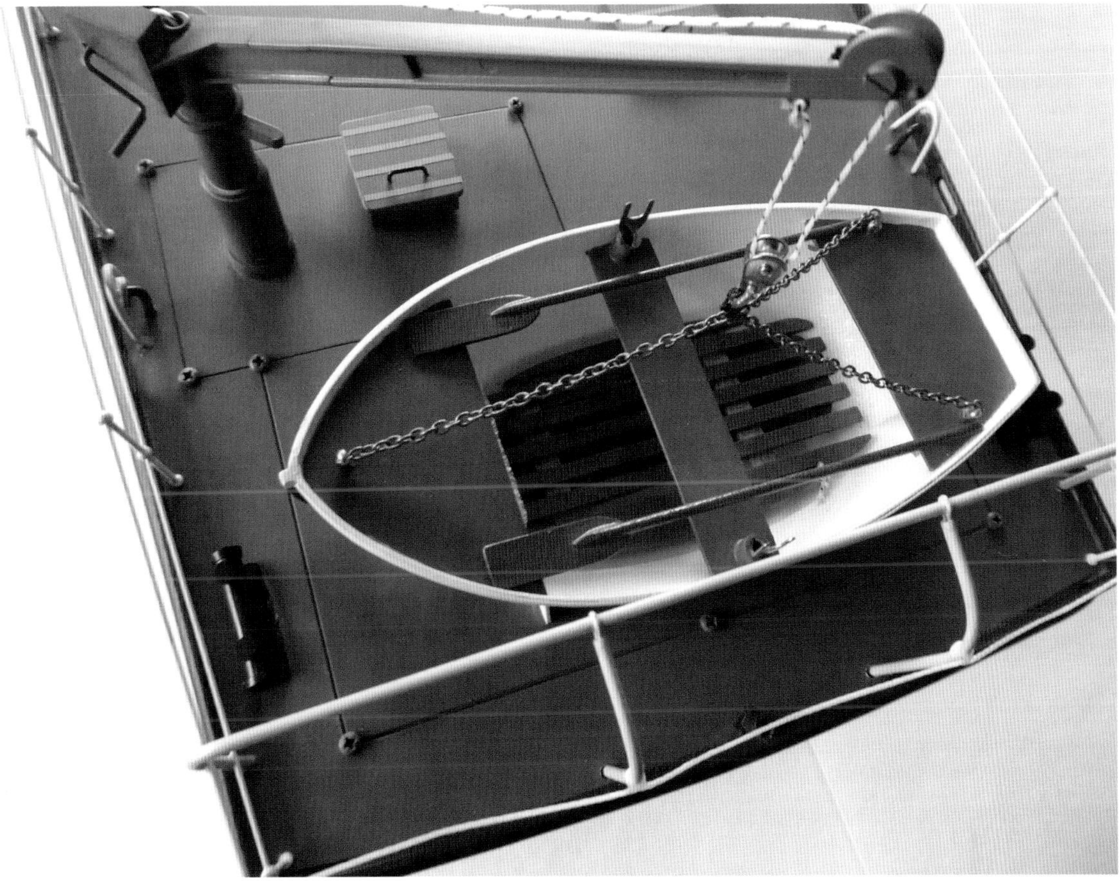

A view looking down on to the stern of the model, showing a removable panel over the rudder assembly. This is an essential feature, as the linkages will invariably become loose at some point, necessitating some maintenance.

internal gears rather than plastic ones, which will wear more quickly.

The linkage on a rudder system can be under considerable strain and vibration, and can come loose, with total loss of control. Ensure that anti-vibration washers or springs/clips are used to stop the turnbuckle coming loose or falling off. Always design a model so that access is possible at the stern to rectify any problems that occur. Never use string or thin plastic rod, as this can stretch or bend – rudder failures are usually down to poorly designed linkage systems.

Servos are often used to move/activate all sorts of movement on a model boat. Whilst small motors may be fine for raising/lowering anchors, flags on poles, or turning gun platforms, when a little more power is needed for a given task, then a servo may be the lowest cost option, particularly if only an arc of movement is required – although continuously revolving servos are also available.

ELECTRICAL CIRCUITS

Protecting Electrical Circuits

Before considering the electrical circuitry of a boat, it is worth looking at what is necessary to protect it. Electricity and water are not good bedfellows, and some thought should be given to ensuring they are kept apart. If a boat hits something and is holed, or waves splash over it, problems will inevitably occur. Always bear this in

General view of the removable superstructure on this model of a fireboat.

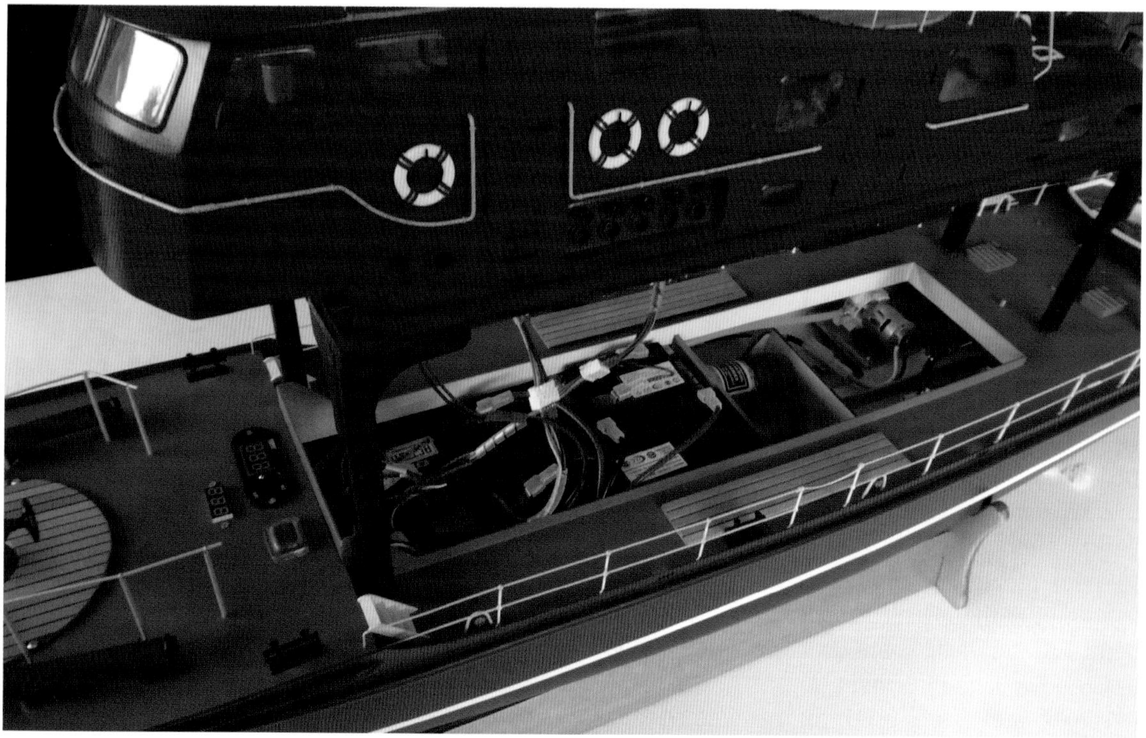

The superstructure is raised on a dedicated exhibition stand, to allow access to the electrics on this complicated model when connecting everything up. Unless there are navigation lights and so on, requiring power on the topworks, then this will not be necessary, and the superstructure can simply be lifted off.

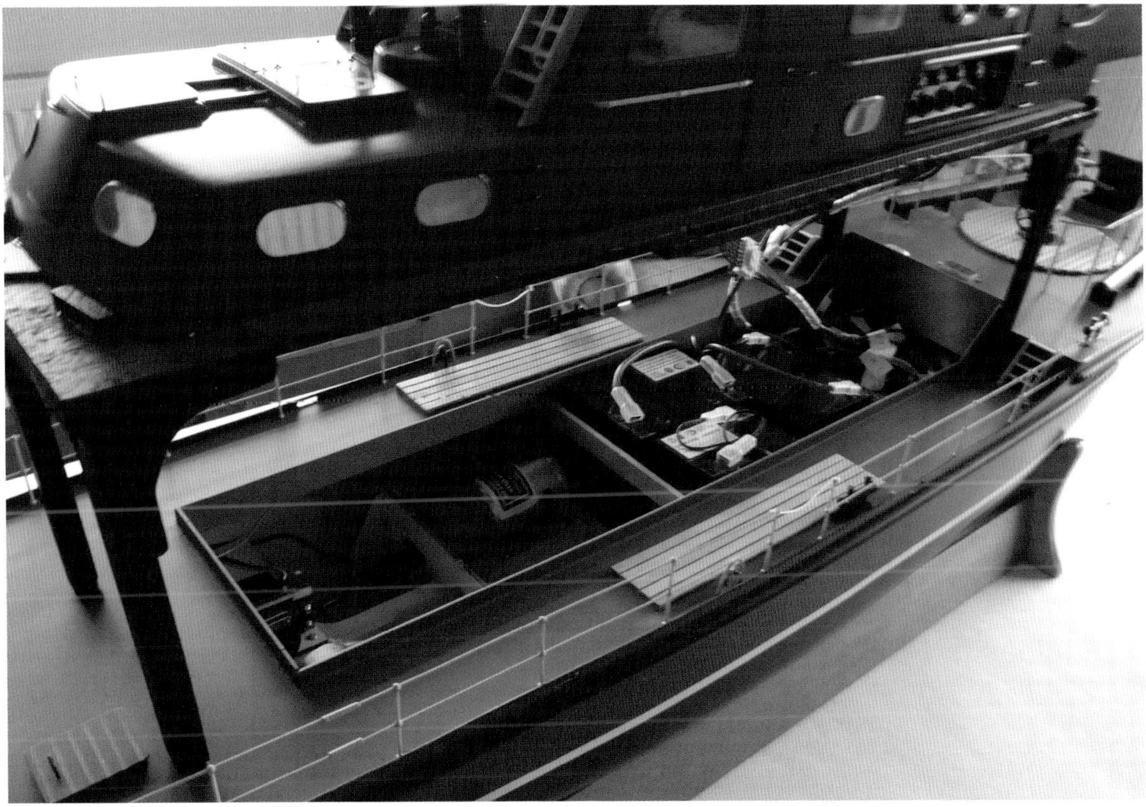

Another view. All the electrics are in a removable panel tucked up under the bow to the right, as far away from the motors as possible to avoid any unnecessary interference. Take note of the high protective coaming around the access hole, to prevent water getting into the 'works'.

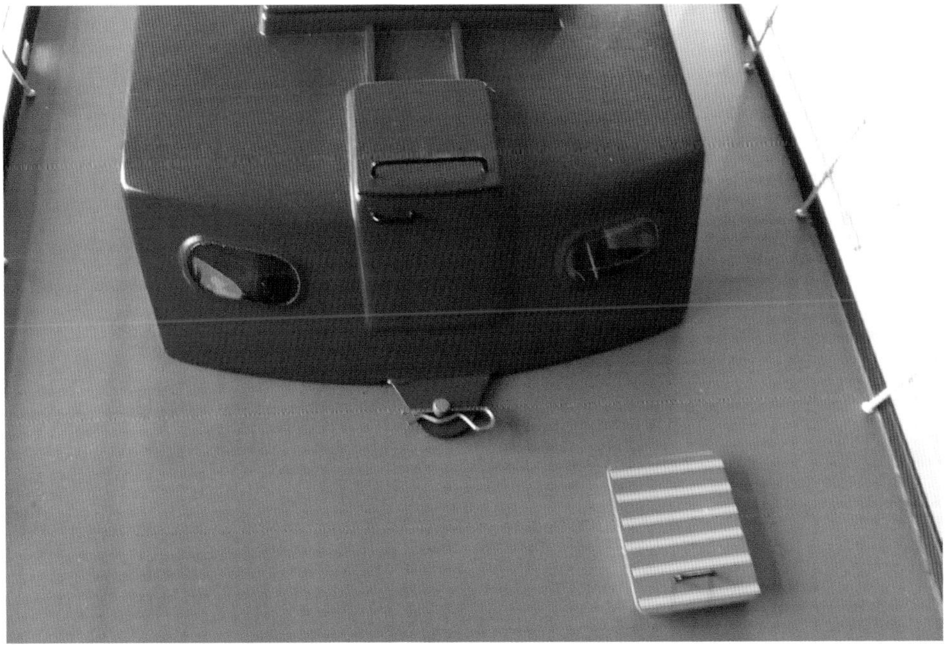

To ensure that the removable topworks do not become detached during sailing, the bow is held in place with pegs, the rear as shown by a simple clip, enabling easy removal.

mind when positioning the various components: some are waterproof, some are splashproof, some will be destroyed in contact with excess water.

Whist the model displayed won a number of awards, it is a kit and the actual design of the removable superstructure is poor as there are no raised coamings around the open area to prevent the ingress of water, which may wash across the deck in rough water. This is an example of a large access area, at the possible expense of damage to the internals. Never assume that because you are sailing on a lake that there will not be some wave motion at some point.

One solution is to use Vaseline all around the edge, although this can prove to be somewhat messy!

Designing Electrical Circuits

Once the main electrical components have been chosen, take a large sheet of paper and sketch a simple square for each component. Next, mark out every connection, and label each module and electrical connection (include the battery and particularly the Rx), taking care to notate every positive and negative lead connection. Draw in the position of every wire, if possible, using the correct colours for each wire. Use a soft pencil because changes will more than likely require an eraser before you are finally satisfied.

A drawing such as this will enable a better understanding of all the parts, where they go, and what they do. Always remember that weight, ballast and balance govern how the model will float and perform – batteries, in particular, may be heavy and may need to be placed centrally and low down in the hull.

When a final design has been decided upon, maybe re-draw it for clarification, if necessary, and keep it safe. In five years, when all the initial wiring considerations have been forgotten, and there is a problem, an old drawing can prove invaluable. If it does not comply with standard electrical symbols, don't worry – as long as *you* understand the diagram, that is all that matters. Either encapsulate it or at least keep it inside a plastic cover – and always take it with you when sailing.

All electrical modules should come with installation/operating instructions of some kind. Study them in detail to ensure you know the polarity

An example of poor design, where there are no protective coamings around the access hole to prevent the ingress of water. The solution was to protect the electrics with a sheet of polythene – inconvenient, but necessary.

Effective under sail on the lake. There is no better feeling than finishing a complex model, and then seeing it on the water, doing everything that it was designed to do.

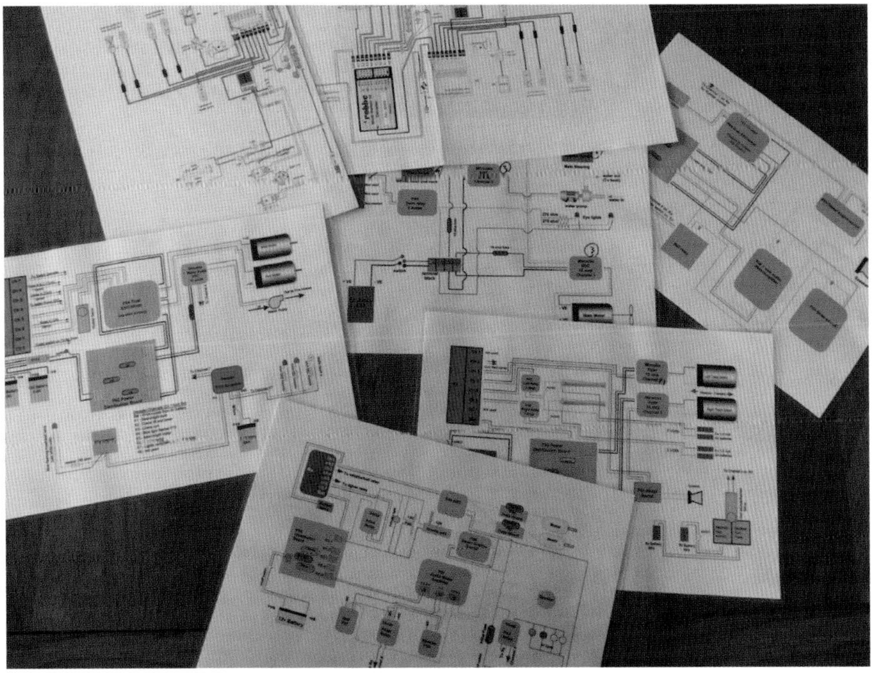

A selection of the author's electrical circuit drawings. They do not have to be this complicated, and are merely for use by the modeller as an aide-memoire in the future, when modifications or additions are envisaged, or when there is a problem.

of every lead and connection. Simple things such as modern LED bulbs will only work one way, so always check, and then check again. There is much information online, so use this source for research when it is available.

Talking to manufacturers, apparently the most common cause of damaged components and their return, is when the customer has not observed the correct polarity on polarity-sensitive modules, and something has burned out.

If you are lucky enough to have access to computer software with a drawing program, then the process of designing the circuitry can be much easier. However, it is not really necessary. The circuits shown were for the author's own use, or supplied with a kit. To better understand any electrical hook-ups, all manufacturers offer written or online guidance to help the uninitiated. It is better to ask what is apparently a stupid question, than to plough doggedly ahead and end up burning out an expensive piece of kit.

Wiring Choice

Apart from being available in a multitude of colours and thicknesses, electrical wiring comes with one of two insulating coverings. The most common is PVC, the other is silicon. PVC wire is stiffer, handles a lower current, and melts at lower temperatures, but is cheaper. Silicon tends to be more supple and will not hold a bend as easily as PVC, so can look untidier if it is not clipped down.

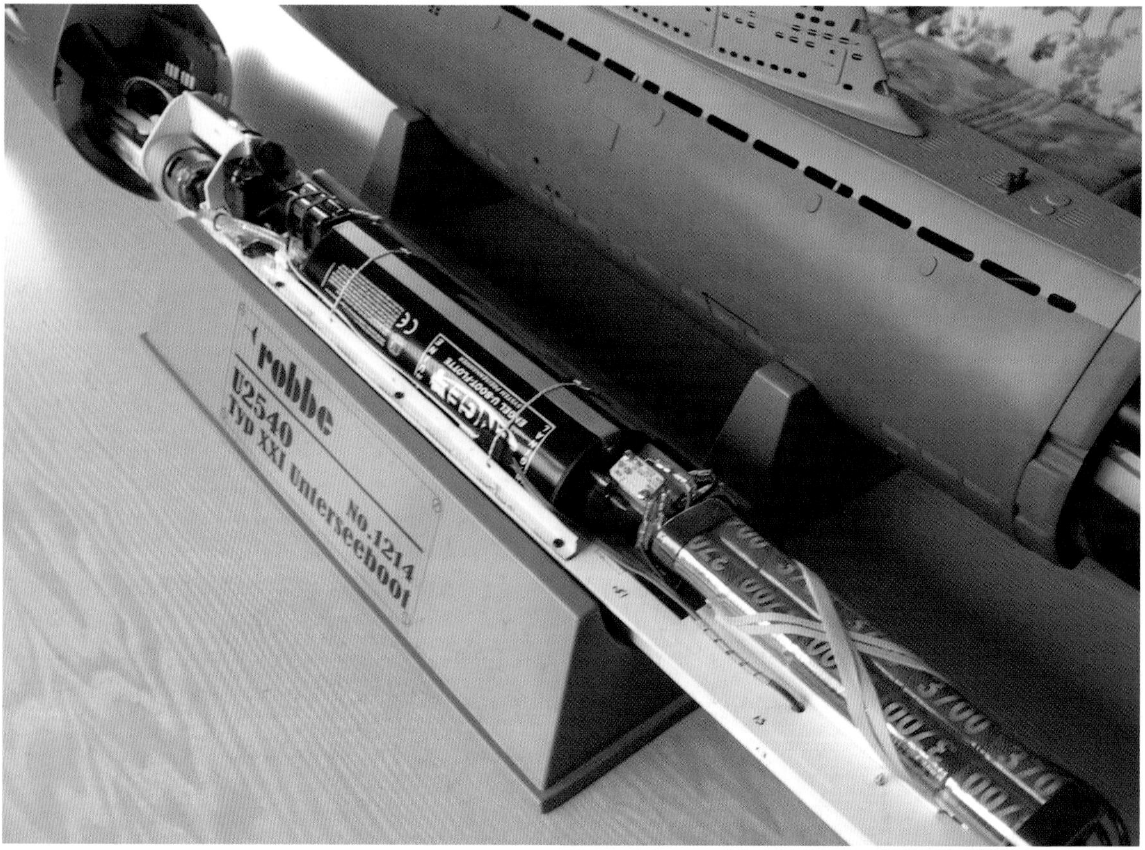

Model submarines are basically a watertight tube, with a cosmetic external shell that looks like a submarine. Consequently, everything has to be very carefully planned to fit inside the tube – it is very congested, yet it must all still be reachable.

Any self-respecting modeller should take pride in their wiring: if it is neatly laid, it is indicative of a methodical, careful approach. If there are problems on the lakeside and a more experienced sailor is asked for help, if the inside of the boat looks like a bird's nest then don't be surprised if there is some reticence on their part to respond!

Wiring Size

A question that is often asked is 'What size of wiring should be used?' This is dependent upon what current the wire has to handle. Use too thin a wire and it may become hot; it may also create a voltage drop and loss of power, and at worst it could start a fire. Too thick, and it takes up more space and weight than is necessary, and is a waste of money – but as a general rule it is better to make the wire a little oversize rather than undersize. The internal copper strands are measured in awg (American wire gauge) – typical wires from a servo to the Rx are 22awg, to give some idea of size.

The following table will give a crude guide to typical wiring available. This is not exhaustive, and is merely offered as a guide for comparison. There are other sizes, and their carrying capacity will be governed by the number and quality of conductors (the actual wires inside the cable).

These figures are for continuous use. Most cables can handle a surge of much higher current

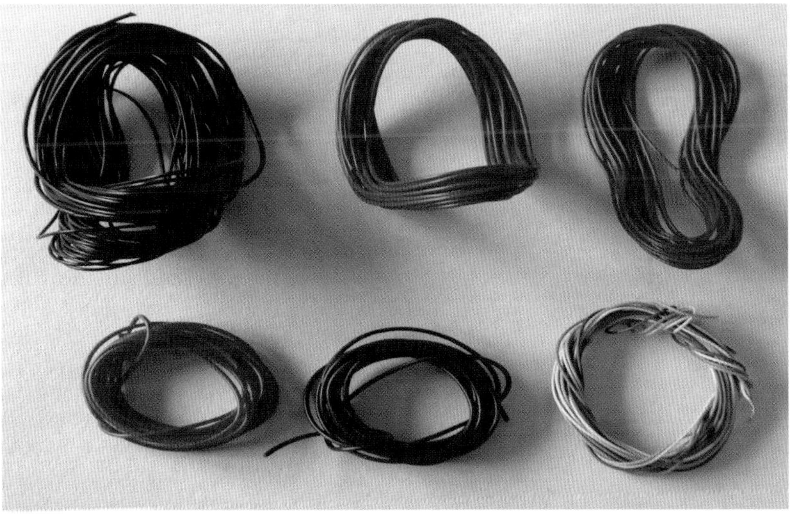

Wiring comes in all sizes and colours, usually available in rolls or hanks, as shown. A good rule of thumb when cutting a length of wire prior to installing it is to make it much longer than judged necessary. There is nothing more annoying than attaching one end, to find after routing that the other end is just too short, simply to save 5p worth of wire.

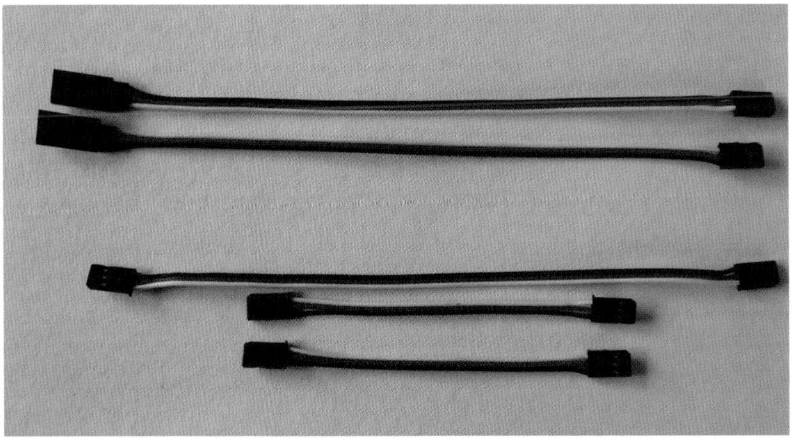

Various Futaba connectors on extension leads to, say, a rudder or other device use this three-wire communication system. The red wire is positive, the black negative, and the white for signal transmission. The top extension lead has the female connector to the left and the male connector to the right. The bottom three are male at both ends. The Futaba connection has a lip on one side of the plug to ensure it only fits in the other socket or Rx, one way.

Typical wiring available

Size	Overall Dia.	Current Silicon	Current PVC
10awg	5.4mm	80amps	–
14awg	3.6mm	32amps	25amps
16awg	3.0mm	22amps	15amps
18awg	2.3mm	18amps	10amps
22awg	1.8mm	7amps	3.5amps
26awg	1.5mm	3amps	1.8amps
30awg	1.2mm	1.2amps	–

briefly. A good quality silicon wire should be capable of being used up to 200°C. For LEDs and similar low-power circuits, telephone wire or similar can be used.

Connector Types

The most common plug types for signal use are either labelled Futaba or JR. Both are made with a profile to ensure that they only fit into the socket one way. Either may be supplied on the end of the servo, or other component, depending on the manufacturer. Futaba connector wires are normally coloured white for signal, red for positive, black for negative. JR connector wires are normally coloured orange – signal, red – positive, brown – negative. Other manufacturers may differ, so check carefully to ensure polarity.

The plug has a tiny window over each internal brass wire attachment. This holds a little clip that, if pressed with a sharp pointer, allows the wire to be withdrawn from the plug housing to release it, if necessary. Sometimes when using a BEC it may be necessary to remove the live red wire if the instructions on the ESC advise this. The same comment applies when using multiple ESCs with multiple motors.

There are many types of plug/sockets available, many made by particular manufacturers, others for specific duties or electrical loads; only the most common are displayed here. For specialist applications it may be necessary to do some research, to be certain that the plug/socket being used is suitable for the duty.

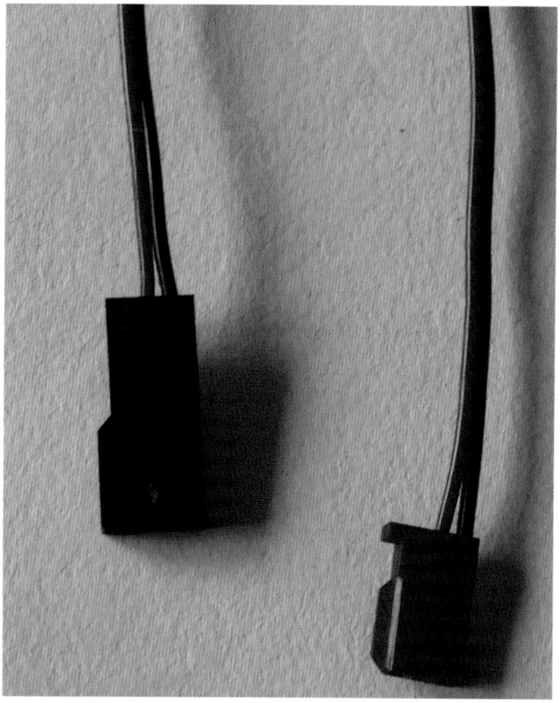

The locating lug is clearly visible on this two-wire extension piece, also useful where there is a colour coding of the plug sockets to differentiate which plug goes into which socket. Often a dab of paint may be applied to each half of the connection so that plugs do not get mixed up and plugged into the wrong socket.

Spare packs of connectors can be purchased to build up any combination necessary. Normally these brass pins are not soldered to the bare wire end, simply crimped tightly. A blob of solder is likely to prevent the pin being pushed into the plug housing. Alternatively spare extension wires/plugs can be purchased in various lengths, already assembled, for less than £1.

A multi-wire connector that will only connect one way is useful where a number of separate signals are required, each with a different coloured wire. Originally designed for use in model aircraft, it is very useful where light electrical loads are being used and where multiple bundles of separate wires are impractical.

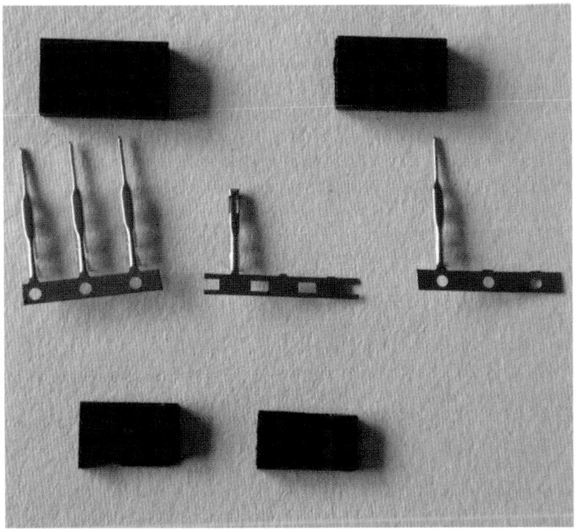

Where there is a need to make up wiring, then a set of plugs and pins can solve a problem.

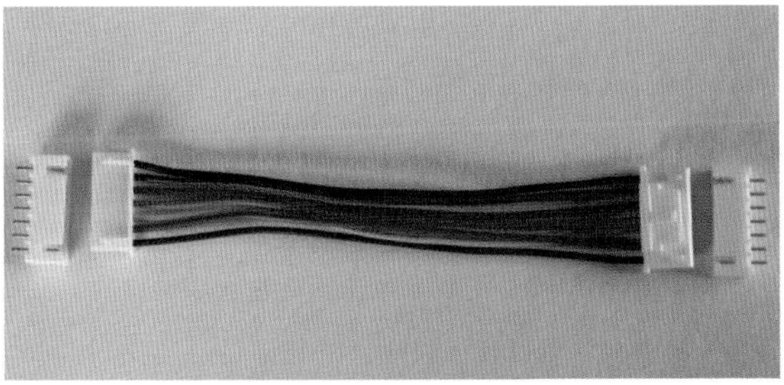

A useful (but short) multi-wire extension, which can help with multi-wire installations to keep everything neat and tidy.

This was used in the author's fireboat, shown earlier, where a number of signals were required, to firehose turntables, radar, searchlights, blue flashing lights and navigation lights, and speakers.

For heavier duties a plug known as a 'Deans'-style plug can be used; it can handle a 14awg wire, rated at least 25amps, and is useful for power supplies to/from main batteries. It will only fit together one way to prevent crossing heavy current wires.

Push-on spade connectors, to connect to the main terminals on the battery, should always be shrouded to prevent a 'short' directly across the

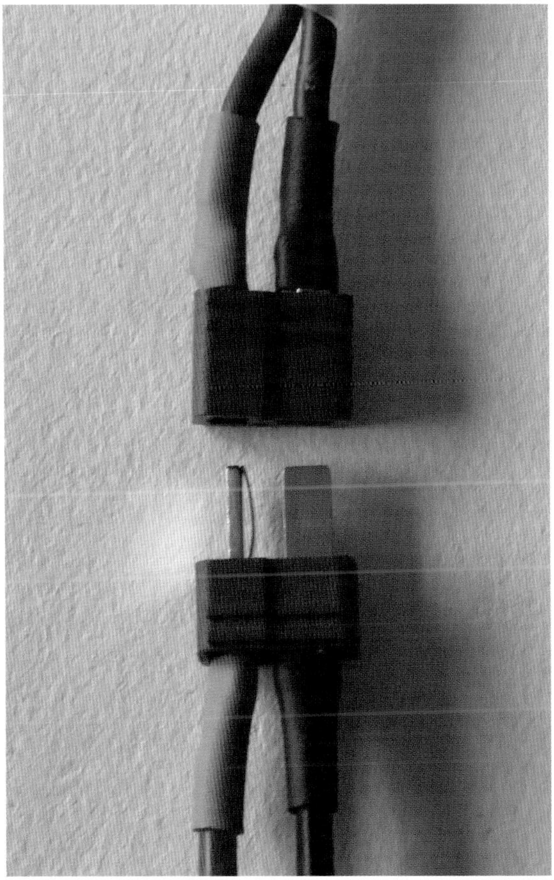

A Dean's power battery connection, illustrating the 'one-way' linking to avoid shorting out the battery.

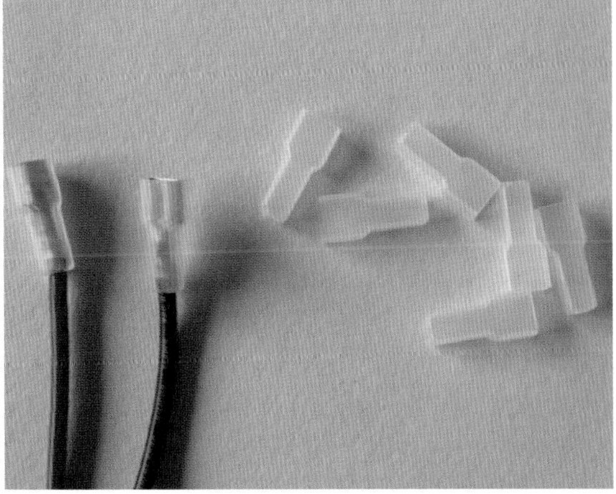

Plastic insulators, again to stop a direct short across battery terminals, where the battery terminal 'spade' slides into the connection.

Tamiya connectors, normally supplied ready fitted to a power wire end, or supplied as a loose kit with the necessary metal terminals that you can attach yourself.

terminals, with potentially disastrous results. After some use the connectors tend to work loose, which can lead to a poor electrical connection. Simply pull back the nylon insulator and lightly squeeze the connectors down with a pair of pliers, to achieve a better grip again. Always ensure that all corrosion, moisture or dirt is removed to get the best electrical contact possible.

Similar to the Deans plug, 'Tamiya'-type plugs and sockets are used in a similar way for carrying main battery power to the rest of the circuits, where the battery leads may have to be disconnected for some reason. They could also be used between the ESC and the motors where a high load may occur. There is a small nylon 'latch' on one side to prevent the two halves separating by accident, and the plug will only fit the socket one way to prevent damage to circuit components.

TROUBLESHOOTING

Keep Wiring Tidy

Earlier the subject of a tidy boat was mentioned. Cable ties that will only operate once are not a good idea, so consider something that can allow the wire (and whatever is attached at either end) to be removed. Coiled plastic is ideal: simply cut off a length as required and wrap it round the cables. More often than not, a single wire will need to be removed for some reason, so bear this

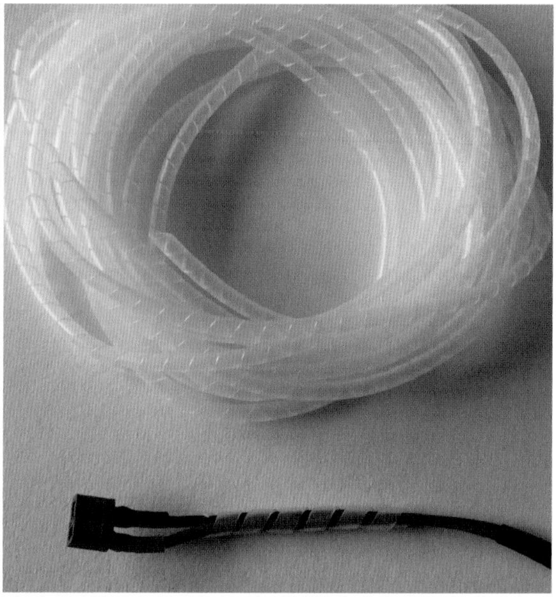

A wire 'tidy' not only looks neat but helps to protect the wire bundles and prevent connections being pulled apart accidentally.

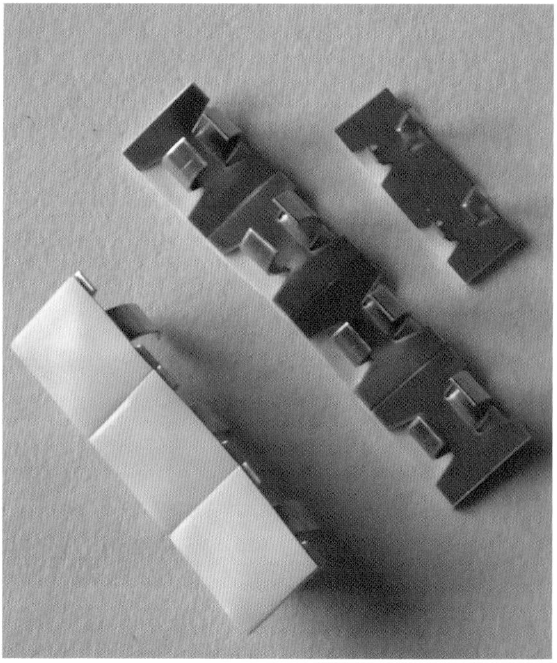

Self-adhesive cable clips in different sizes. Made from soft aluminium, the two arms are folded over the wires once installed, and can easily be pulled apart to remove a wire, if needed.

in mind, use short separate lengths of the coiled plastic, and keep it to a minimum.

For wiring that has to be actually anchored down, then aluminium clips do the job quite well, and can be opened again if necessary. Available in different sizes, they can hold a large number of small wires permanently, once the self-adhesive backing is removed; they do stick better on a smooth plastic surface than a rough wooden one, or GRP.

Heat-Shrink Tube

There are many different sizes and colours available of heat-shrink tubing. It is used to insulate bare wire joints, or even bundles of wire as a simple retainer (before anything is attached to either end, preventing the tube being slid along the wire). The length required is placed over the joint, and then heat is applied with a hair-dryer until it has reduced in diameter and shrunk to the required size. If it needs to be removed, then normally it will have to be cut off and a new piece used.

Velcro Tabs

All electrical components should be held in place with Velcro tabs, or similar, so that they can be removed if necessary. Only items such as motors, servos or heavy speakers should be screwed down where movement, vibration or leverage is experienced. Double-sided self-adhesive tape is often suggested, but can be difficult to remove, although it is somewhat more 'permanent' than Velcro.

Fuses

Earlier in the book, a simple circuit was used to illustrate the connections between the battery,

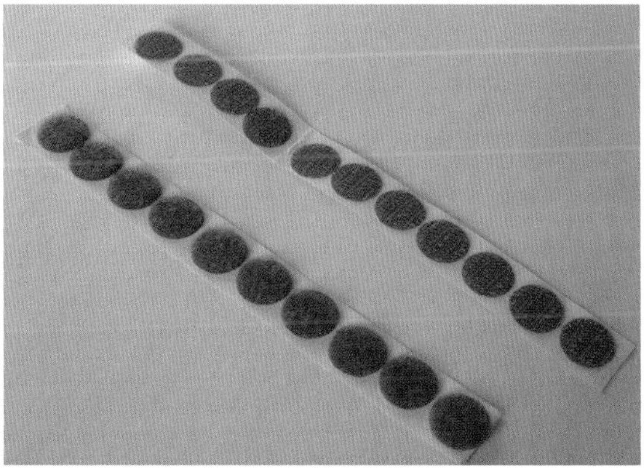

Velcro, or similar, tabs are a better solution to holding components in place than double-sided sticky tape, as it enables easy removal, if necessary.

Heat-shrink tubing, available in every size and colour needed. Simply cut off what is required to cover a bare wire joint, allowing a reasonable overlap at both ends, and apply a hot hair dryer for 30 seconds or so.

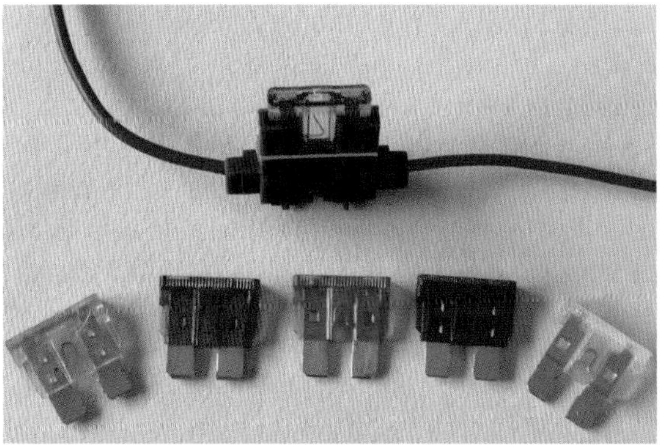

Fuses and an in-line fuse holder. The colour of the fuse denotes its rating. Always check out the maximum number of amps that a device will use, and then go to the next fuse value above that. Some power distribution boards also use the same type of automobile fuse, so again ensure it is suitably rated for the circuits in question.

the ESC and the drive motor. An often overlooked component is the fuse, to protect the system. Modern houses use circuit breakers, which operate faster and are safer than fuses, but every plug in every appliance in the house will still have a fuse. The fuses shown and the in-line fuse holder are normal automobile fuses, available from any car accessory outlet, or model electrical component suppliers.

Always research the maximum power requirements of the motors, speaker amplifiers, or whatever components will use electrical power in the model. Whilst the simple circuit shown did not need any other power outlets, often far more are required, and a power distribution board is the solution. The battery is connected to this board via an isolating switch, and there are a number of terminal outlets that can be wired to other components, each individually fused. More often than not, it will also have a flying lead to plug into the Rx as a BEC so that additional supplies/batteries are not required to power servos via the Rx.

Testing

There are a number of LCD digital multimeters on the market that are not too expensive, and they can offer the ability to troubleshoot a number of different scenarios, including battery health and voltage. Many commercially built units, such as power distribution boards, will have additional lights to indicate they are 'live', but sometimes a little detective work is required to identify a problem. A multimeter can be used to check wiring for dry joints, or other breaks in the circuit that quite easily create a loss of power.

Simpler, less costly battery checkers are also available, although they are obviously less versatile. When using Li-Po batteries always remember that a low-voltage alarm/checker should be included in the circuit. They only cost £3 or £4, and could save a great deal of money and heartache at some point.

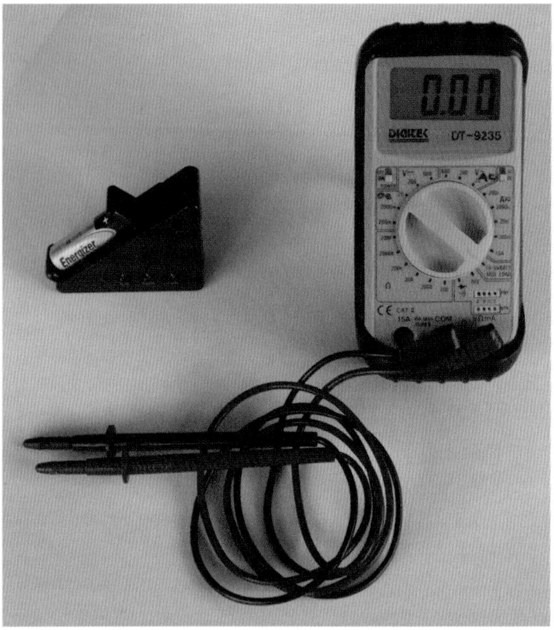

A digital multi-meter and a simple battery checker, each useful for establishing why a model is not performing properly.

Soldering

Before two wires can be soldered together, or a wire soldered to an electrical component, the wire must first have the outside insulation 'cleanly' removed to expose the bare internal copper wire, the electrical conductor. Using wire strippers such as those shown, or similar, not only makes the task easier, they do it much more neatly than trying to strip a wire with a sharp knife (usually against the thumb – with painful results).

Solder is basically a low melting point alloy of tin and zinc. It used to be an alloy of tin and lead; however, lead is now frowned upon for health reasons. Although termed 'low melting point' it is still very hot, and care should be taken to ensure that molten solder does not fall and mark sensitive areas – or skin! – as it will burn. The same thing applies to the use of a soldering iron – always 'park' it so that it cannot roll over and burn/melt something, or in a worse accident, set fire to surroundings.

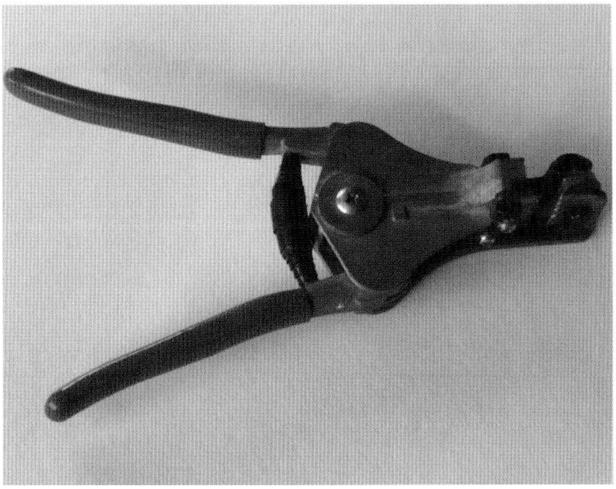

Wire strippers can save a great deal of time during the wiring-up phase of a model.

Various mains-powered soldering irons, each with a different 'bit' for fine or coarse activity, rated from 20amps to 30amps; these are usually more than adequate for fine soldering.

Do not confuse this style of soldering with 'silver solder', which is used for much stronger joints in metal sheeting or similar, and at a much higher temperature, using a blowtorch.

The basic sequence of operations when using solder is as follows:

- First remove any insulating covering and check to see it is clean and not corroded.
- Apply a small amount of flux to the surfaces to be joined. This helps the solder flow and keeps the surfaces clean.
- Ensure the soldering iron is hot enough by touching the tip of the iron to the end of the roll of solder – it should almost instantly melt the solder, allowing some to deposit on the hot end of the iron.
- 'Tin' the end of the wire by holding the iron against it until the solder flows into the wire. Do the same to the other surface to be joined, be it another wire, or a terminal.
- Hold the wire against the other surface and touch it with the iron to allow the heat to melt the solder again until the two fuse together. Allow the join to cool before wiping off any excess flux.

If two wires are being joined together, remember to slide a piece of heat-shrink tubing along the wire *before* making the join. Always keep it well back from the join or the heat from the iron may accidentally shrink it too soon.

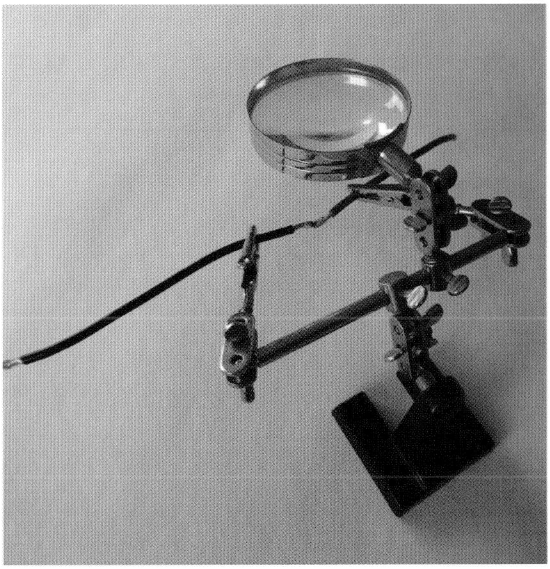

The 'helping-hands' tool is extremely useful in providing a 'third' hand when trying to hold parts together whilst juggling with a hot soldering iron.

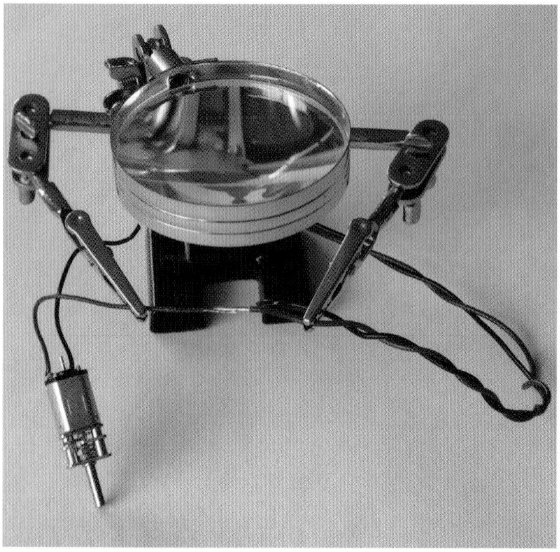

The 'helping-hands' tool can be most useful for the very fine wires in small motors such as these.

It Won't Start?

The following quick lakeside checks can be made when something appears to be wrong:

- Is the battery charged and switched on, also the ESC?
- Have the connections come loose?
- Are the power lights on?
- Will the rudder work?
- Is Tx switched on with enough power, and was it switched on first before Rx?

A more complete troubleshooting guide appears at the end of the book, but the above checks only take a minute, and may save the day.

Chapter Six

Non-Essential Accessories

LIGHTS

Navigation Lights

It is not necessary to have any lights on or in a model; however, if a night sail is planned at any point, then some lighting is essential, or the model is likely to sail off into the darkness, never to be seen again! Many models are finished off with dummy lights simply painted red and green to indicate port and starboard navigation lights, but working items look so much better.

Port and starboard navigation lights are designed to be seen in an arc of 112.5 degrees from the bow to just behind either side amidships, so from the rear they will not be visible by another approaching vessel, but will be visible on either side and forward, so aim to fit these inside a holder to give this arc of visibility approximately. White or yellow lights for larger powered vessels use the same arc reversed, but either towards the bow or stern, depending on their position – although generally for models they tend not to be shielded to give a visibility arc, and shine through 360 degrees, unless it is felt necessary for extreme accuracy.

Two views are shown of HMS *Envoy*, a naval tug used during World War II. It is made from a kit with a number of additions – lights, sound, smoke, and so on. It is necessary to research any original material pertaining to the model (or class if it's a naval ship). Depending on the size, in addition to the red and green lights there are port and starboard lights, bow and stern lights, plus mast lights, that may be required to do the job properly. The number and position of white lights depends on the size and type of ship, and also what activity it is engaged in. It may be worth trying to find an old copy of the *Admiralty Manual of Seamanship Vol. 1* for naval details, where other sources may not provide an answer.

Other Lights

Other internal lights can be used as indicators, linked to, say, a smoke generator, so that it is obvious that the smoke generator is switched on, from a distance. These could be either behind glazed portholes in the hull, or, say, an internal wheelhouse light.

Consider fitting flashing blue lights to emergency service craft, or then again, maybe searchlights. Most trawlers have a number of floodlights for night fishing, which look spectacular on the lake at dusk, or for night sailing. Another feature that spectators find fascinating is a working Aldis lamp used for sending Morse code, linked to a sound card that emits Morse code via a speaker – but that is perhaps for a future model.

Sometimes actually running the wires to a light can be troublesome, especially if they are somewhere on a mast, and concealing them is difficult. One way around this problem is to make the mast from brass tubing, with one wire inside it. The tube can then become part of the circuit. If

When installing navigation lights, choose the ultra-bright version, rather than the standard one, as it will show up better in sunlight. The port (red) light is always on the left looking towards the bow. 'Is there any red port wine left in the glass?' is a good aide-memoire, if the correct colours and positions cannot be remembered.

This naval tug also displays a number of mast lights. Note that the surrounding to the starboard navigation lamp is also painted green to help reflect that colour.

there is more than one light, make the positive side the (red) wire, and the brass tube the negative side, with any resistors necessary inside the tube – remembering to insulate any bare wire, or soldered joints.

Control of Lighting

The simplest way to control lights is to have a battery linked via a switch to the lights, where they are switched on before the boat is launched by the owner. The model is then sailed around with lights on, until it returns to shore and they are manually switched off again.

However, if there is a spare channel on the Tx, preferably a switch rather than a full proportional control channel (although that could be used – it is a waste when it could proportionally control something more dramatic), then by using a relay in the model connected to the Rx, instead of the manual switch mentioned earlier, the model lighting can be remotely switched on and off at will. More about relays later.

Choosing and Fitting Lights

Modellers have used lighting in model boats for many years; originally these were hand-torch bulbs, however, the lights used in the past were miniaturized versions of the old tungsten bulbs used for house lighting. Later they became even smaller and were termed 'grain of wheat' or 'grain of rice' bulbs – and just like a house light they became hot in use, which in the enclosed space of soft plastic or wooden wheelhouses could present a problem.

Now LEDs (light-emitting diodes) are available in a number of sizes and colours; these use almost no power and do not get hot in use, are very cheap to buy and easy to install, so are ideal for modelling use.

But unlike the old tungsten bulbs, which had no polarity such that they could be mounted either way round, LEDs are polarity sensitive and must be connected the correct way and at the correct voltage. There are two leads attached to the base of the LED: the longer one is the positive ($+^{ve}$) connection, and must be connected to the positive side of the battery, or distribution board, or relay.

The second consideration is that different colours use different voltages of 1.6V, 2.0V, 2.4V, 3.3V, and so on, so the port and starboard (red and green) navigation lights will require a different supply, as will a clear masthead lamp, or a wheelhouse lamp. However, this is not as

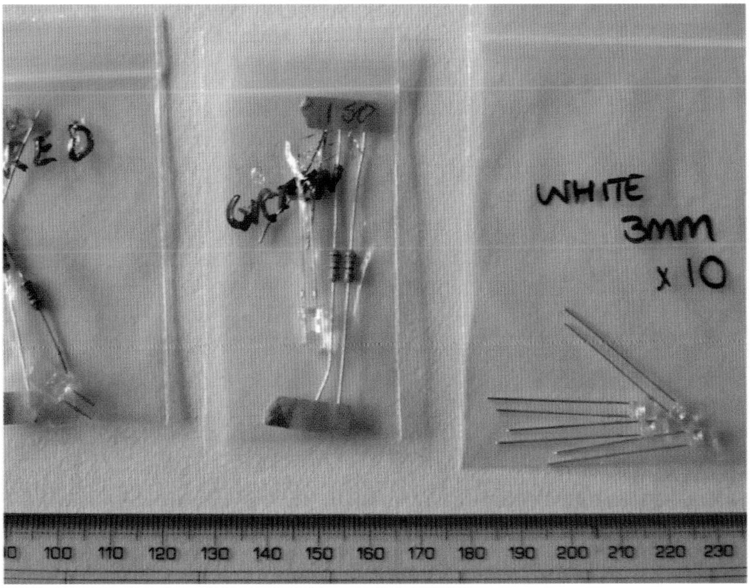

A typical set of lights. The green and red LEDs will only display their particular colour when wired with the resistor enclosed, so it is always necessary to label them to avoid confusion. The white LED has separate resistors, not included here. All the resistors will be dependent on the battery voltage – refer to the formula shown.

complicated as it sounds, as a resistor is simply wired into the positive side of the circuit to give the voltage required.

Whilst LEDs can be purchased with a coloured housing or lens, some of the colours are obtained with a lens that is clear, and the actual voltage (and resistor) gives the colour, although it is not possible to generate different colours simply by changing the resistor for any particular LED. They are made to give a specific colour.

The size is measured by the diameter of the lens, typically 3mm, 5mm and 10mm, 3mm being the most popular. Apart from colour, there are bright, ultra-bright, flashing, flickering, also micro, and sub-micro down to 1.3mm. So there are plenty to choose from.

Resistors are all colour coded to indicate their value, and measured in 'ohms'. To work out the value needed for a specific LED, use the following formula:

50 × (battery voltage – LED voltage) = the required resistor

For example, assume a resistor for a white LED is required, and the battery in the boat will be 6 volts. By looking up the manufacturer's table, it can be seen that a white LED runs on 3.3 volts. Therefore the resistor required = 50 × (6.0–3.3) = 50 × 2.7 = 135ohms. Now 135ohms is not readily available, so always size up, rather than down – that is, choose 150ohms, and solder it to the longer of the two leads.

Another scenario could be a string of lights, say, down the side of a hull at various portholes. The individual lamps should be connected in 'series', one after the other, or 'daisy-chained', such that the short lead is connected to the battery negative terminal (via a length of fine wire) and then its positive lead to the next negative LED lead, and so on until the last LED, the positive lead being connected to a resistor, and then to the positive lead of the battery (only one resistor is required). The formula now becomes:

Required resistor = 50 × (battery voltage–1st LED voltage–2nd LED voltage)

For example, assume two white LEDs with a battery at 12 volts:

Required resistor = 50 × (12–3.3–3.3) = 50 × (12 – 6.6) = 50 × 5.4 = 270ohms

It is possible to see that a number of LEDs could be added, but not more than the sum of all the LED voltages, which cannot exceed the battery voltage, or they will not light. As LEDs use very little

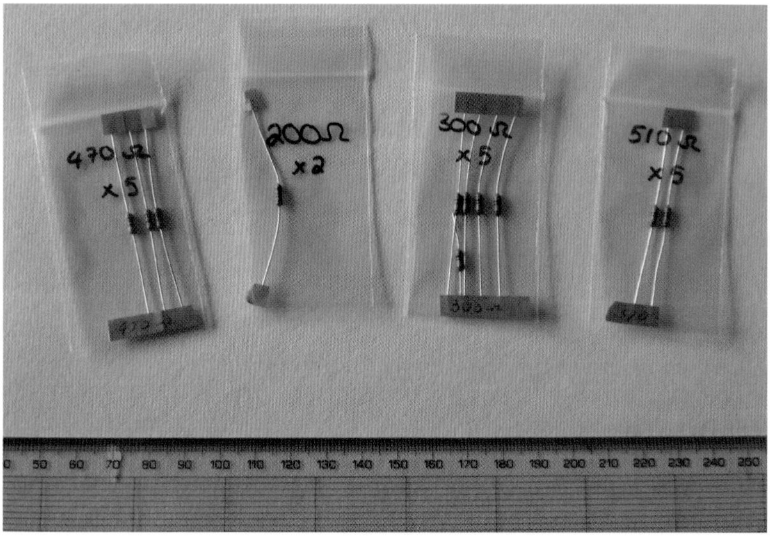

All resistors will be colour coded as shown here, with their specific resistance in ohms.

current, a very fine wire can be used – a multicore security system wire is ideal for this, or telephone cable wire.

For further information, this subject is covered thoroughly in the Component Shop catalogue – their contact details are at the end of the book.

RELAYS

To remotely control any feature on the model, a Tx channel will have to be used. For modulating the speed or controlling the rudder it has already been explained that a fully proportional channel is required, which can be positioned at any point between 0 and 100 per cent.

However, simply turning lights on, or sounding a horn, say, only requires a switch that is either 'on' or 'off', on the Tx, with the appropriate free channel on the Rx. If a number of 'switched' items are required this can take up a lot of channels, which probably will not be available. One answer is to use one channel and a device called a 'decoder' plugged into the Rx, which effectively gives up to eight extra switches, although this can be an expensive solution.

Another consideration would be where the feature requires some power – say, a smoke generator – some of which have a heating coil in them and require a switch that can handle around 3amps. The Rx would not be capable of handling this without damage, so another 'more robust' switch would be required. This could be achieved using a microswitch rated to 3amps, a servo with an arm to trip the microswitch, and a proportional channel to move it, although this is now regarded as a rather old-fashioned approach.

Better still, a relay could be used, rated at 3amps with an on/off switch on the Tx to operate it, via the Rx. The relay is basically the same thing,

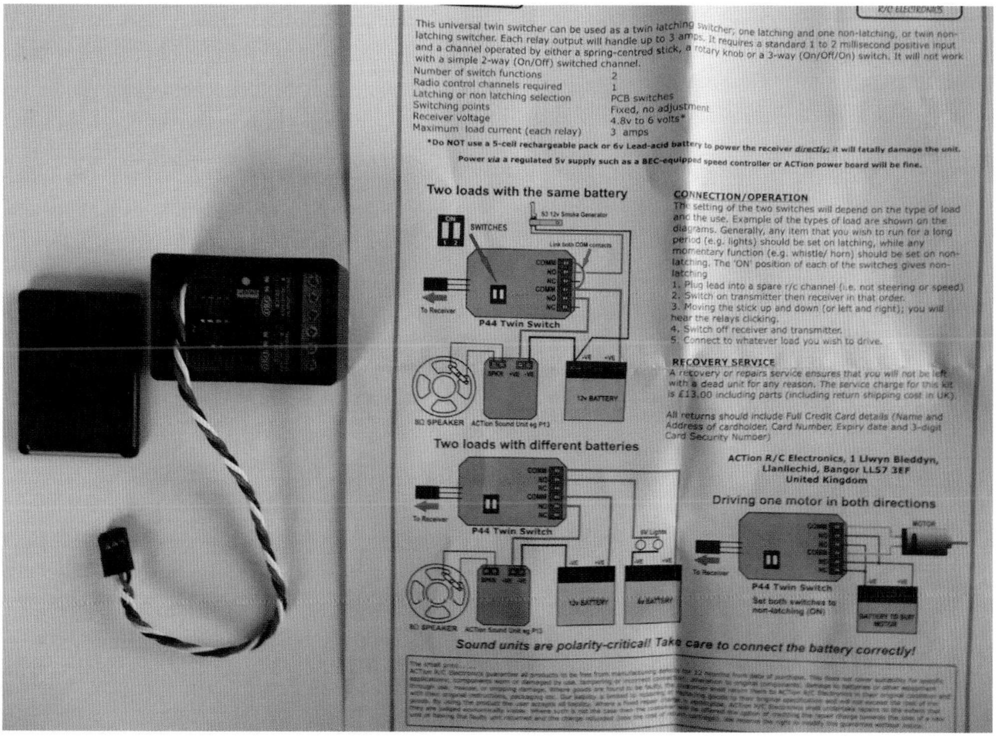

A typical double relay, showing the detailed installation and wiring instructions. Most electrical units will include something like these, and it is essential that they are carefully studied, and all terminals correctly identified, before making any connections and applying power.

with a microswitch embedded in its circuitry, and overall is smaller. Thus it is possible to switch on and off an item, which in itself requires more power, yet only uses a simple switch on the Tx. But always check that the relay is rated to the maximum current required, as the fuses in the distribution board or elsewhere may not provide enough protection before a fire has melted part of the relay circuit.

Many manufacturers make a switching relay, either as a single unit or as a double, quadruple, or even eight-channel switching, within a single case; each will come with a set of wiring instructions to enable the required connections to be made, and how to control it.

Voltage Regulator

Many accessories work on voltages other than the main battery voltage, as stated earlier. Should this be the case, then a small voltage regulator can be installed, set to the requirements of a particular item.

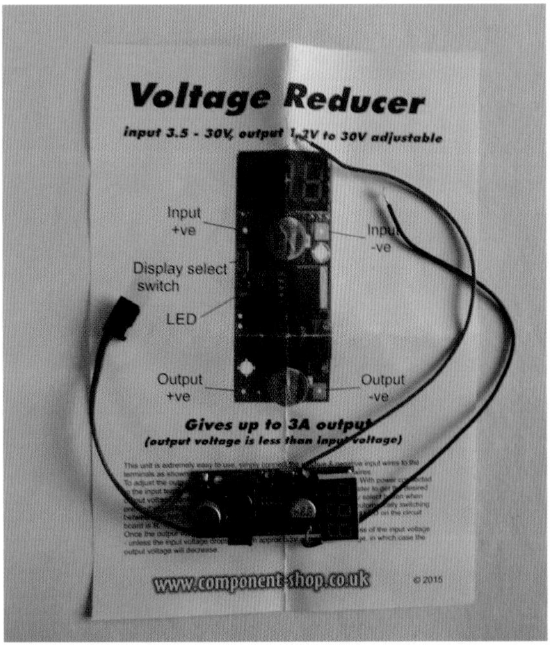

This simple voltage regulator is the solution when incompatible units do not match the battery voltage, assuming that there is no other alternative.

POWER DISTRIBUTION

Sometimes getting power to where it is required is easy, say, with the simple set-up earlier described where there is only a battery, a servo to the rudder, a Rx, an ESC and a motor, because they all tend to work together. But if there are three or four motors – a sound system, smoke generators, lights, bells, horns, working winches and so on – then use a power distribution board.

In its simplest form this is a bus-bar connected to the battery with multiple take-off terminals to the individual items; if this is used, then consider where fuse protection is likely to be needed, particularly with those items drawing a high current (amperage). Better still, use a commercial power distribution board with built-in fuses, LED voltage indicators, and a BEC.

The board on the next page is to the left and a small smoke generator to the right. Much of the wiring loom (with labelled plugs and sockets) is also visible, with additional items underneath the power board. As the smoke generator can get hot it is shrouded to protect the wiring, and positioned away from everything else. As can be seen, the whole thing is designed to be removable for maintenance.

Power to the motors, in the lower image on the page opposite, is supplied by extra fuses and 'direction of rotation' LEDs within the circuit board. Again, everything can, if needed, be removed.

Self-Contained Machine Gun

Sometimes it is useful to keep a function totally separate, and all that is needed extra here is a servo and single channel. The servo arm sweeps across two mounted microswitches, one to operate a very realistic multiple machine-gun sound via its own speaker, and the other to operate flashing lights somewhere. If the lights (up to four) are shrouded inside some shrink-wrap tubing with an attached 1mm fibre-optic plastic cable, the other end of this can be fed down the inside of a model gun barrel so that the end is just visible, and a very real machine-gun effect can be generated.

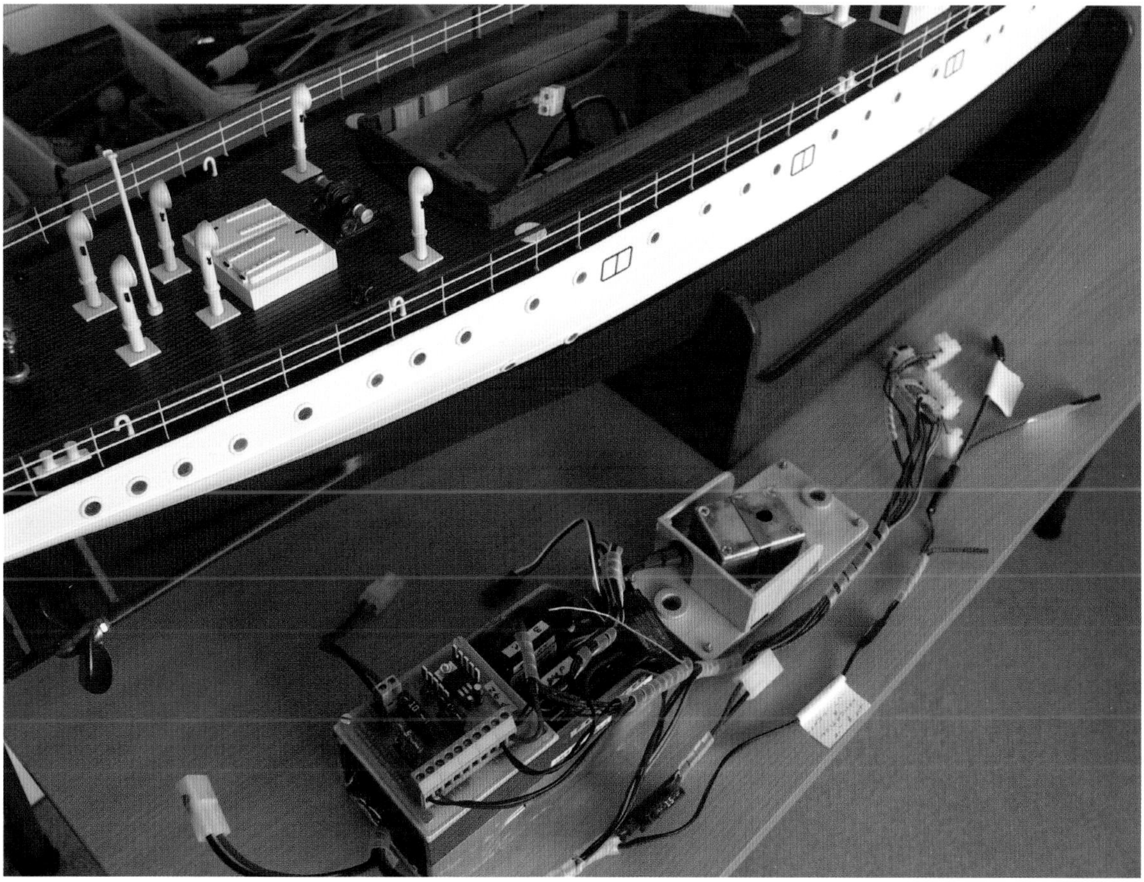

Part of the wiring loom and electrical units to be installed in Komet. The distribution board is at the bottom of the picture, followed by other units, with a smoke generator at the other end. The hole is where the 'smoke' is emitted, via a brass tube in the styrene funnel. Note that each wire is labelled, and the whole unit is removable.

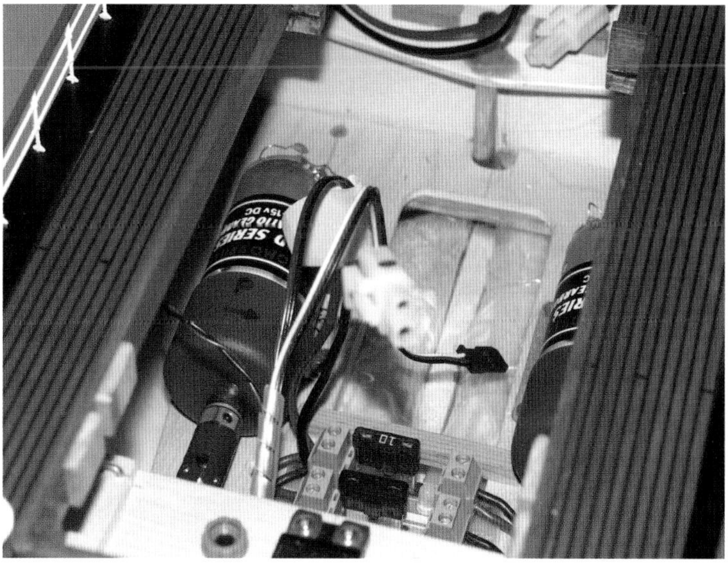

Individual 10amp protective fuses for each motor are displayed. Also note the lead shot retained in polythene bags, on either side of the keel, as ballast. The direction of the motor, and thus propeller rotation, is always marked with indelible felt tip as a reminder, assuming the boat is moving forwards.

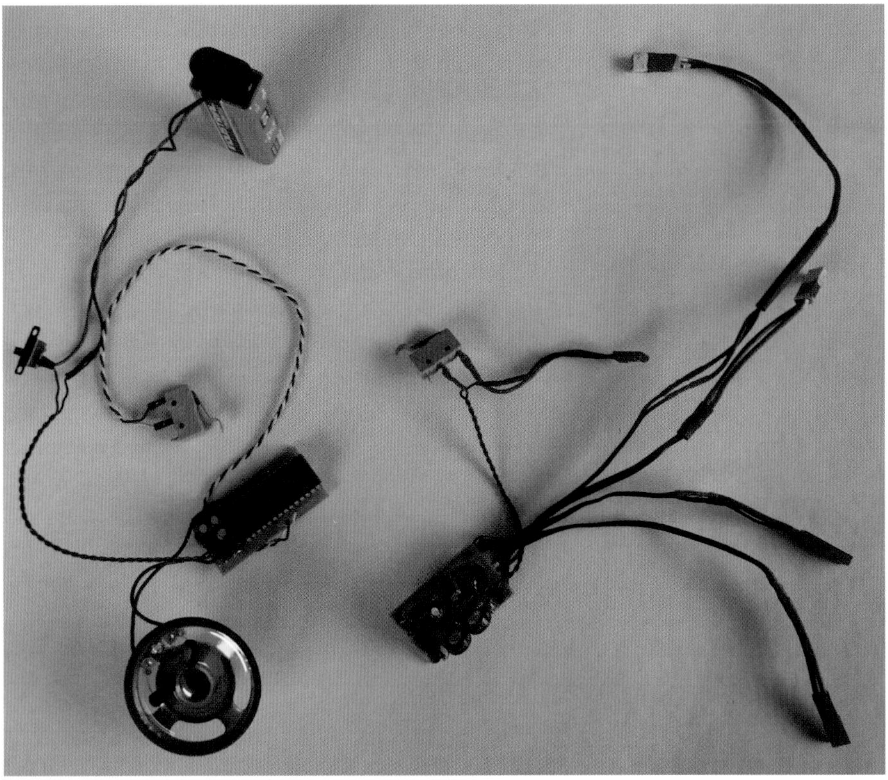

Two self-contained units to provide a machine-gun sound, and lights to provide the flickering of gunfire. The little blue microswitches activate the effect via a servo.

Working Guns

Guns on naval ships can easily be made to swivel and elevate with additional servos under the deck, but they can also be made to actually fire quite realistically. Using the same de-natured black powder that is used in ancient muskets at countryside battle re-enactments, it is possible to ignite it using a glo-plug from a model diesel engine screwed into the back of a robust metal tube (the barrel).

Use about 1cc of black powder and 'lightly' tamp it down, and plug the barrel with a rolled-up piece of tissue paper (small pea size). Using a relay attached to a switch circuit on the Rx, and about a 2-volt supply – or enough to make the glo-plug actually glow – will produce very little power, but a very satisfying bang and a great deal of smoke. It should be stressed that this is not a toy, and should only be used out on the lake, away from wildlife and other lake users, and any permission necessary should be obtained beforehand.

You will have to produce identification, home address and so on in order to buy black powder, so ensure that they are available, should this extra facility be used in the model.

SOUND EFFECTS

With the advent of small memory cards there is now an enormous range of sounds that can be incorporated into a model. The most popular is to link the motor ESC to a dedicated sound circuit, such that the engine sound, which may even be a recording of the real thing, will increase and decrease its 'revs' even including a 'start up' and 'stop' routine. This naturally requires a speaker, and waterproof versions with a plastic cone are widely available. Depending on the output wattage required, an amplifier may be necessary, although some units have them built in already.

This 4in (100mm) speaker had to be mounted as low as possible because of its weight in a narrow, unstable hull.

Always try to buy a complete system where all the components are matched up before you buy them. A number of systems can also have other sounds built in, such as an anchor winch, bells, hooters, seagulls, sirens, noisy chains, asdic, whistles, and so on.

It is necessary before starting that a decision is made about what sounds are required, whether a single sound, or a multitude. Single-sound simulators cost around £20 each, while a programmable system with multiple sounds is £80 to £100. For many years units such as these were supplied with a plain plastic box, and the modeller had to cut the required holes for terminals and wires; however, with the advent of 3D printers this is changing, and dedicated boxes are now available, with all the necessary holes already in place, saving much time in drilling and filing slots in the casing.

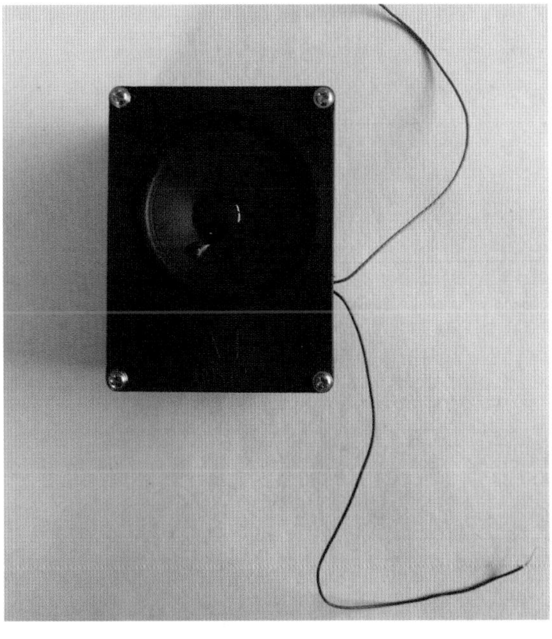

A speaker mounted in its own dedicated sound box – a good idea if there is enough space. This particular one measures 2 × 3in (50 × 75mm), and is 2in (50mm) deep. Failing that, it is normally bolted directly under the deck.

Some consideration has to be given to the speaker position. Ideally it would be up on deck and preferably aimed in all directions (multiple speakers), but clearly that is not a practical solution, and a speaker is generally hidden away,

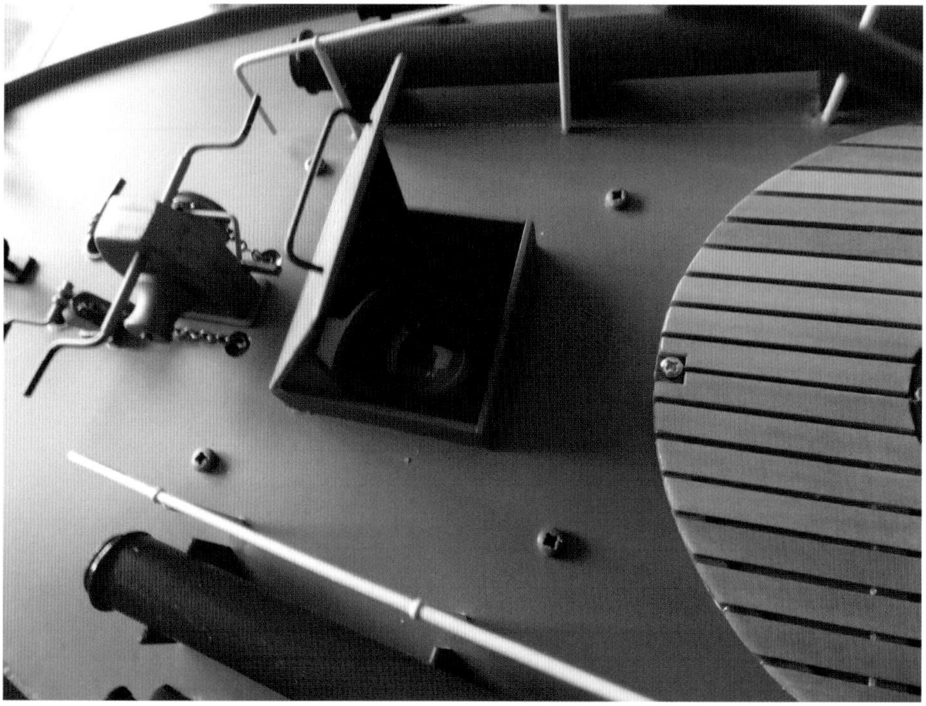

A speaker placed under the deck, and a fake hatchway built to allow the sound to be broadcast. In this case the sound is projected upwards – it is reflected back off the hatch cover and then hits the front of the wheelhouse, and thus is able to spread in all directions to be heard.

A similar arrangement where all the skylights are open to allow sound out from the engine compartment roof.

In this case there are convenient large holes in the stern of Lady Lesley *for the fishing trawl nets, so the speaker is installed on a bulkhead behind the fish hold.*

either below the deck level or in a wheelhouse, or maybe a gun turret.

Speakers produce a better sound if they are in a box, but from a practical standpoint there may not be enough space. As a general guide a 2in- (50mm-) diameter speaker will give an adequate output, although if there is enough space a 4in (100mm) could provide some spectacular sound, given a good amplifier back-up. There is a heavy magnet in a speaker, so if it is planned to install a large one far forward under the bow, say, consider what effect this will have on the trim balance and buoyancy.

SMOKE GENERATORS

Smoke or steam generators come in all shapes and sizes. Some use water as a medium, others use a thin oil, most also use a reasonable amount of power – so if a smoke generator is a consideration, ensure that the chosen electronics will be able to cope with the power demand. Also, as some can get quite hot in operation, ensure that they are kept well away from any part of the boat construction that could be damaged.

Some include a fan to force the 'smoke' where it is required to go – that is, up a smoke stack; if not, then the small fans used to cool computer chips can be used as they already work on the normal voltages in the model, and they will also help to cool the smoke generator casing somewhat. Often the smoke stack in a model is a plastic forming, so a brass inner false funnel may help protect the plastic from deforming.

It is a good idea to whip the inner funnel with a coarse string as an insulator, if it has to be removed to disassemble the model after sailing, as the brass tube can get quite hot and burn fingers.

A simple solution if a smoke effect is required is to have a metal internal in the smoke stack, a cigar tube maybe, and burn an incense stick, or similar – but beware of strange looks from passers-by! Alternatively, explore the world of model railway enthusiasts, who have designed some very effective miniature smoke generators for their passion.

MOTOR MIXERS

When multiple motors are used, particularly in naval warships where the hull is long and narrow to give good design speed, unless large out-of-scale rudders are employed, then a 'motor mixer' is worth consideration. It is connected to the rudder and the motor ESCs to enable the model to turn in a tighter radius.

This is achieved by modulating the speeds of the motors as the rudder is turned. With a turn to port (left), the starboard motors increase speed whilst the port motors reduce speed, thereby pushing the stern around more effectively.

Another way of achieving high manoeuvrability, apart from using bow thrusters, mentioned earlier in the text, is by operating a paddle steamer with independent motors, rather than a common shaft connected to both paddles. The shaft is then split with a toothed pulley drive to two separate motors that can operate together, or in opposite directions, the result being that the model can be made to rotate about its own centre point, almost making the rudder superfluous.

A device called a 'Kort' nozzle, which shrouds the propeller, can be made to swivel vertically on a right-angled propeller drive. They are used to great effect on harbour tugs where great manoeuvrability is essential, but do require some engineering skill from the modeller. Likewise, rudder systems that are double hinged to give greater 'bite' to the rudder, called a 'Becker Flap' rudder, could be an interesting challenge for a future model.

The paddle steamer Glasgow, *suitably modified to have separate driveshafts and motors to each paddle, to allow better manoeuvrability. She had to be very accurately balanced across her beam, to ensure both paddles had the same 'bite' in the water.*

CAMERAS

With regard to model boats on the water, there is little need for still cameras to be placed in the boat itself, as it is much simpler to take pictures with a telephoto or zoom lens from a distance, if that is what is required. However, if pictures of the model itself are wanted, always try to get as low down as possible, to gain the same perspective as would be the case when viewing the real thing.

If taking a video of a model boat in motion, remember that in effect time is at a different pace – that is, it is speeded up. A model easily rocks about in the small waves on a lake, and if this is translated into the movement of a full-sized boat, most of the passengers would likely be thrown overboard by the motion. Consequently, if it is possible to slow down the video, then the movement of the model will look far more realistic.

The first photograph is typical: if this were a real motor torpedo boat, then this picture would have to be taken from a helicopter or a drone, whilst the second, as a close-up, is almost real.

Today there are many tiny video cameras, and these can make a very interesting hobby in their own right. The resulting movement and low-down perspective when mounted in a model boat or submarine (with a waterproof camera in clear water) can produce excellent results. The swan in

A good picture of a model motor torpedo boat, which would have been much better at a lower angle.

A close-up of the bridge on the motor torpedo boat. The figures are around 2in (50mm) tall, to offer some idea of scale. Including detail such as this can really bring a model to life, as long as the scale of all additions are the same. Putting a 'giant' figure into the model just because it is available simply looks ridiculous.

This miniature video camera fits inside the little cygnet attached to the back of the swan. It provides good close-ups of wildlife, although the camera has to be turned on before putting it on the water, so a lot of editing is necessary. The alternative would be a much more complex remotely controlled system.

'Cygnet-cam' on its way to try to approach some other waterfowl.

the photographs is an example, where the camera is concealed inside the little cygnet (for anyone who is an avid bird watcher it is actually a duckling, as unfortunately a model cygnet was not available).

The swan enabled the camera to approach any wildlife on the lake and get close-ups that would normally not be possible, although it is necessary to video when the lake is flat calm with little wind, to keep the camera steady.

FIGURES AND SCALE

Today it is possible to have virtually any figure or item included on a model to supply greater detail and interest. What is more important is to ensure that whatever the item, it is at the same scale as the model. Even some fittings actually supplied with a kit can on occasion be to the wrong scale.

If inserting military figures that have to be painted, check out the insignia and uniforms before painting, so that it is correct, as often they will be supplied unpainted. Food and cutlery items, normally used by enthusiasts for model dolls' houses, are a ready source of inspiration. Likewise fish and fish boxes for trawlers, fuel drums, coiled rope, ammunition and so on, can be had from specialist model makers. Better still, make and design your own – it can prove to be a great deal less expensive, and provide an enormous amount of satisfaction.

Even a good kit manufacturer can supply the wrong scale item at times – obviously this ship's wheel was never going to fit inside the wheelhouse. If a kit is made in the UK, it is usually very easy to get a component replaced, although sometimes if it comes from overseas then it may take some time.

An overhead view, looking into the wheelhouse of Lady Lesley, *with the roof removed. The crew are busy making a cup of coffee to wash down the pasties, whilst the ship's dog looks on expectantly. All these items are available at reasonable cost and really add life, and fun, to the scene.*

Always check the scale of any figures so that they match the scale of the model. Many are either oversize or undersize and will not look correct to the eye. Most scales are catered for throughout the normal range of models.

Chapter Seven

Building an Off-the-Shelf Kit of the Steam Yacht *Komet*

CONSTRUCTION OF *KOMET*

Most models will have a history, and in fact many are built *because of* their history, either to the modeller, or as the result of some historical battle or era. Combine this with an elegant hull design and a fascinating period in time, and it is immediately apparent why there is a kit for this elegant steam yacht.

Komet was built in the shipyards of Bremer Vulcan in Vegesack, Germany, in 1911. She was built for the Governor of German New Guinea to control the various local islands of the German Empire of the time. At the outbreak of World War I she was commissioned into the German Navy, although she should have been surrendered to the Australian forces. Instead, she went into hiding, but was soon discovered by a passing gunboat, the *Nusa*. Without a shot being fired she was captured and recommissioned into the Royal Australian Navy, as the sloop HMAS *Una* for the rest of the war.

Little used, apart from being the official yacht of the Prince of Wales in 1920 to inspect the Australian fleet, she was sold as a pilot vessel in 1925, and yet again renamed *Akuna*, until 1953. In 1954/55 she was broken up for scrap. All that now remains is one of her original anchors as a memorial on the foreshore in Queenscliff, Victoria, and there is a ship's wheel in Wyuna, donated by the Port Phillip Pilot Service.

The Kit

It is not suggested that this kit is a 'starter' kit for someone who is new to making model boats – in fact even the manufacturers regard it as only suitable for a very experienced modeller: so take care, it should not be a first choice. However, the same principles apply to more modest models as to complicated ones, which is that they will simply take longer to build. The only difference is that there is more to consider, when previous experience and skills may need to be called upon. Start off with a single motor, and leave all the 'bells and whistles' to a future model. The aim here is to show what a newcomer to the hobby can achieve with a little knowledge and experience, using this build as an example.

This model is 58in (147cm) long, from the end of the bowsprit at the bow to the stern, so it does need quite a lot of room. This is a consideration when transporting any model in the car.

As is typical of a kit, there will be a moulded bare hull, decking, superstructure, brass-etched sheets, white-metal castings, wooden dowels, laser-cut styrene or plywood sheets, and a large plan and printed instructions, which can vary considerably from one manufacturer to another.

The kit laid out to reveal all the parts. Count and check everything carefully when the box is first opened; identifying and labelling all parts before beginning work helps familiarize the modeller with all the components.

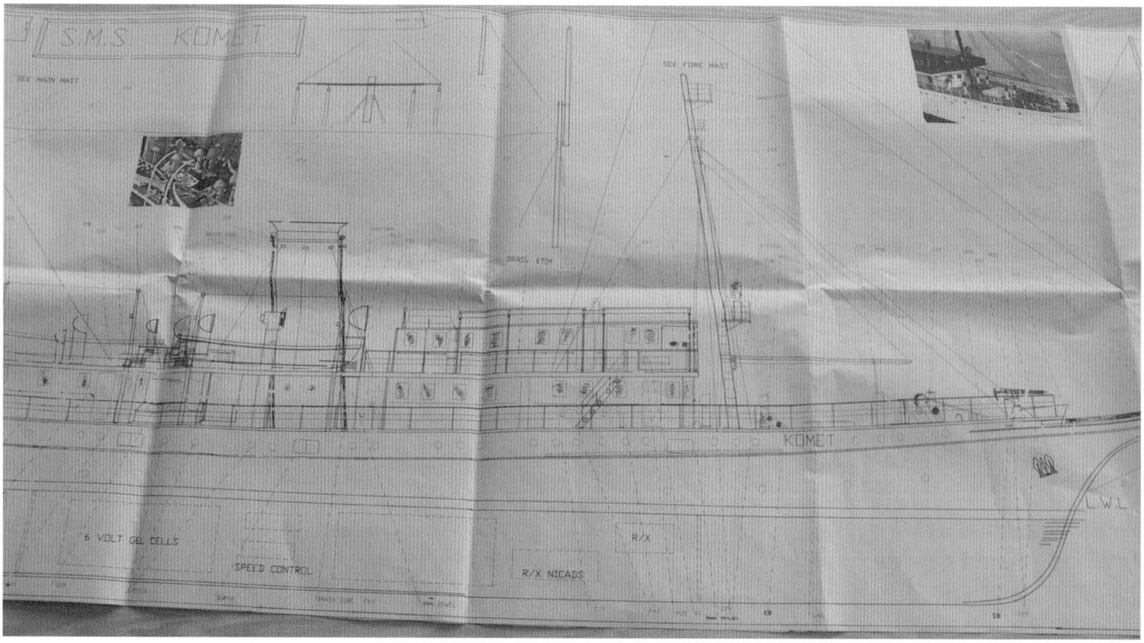

A large drawing can be daunting at first, so study it carefully to identify part numbers or names before starting. If it is printed on thin paper, reinforce all the folds now; also read the instructions for cross-reference.

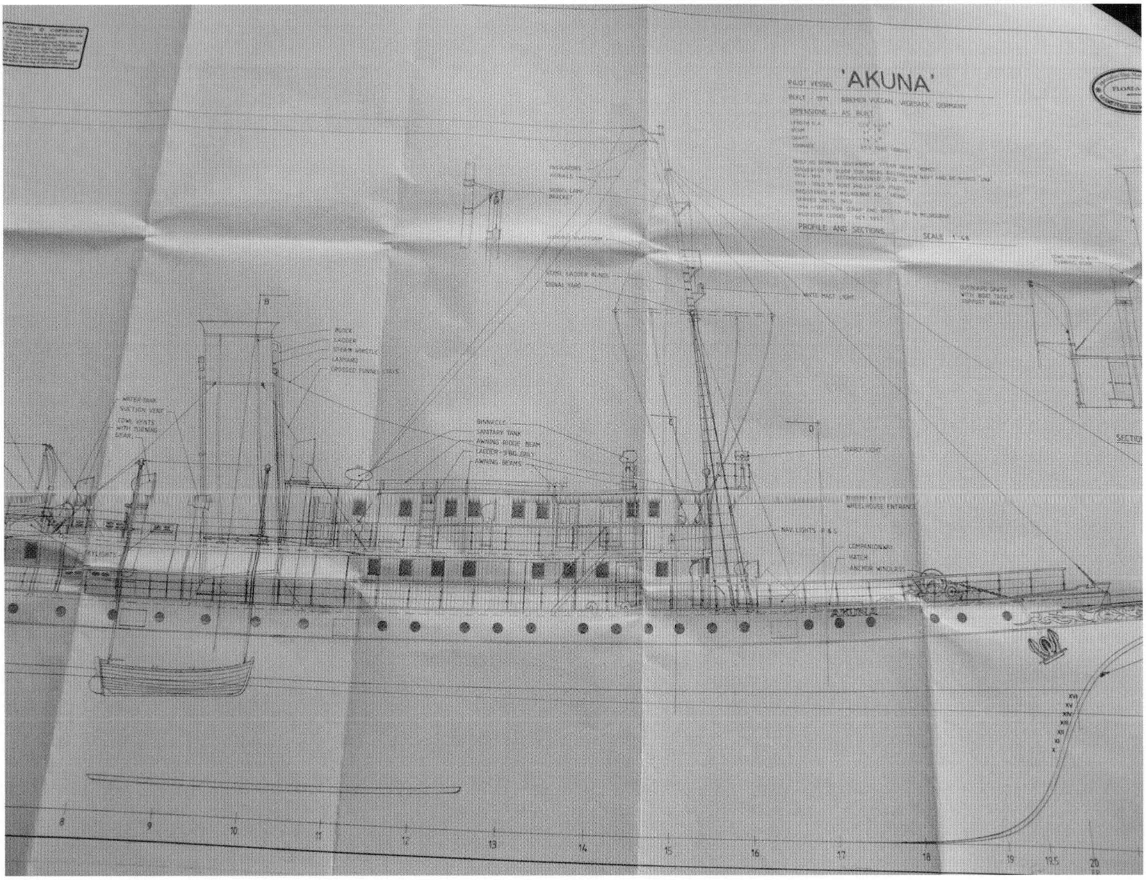

With a little research, often something better than the information supplied with a kit can be found, if greater detail is felt necessary.

On foreign kits, do not be surprised if the English grammar or translated wording is strange, such as 'fuselage' for 'boat hull', for example. It makes the actual challenge of building the model a little more thought-provoking – not to mention the fact that quite a number of words on the plan may be in the home tongue, so it could offer even more interest.

In order to get greater detail than was supplied on the plan that came with the kit, it was possible to obtain copies of original drawings of *Komet* when she became *Akuna*. Whilst these were produced at a later date in her evolution, and had to be obtained via an Australian model shop, it did provide much needed greater detail for the proposed model, and was worth the extra effort involved on-line to source them. A CD was also available from the kit maker as another reference.

ADDITIONAL ESSENTIAL ITEMS

There will be many items not included with the kit as shown, apart from the various adhesives, paints and so on required to complete it. So apart from the initial cost of the kit, all these extra costs need to be taken into account, which can total hundreds of pounds if care is not taken.

In addition to all the above items, extra plywood, styrene sheet, strip, epoxy, twine and so on, will

The 'extras' can double the cost of a kit, so try to keep them to a minimum at first, and stick to essential items.

probably be required. Over time this does not matter, as there will invariably be material left over from earlier builds that can be incorporated, but initially it will be a consideration. Only purchase what is necessary at the time.

DESIGNING THE ELECTRICS

Designing the electrical circuits should start with a list of what is essential – such as motor and battery – and then a 'wish list', with the cost of each item alongside it. This enables the modeller to budget for the costs involved, and to whittle down the list to practical limits. A crude sketch of all the terminal connections to the various items, followed by a clean drawing, will enable the final ideas to crystallize, and provide a future reference when needed.

The manufacturer of the various electrical components may also provide invaluable help during this design process. It is a sound idea to adopt a policy of making up a folder for each model, containing all the installation material, electrical wiring and maintenance literature that comes with the parts, and the kit, for future reference.

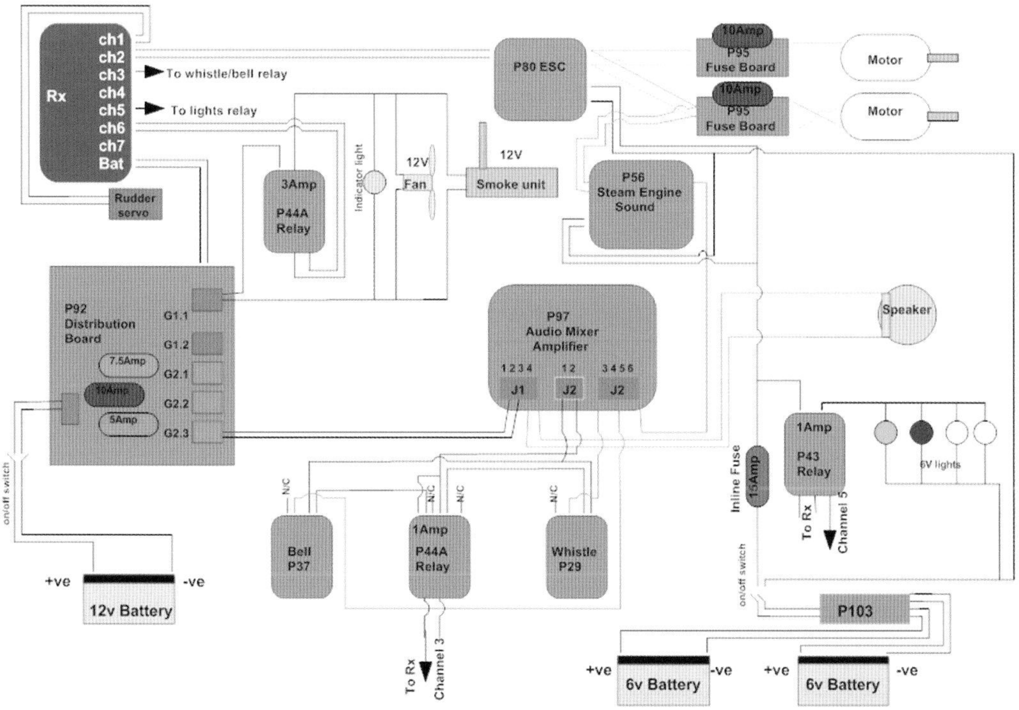

The wiring diagram, originally made as a composite from many individual 'hook-up' instructions supplied with each electrical function. It may take a few days to draw this, and it does not need to be as detailed as shown, but it is really worthwhile in order to understand the circuitry.

INITIAL TESTING

Always test the major items before they are fitted, and even then, make them removable. The motor mounting board has a three-screw attachment point, plus the motors are screwed to the board, so that everything can be taken out, if necessary. Here all items from the battery, Rx, ESC, distribution board and motor board can be tested easily.

FITTING THE MAIN COMPONENTS

The first thing to do, after checking all the components of the kit to ensure that they are there and not damaged, is to thoroughly wash the main fibreglass hull and superstructures in warm water and washing-up liquid to remove any silicon spray that will likely have been used to aid in the release of the parts from the mould. If this is left on the surface, then paint or adhesive will not adhere properly. All inside contact points for epoxy and so on, should be roughened with a fine file or grinder to give a better 'key', or with a fine wet-and-dry sandpaper if it is on an external surface.

Making a Stand or Cradle

The next thing to do is regarded as an irksome task by most modellers, and that is to make a stand, or cradle, for the hull to sit in. It is almost impossible to work on a hull unless it is flat bottomed, because it will roll about, and this item is very necessary to hold it steady. Some kits offer the materials and hull profiles to do this, others do not. Refer to Chapter 9 for further details of how to make this item.

Shaping the Hull

The bare hull has now been braced with additional cross supports in pinewood, and a softwood

Some of the more important items being bench-tested. This is very necessary to understand the range of control, via the Tx, and to be sure that the right wire goes to the right terminal. Each function is tested in the same way, before being fitted into the hull.

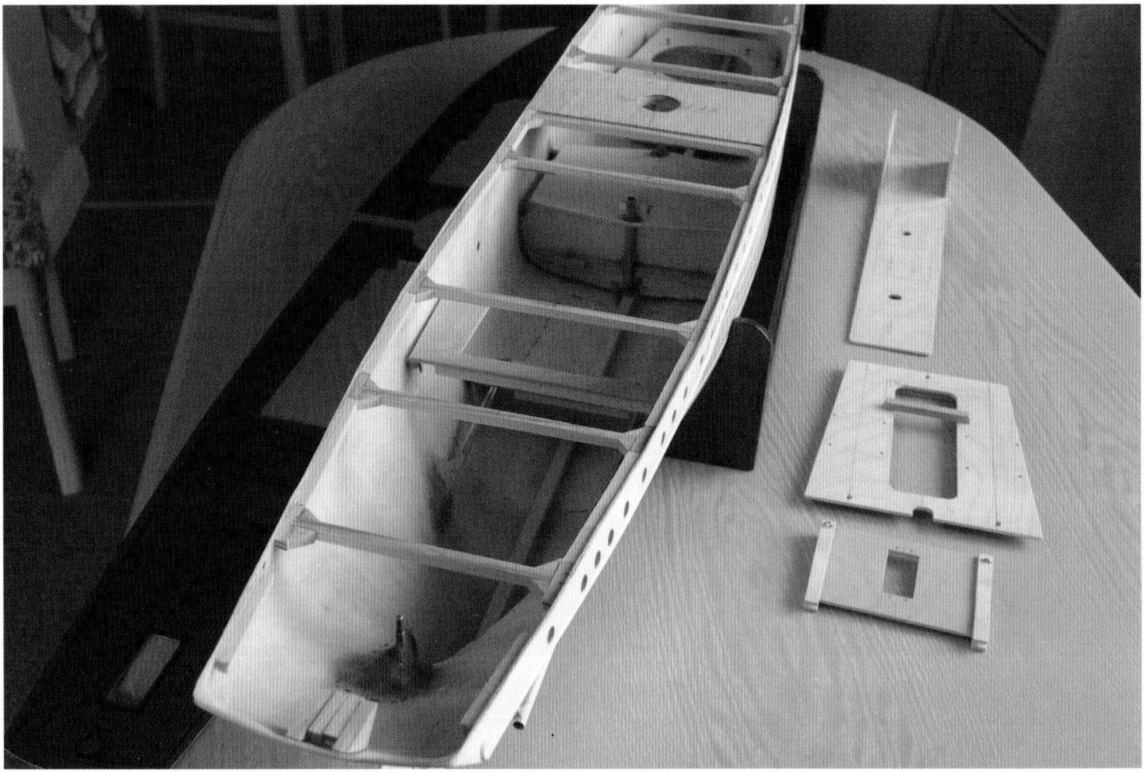

The hull has some of its internal fittings fitted, such as the rudder and propeller shaft. The basic mounting boards are to the right-hand side, from a servo board in the foreground to a motor board, and then to an electrics board at the rear. None of these are part of the kit, and all must be designed and made up.

(such as balsa) stuck all around the upper edge to support the rim of the decking when it is finally glued in place. Frequently a fibreglass hull will warp after it is taken out of its mould and stored somewhere until sold. By warming it with a hair dryer it is often possible to correct any mis-shape, so don't worry if it is a little out of shape.

Ensure that the final length of the supports are taken off the plan and decking to give the correct width of the deck, rather than using the width of the bare GRP hull, which may not be correct if it has warped.

The stiffeners and supports can all be glued in place with a two-part epoxy, always using the deck itself as a template for the final finished hull shape; this is to obtain the narrowest of gaps between the edge of the deck and the inside of the hull, which will have to be filled in later to make the hull watertight.

It is also worth noting the pink fibreglass reinforcing around the vertical rudder shaft, providing support and water tightness. All the additional mounting boards for the various electrical items can now be designed and cut out; usually 3mm plywood gives adequate strength, without increasing weight too much.

Decking

Depending on the model, there are a number of ways to make a wooden planked deck; generally they start with a thin plywood sheet, which is effectively shaped as a plan view of the model. The planks are then either already engraved/printed into the plywood, or the modeller can use ink or a soft pencil to draw them in. This will still mean that the overall grain of the plywood will carry on across the deck and each plank, which is visible and not very realistic.

A much better way for a serious modeller is to plank the plywood sheet with, say, walnut strip planks cut to the correct scale. This will take longer but the end effect is so much more satisfying, and once varnished will look superb. Always remember that trees are not infinitely tall and planks were made in short lengths, so there should be a join every 2–3in (50–75mm) or so, depending on scale.

> **CAUTIONARY TIP**
>
> Always remember that once the deck is glued in place, it is almost impossible to have full access inside the hull, so ensure that nothing is overlooked at this stage. Check that all the boards that may need to be removed will actually come out with all their components in place through whatever access holes there are in the deck. If anything is screwed down, can a screwdriver or Allen key still reach the screw head, or a spanner reach a nut?

BATTERY

In this case there were two separate circuits, one at 12 volts for the motors, and the other (for some accessories) at 6 volts. This meant that separate SLA batteries were required for each circuit, or a voltage reducer for some of the accessories. The choice was made to use extra batteries due to the ballast weight being required, and also that the hull was narrow, making it difficult to install one larger battery.

MOTORS

The motors were contra-rotating (by wiring their terminals opposite-handed) with quite large propellers, so a gearbox was chosen with a 2.5:1 reduction. This provided a good scale speed on the water without throwing too heavy a load on the motor, such that it could tend to overheat. A universal joint was needed for each motor, although the propeller shafts were included with the kit.

Scale Speed

From time to time this subject comes up amongst dedicated modelling enthusiasts. Just as the scale time needs to be slowed down for a realistic effect when filming, so does the actual speed of the model. Whilst this is almost irrelevant at this stage, it is worth mentioning as inexperienced modellers want to know how large the motor and propeller should be for a specific model. *Komet* would look extremely odd careering around the lake at high speed, which the original would never have done.

The formula for scale speed is generally calculated by taking the square root of the model scale and multiplying it with the real full-scale speed. Using *Komet* as an example, the scale is 1:50 and the top speed of the original yacht was around 13 knots.

So the square root of 1:50 = 0.14 multiplied by 13 knots = 1.84 knots – say, around a slow walking pace. This proved to be quite accurate on the lake, and she does look relatively realistic under sail.

PROPELLER SHAFT AND PROPELLERS

In order to ensure that the motor shaft and the propeller shaft are lined up it is essential to spend some time on this task. If they are not aligned then additional wear, friction and load on the motor will occur, resulting in extra battery load and shorter sailing time – or no sailing time if it is that excessive!

The device shown below replaces the universal joint, and keeps everything lined up whilst pre-fitting. The board on which the motor is mounted will normally have to be packed to get the correct angle, an important chore that must not be rushed. Care taken now will repay itself many times over in the years to come.

Two white-metal 55mm-diameter propellers were provided for use if the model was built as a static display model, but these were impractical for actual model sailing and were replaced by brass ones. Thus it was simply a matter of copying the pitch, diameter and number of blades, one left-handed, one right-handed, as earlier discussed. In general, high-speed boats have more blades set at a finer pitch, because the motor will revolve faster, so always be guided by the drawings and instructions, and do not try to make a model do something it was never designed to do.

Many propeller shafts have to be extended a long way beyond the hull to ensure the propeller does not hit the underside of the hull, and will

A useful little tool to ensure the motors are lined up with the propeller shafts on their mounting board, which is angled to fit.

Long hulls need large rudders, with plenty of support; also long propeller shafts require the same mechanical 'A'-frame additions. It was also felt necessary to replace the bottom support for something a little stronger.

require some kind of support. This is a typical white-metal 'A' frame, which again must be carefully installed so that everything lines up perfectly with the propeller, shaft and motor. Note also that the bottom of the rudder, due to its large size, has a brass support to replace the white-metal unit originally supplied, to give extra strength.

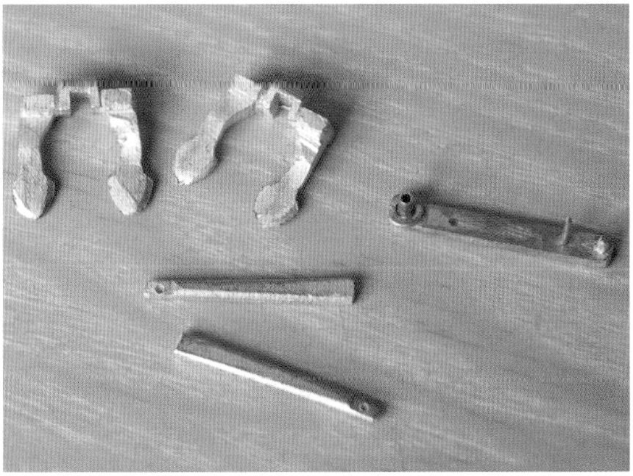

The original rudder support and anchors, both replaced for aesthetic reasons.

THE HULL AND TOPWORKS

Anchors

There are many different anchors in use today, each offering a means of anchoring where different bottom conditions give them a particular advantage. The Navy uses the modern naval, Admiralty pattern, or Stockless anchor as it is termed, but there are also Danforth anchors, CQR, Hall, kedge and mushroom anchors, to name but a few.

Komet's real original anchors were in fact an old-fashioned traditional cast-iron Admiralty pattern or stock type, with curved arms and a fluke at each end, and with a movable stock; however, these were somewhat impractical to use in the model.

The anchors supplied were from a later period, more like the modern Navy Stockless, but it was decided to replace these with other commercial items with better detail, rather than spend time filing them down to a more reasonable shape. This illustrates a point often encountered with model kits: do you accept the parts given, or choose to upgrade to something better? It is a personal choice, and is down to what additional cost is thought worthwhile, or maybe what the modeller has already accumulated in the workshop from earlier model spares.

Anchor chains are run out from the chain locker below the deck at the bow, via a winch winding and brake mechanism, and then down a hawse hole to enter the sea. When stowed, the anchor sits clamped to the end of the hawse hole, with the stock inside the hawse pipe. Always check that the chain is approximately the correct scale for the model. It is normal to break the end link so that it can be connected to the anchor, and then carefully bend it back into shape over the ring in the anchor stock.

Winches

Most ships have anchor winches at the bow. Usually they are supplied as a kit of parts to be assembled by the modeller. When scratch building, take some time to ensure that the winch kit is appropriate for the model, and that it is to the correct scale. Completely paint them with all necessary detail prior to fitting them to the model, rather than waiting until they are in place.

The Hull

The edge of a GRP fibreglass hull can often have small air pockets, which can be either filled in with an epoxy filler, or, as in this instance, covered over with a cosmetic styrene strip, prior to painting.

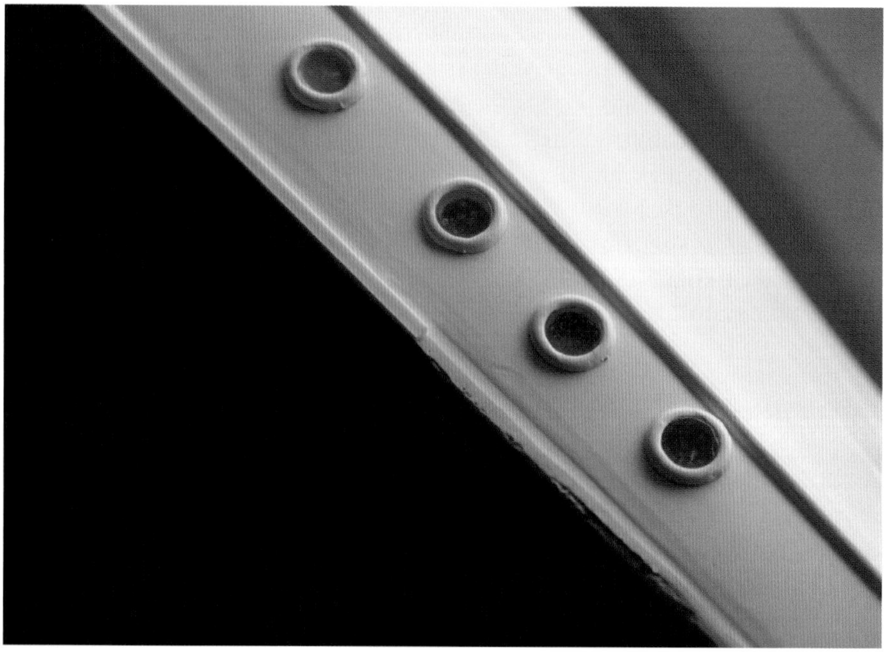

A cosmetic addition to the edge of the hull moulding; this is a common problem with fibreglass mouldings, and is simply disguised with a narrow styrene strip.

Many old-fashioned ships had rivetted metal plating. Should it be desired, this can be replicated by using thin card to represent each plate and PVA adhesive to fix them in place. One step further is to impress each rivet head into the card on the back using a centre punch or sharp scriber, leaving a raised effect on the front face. A rotary-toothed leather marker may also produce the desired effect, or even a small spare gear wheel.

Portholes

There were some seventy-two holes to be drilled for portholes in the hull of *Komet*, plus many others in the superstructure, and larger rectangular windows in the upper deck works. These were supplied as brass-etched flat circles, similar to little brass washers, and it was felt that something more visible would be better. Consequently, milliners' eyelets were used instead, which effected a reasonable stand-off scale compromise (stand-off scale refers to the view from a distance where much of the detail loses its definition, or can be left out). A number of dedicated suppliers make small white-metal portholes, but these would have been expensive in these quantities.

The eyelets were backed with a Perspex window that was held in place with two-part epoxy, as LEDs were placed behind most of them to give the effect of internal illumination.

Many old ships had what were termed 'rigols' above portholes to divert water away, also called eyebrows, which were narrow curved gutters. To replicate them some modellers use a small bent piece of wire above the porthole, which from a distance can look quite effective, or they may be supplied as a small brass-etched item. They do require some patience to fit correctly, so think carefully before embarking on such fine detail.

Funnels

Large funnels are often made from blown or vacuum-formed styrene sheet, which is then joined with another styrene strip inside as a flange, and the two halves glued with styrene cement. Alternatively they may be supplied as a complete

A blown or vacuum-formed styrene half-moulding for the funnel, the two halves joined to form a single funnel.

The finished funnel, complete with end flange and steam piping, painted and ready to be fitted to the decking.

tube, or as a fibreglass moulded item. If there is a join, then this must be filled in with epoxy filler as before. Always prepare and undercoat, then topcoat each item, before fitting it in the model: do not attempt to paint it in situ.

The Superstructure

Part of the superstructure is made from Plasticard styrene sheet. Sometimes this is printed and the modeller has to cut out each piece, but usually nowadays most items are laser cut, and consequently are square and true, enabling assembly and gluing to be much more accurate. When assembling large cabins and topworks such as are shown, take time and do not rush things: check each join with a set square, and always build on a flat surface.

If it is printed, remove any print with methylated spirit after cutting out before it is all glued together. If left until later the print can appear through the adhesive or paint and be impossible to remove. If it is laser-cut, rub down the edge with glasspaper to remove any sharp edges. Sometimes laser-cut plywood has a 'burnt' edge, which can discolour paintwork if left in place.

This particular kit had self-adhesive mahogany-finished plastic sheet for the upper superstructure sides, which proved very effective. Something similar can be purchased at any DIY outlet, to give

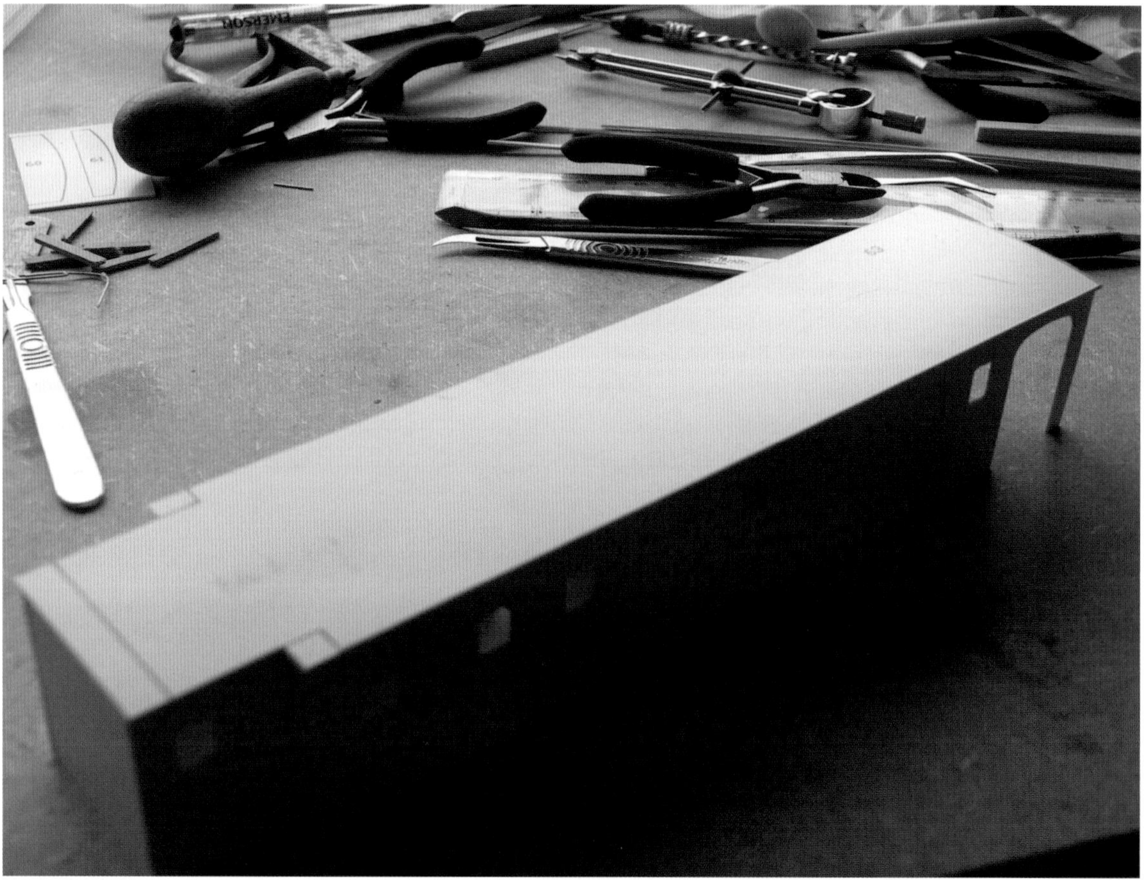

Part of the top deck superstructure, built up from printed Plasticard; note the adjustments to ensure it fitted properly to accommodate the modifications made to fit the extra functions.

The base of the upper deck cabins, again modified to suit the extras with a strong fibreglassed-in pair of supports. This provided additional rigidity when the topworks were removed for the assembly/disassembly of the model.

The mahogany plywood decks are now in place, ready stained and painted, to give an aged appearance in this bygone world of elegance.

the bulkheads, for example, that more realistic panelled wood finish.

Masts and Tapering

One of the attractions of this model are the raked masts, and it is quite easy to take the angle from the drawing to make a template; however, the decking is curved downwards from stem to stern so an individual template is needed for each mast.

Here again a choice can be made: does the modeller want the mast to be permanently fixed in place, or removable? The author's choice was to make it removable, so a brass sleeve was fitted to the base of the mast, and another brass sleeve fitted over it, slightly larger as a push fit; this was then securely fixed in place with Araldite into the deck.

Most models will have some form of mast. The older it is, the more likely it is that there will be more masts, booms, yards, flagstaffs and so on, all of which are usually tapered, from bottom to top. As the dowelling supplied in a kit, or for a scratch-build, will be straight when purchased, it is necessary to taper it as part of the build.

Try and start with a dowel that is longer than required, so that the bottom (thicker) end can be gripped more easily. Using a small hand electric drill and a sanding disc, start to taper a flat line down the length, concentrating more effort on the narrowest part (the top). It is probably better to do this on a workbench or other flat surface to avoid snapping the dowel. Then turn it 180 degrees and repeat until both sides are the same level of taper. Then turn it 90 degrees and repeat

A simple template, the correct angle being taken from the drawing to give the correct rake and appearance of the mast.

again until the dowel is a square cross-section. Then sand down the corners using a sanding block and fine glasspaper, until it is circular again. Finally a smooth finish can be obtained using only a fine glasspaper curled around the dowel.

Another item that can cause difficulty are the davits that support small ships' boats, or lifeboats. The davits should in most cases have a taper towards the top. If they are in a kit, then they are likely to be cast in white-metal as a finished article, otherwise a bent brass tube may be necessary for a home-built item – this doesn't look quite right, but will suffice from a distance on the boating lake.

DECK FITTINGS

There is an annoying paradox with deck fittings, in that the more there are, the more realistic the finished model – but the more there are, the more likely it is that they will be knocked off at some point, so typically most modellers aim for a mid-point to be practical. Whatever deck fittings are used, whether metal or plastic, ensure that they are cleaned with detergent or methylated spirit to remove any release agent used in the moulds, otherwise any adhesive or finishing paint may not stick properly.

Most fittings will be manufactured in a two-part mould so there will invariably be a thin layer of 'flash' where the two halves meet; this must be removed with a sharp scalpel or a fine rat-tail file, prior to fitting or painting.

Wooden parts will require sanding down, and then sealing or undercoating before a final topcoat of paint is applied, depending on how porous the wood is, or what type of wood is used. Hardwoods are naturally harder to shape but do not absorb as much paint, and typically produce a better finish.

Larger components will typically be either resin or GRP, simply to ensure that the total

The ship's boats being prepared to give a more realistic 'planked' effect using strips of carpet tape.

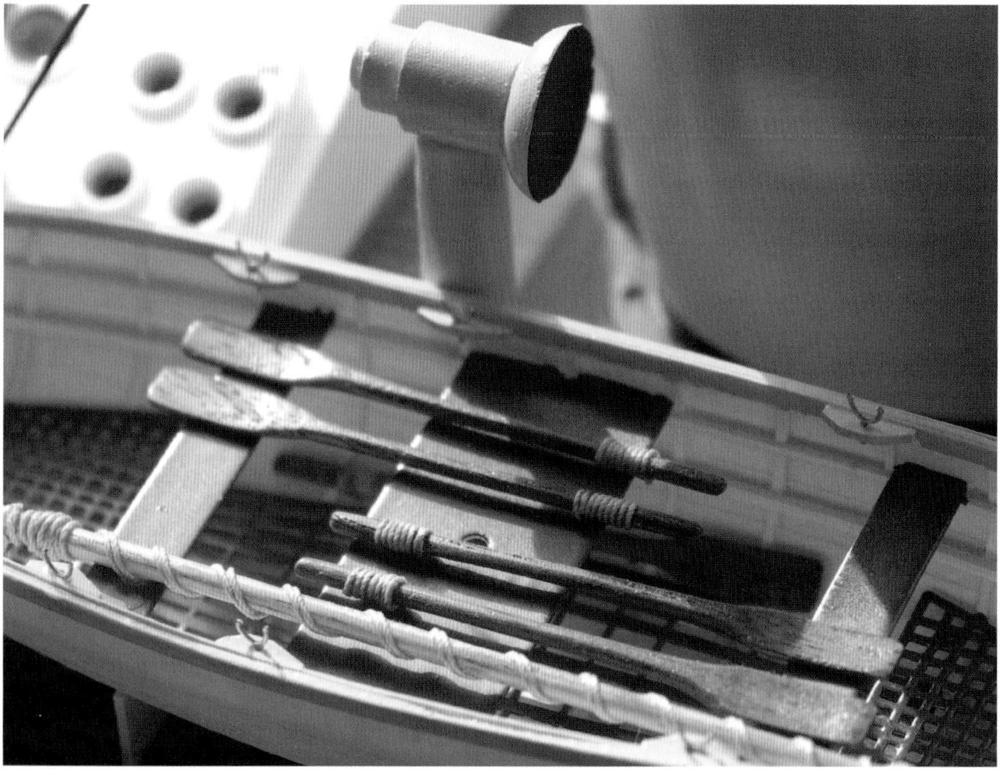

The addition of oars, rope and mast may be a little fiddly, but is well worth the effort.

Note the boat is also taped internally and thin styrene ribs included, plus deck boards.

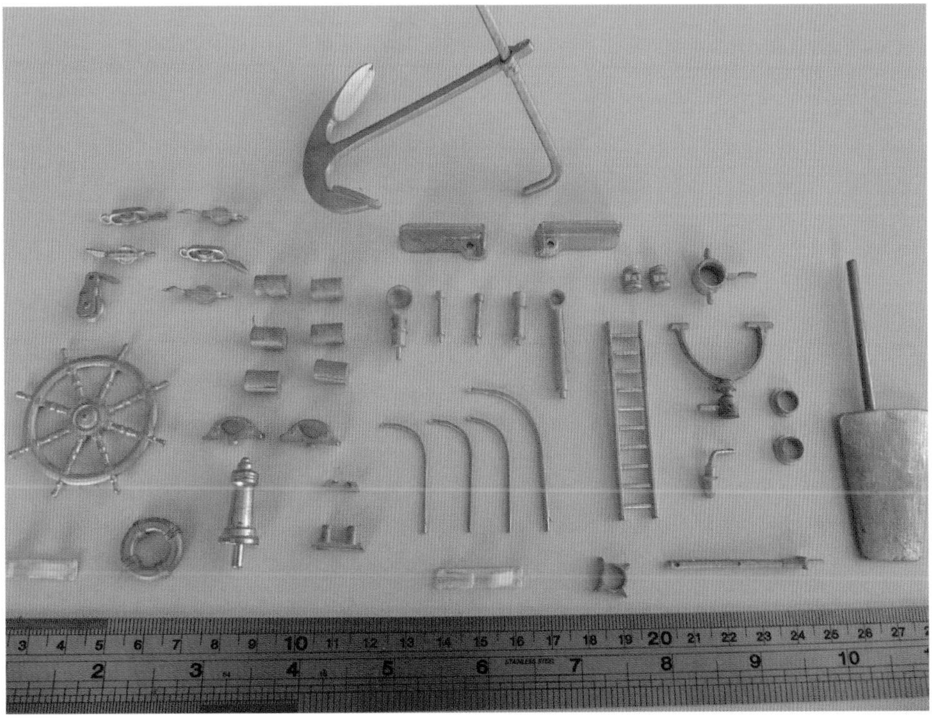

Most small parts will be made from white-metal, where the weight is not important; typically they can be fixed in place using a small dab of superglue.

Often the larger fittings are made from resin to reduce weight; these are best joined with an epoxy resin. The smaller styrene parts can use a styrene adhesive, or again, superglue.

A typical gun platform made from a white-metal base, and then provided with finer detail with a brass-etched top layer.

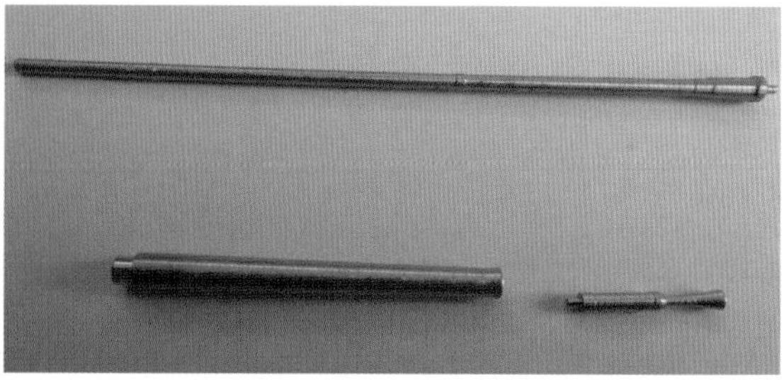

Gun barrels or flagstaffs turned from solid brass offer a better choice and finish than those that are simply made from wooden dowelling, but at greater cost unless the modeller is fortunate enough to have access to a lathe.

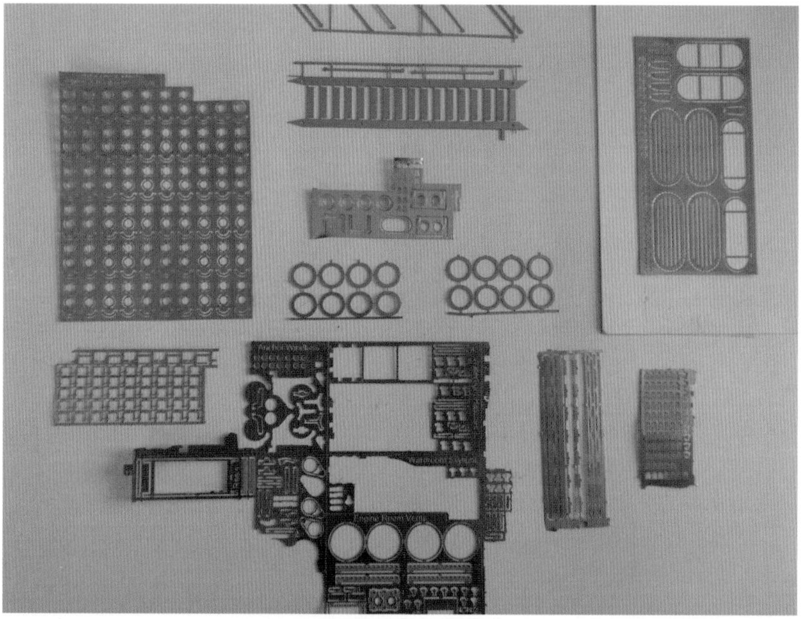

Many kits use brass-etched sheets for small parts, which may be assembled using superglue on the end of a toothpick to ensure accurate placement of the adhesive. Note that there is also a stainless-steel etched sheet in the centre of the picture: this is not common and is much harder to work with, although it offers finer detail and greater strength than brass.

Always use chain to the correct scale for the model – if necessary, paint it before attaching it to the model. Often you will need to split a link with long-nose pliers to attach an anchor ring or similar.

HELPFUL TIP

An easy way to get a 'planked' effect on the ship's boats is to use carpet tape: cut into the required strip width of a single plank, and starting at the keel, work your way upwards on the outside of a smooth-blown or vacuum-formed styrene hull, overlapping each plank slightly. These can then be painted to look like a genuine planked and rivetted old wooden rowing boat.

weight is kept within the displacement weight level of the model.

An observation is that many models are ruined at this stage of preparing and placing the various items on deck because of a modeller's desire to rush things to get finished. This is a great mistake after all the hard work before. On this model there are a number of ship's boats, all highly visible, and it is well worthwhile spending a little extra time on these.

Handrails

Handrails can present a headache in that there are usually a great number, and it is better to make and assemble them before fitting them to the deck, rather than later. Generally it is better to fit the stanchions to the deck unpainted (square and superglued to the deck) and then carefully thread each railing through the holes – this can take some time and patience. Once everything is in place and squared up, superglue each joint. Lastly each section can be carefully hand painted to the required colour.

Ladders

There are two kinds of ladder: those that may be premade with steps, either in plastic, brass etched, or wood; and those with individual rungs that are

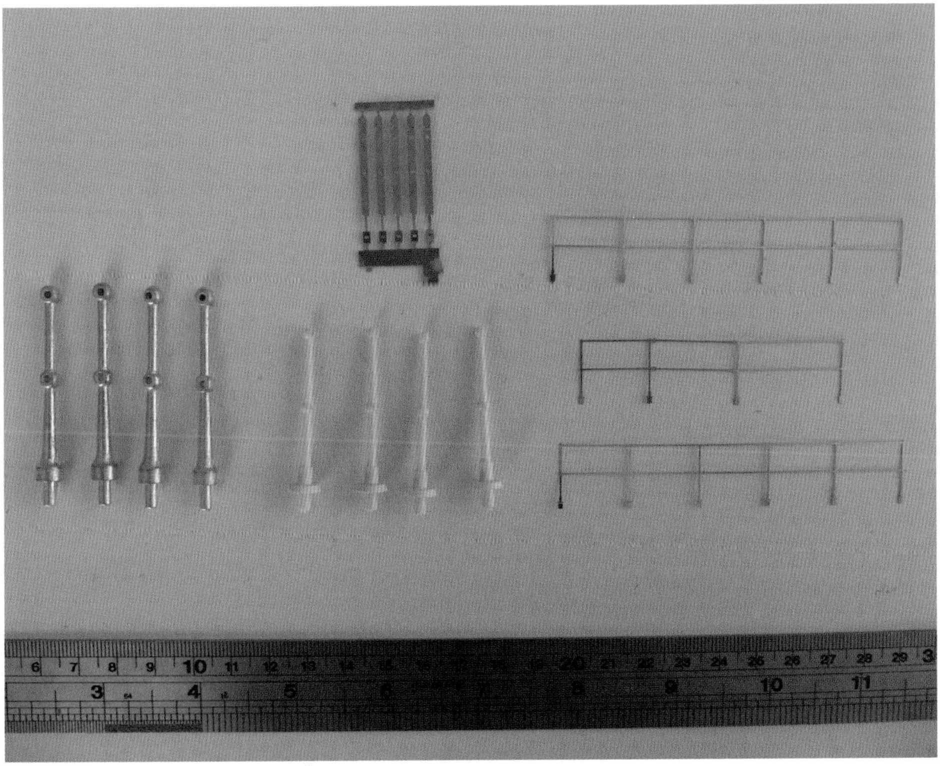

From left to right, a selection of stanchions and handrailing: white metal, brass-etched, styrene and stainless-steel etched, all to different scales, but similar in the method of construction.

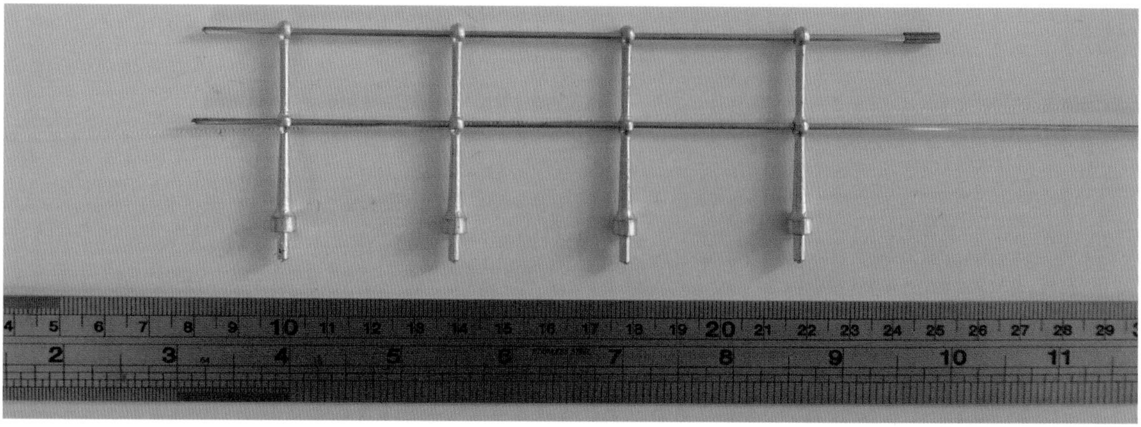

A sample of a white-metal and brass rod handrail: note the small brass tube connector – leave this loose until all sections have been placed on the deck.

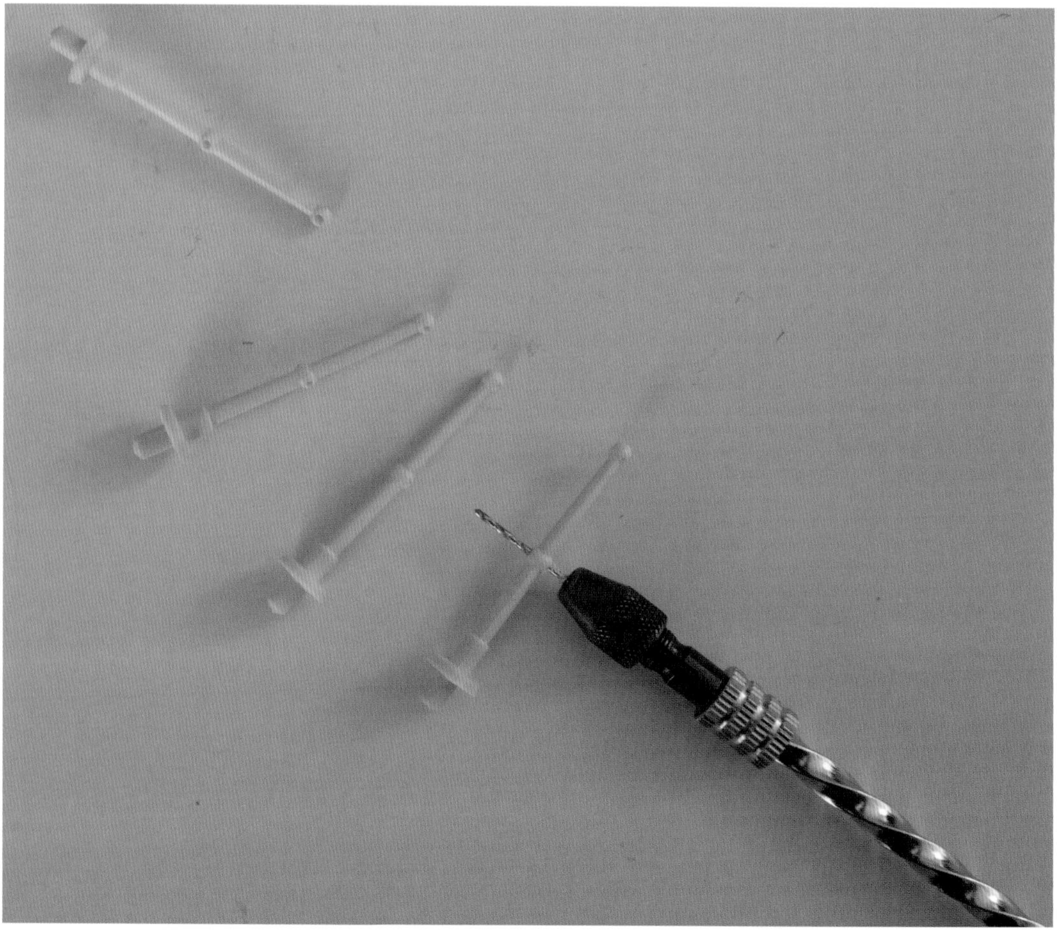

Often it is necessary to drill out the holes for the railing: always try for an oversize hole, rather than a tight fit, so the rods can be slid into place, prior to fixing. If the stanchions are fitted first, it is vital that all the holes for the railings are in line; sometimes a piece of scrap rod between the separate stanchions can assist with this process.

All loosely assembled to ensure a correct fit, before fastening to the deck. Note again the small joining piece. Every deck orientation is different and will require a modification to the assembly and fitting. Patience is a virtue, and it is worth taking time and care with this part of the model build.

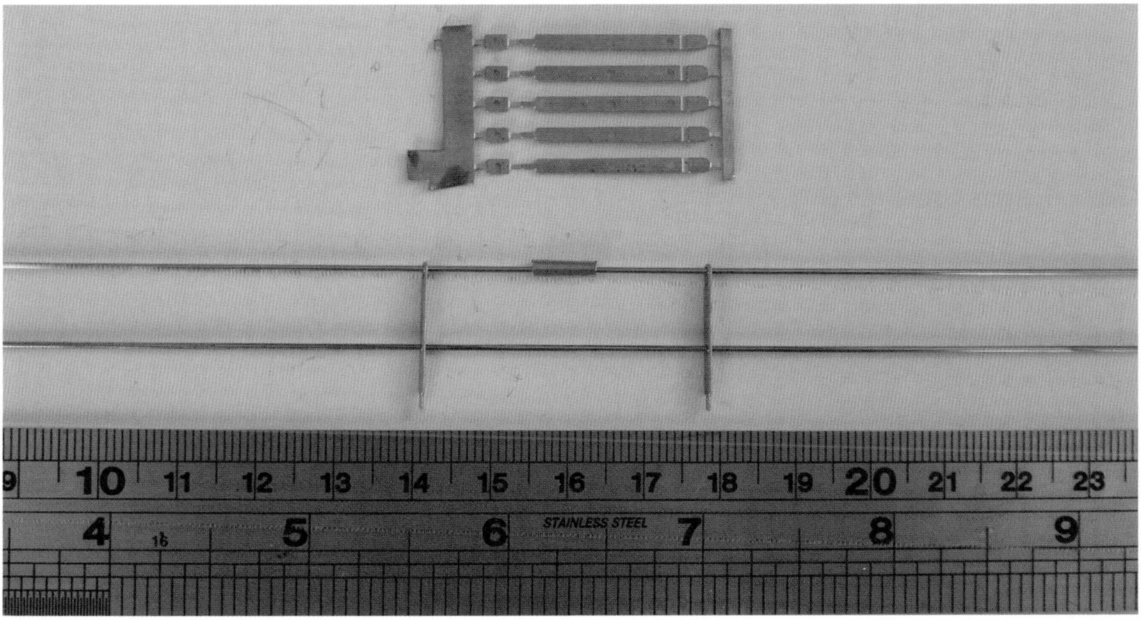

Smaller brass-etched stanchions will require a smaller diameter rod, though this can be accidentally bent out of shape more easily. The smaller the scale, the less strength there will be, so the more care will be required in the assembly.

Again, with a brass-etched stanchion it is sometimes better to spray paint these small parts prior to detaching them from the sheet – this can be a much quicker solution.

designed to go on a vertical surface, say up the mast, or the hull superstructure sides, which are a square 'U' shape. These more often than not will have to be made from brass rod, so make up a square former to bend each rung around before cutting – that way they will all be a uniform width.

Door/Hatch Handles

Usually at their simplest, these handles are an 'L'-shaped piece of bent 1mm brass wire, fixed in with superglue; better still they are a white-metal casting. Whichever is used, always attempt to fit them at the correct height and opposite the hinged side, which might sound obvious, but some naval ships will have them all the way round the outside of a watertight door. Hatches often have a lifting handle, much like the 'U'-shaped ladder rung described above.

Grab Rails

Grab rails are normally a fixed feature along the superstructure walls, next to a walkway. Again, they are made from 1mm brass wire, and are likely to be fixed every so often by small brass eyelets – these can be made using round-nosed pliers, if they are not supplied with a kit. Similar to external handrails, these often need to be threaded along the rail, and then the complete unit can be stuck in place, after adjusting for curves. It is better to make these in short lengths and fix them together with a small piece of tubing, rather than try to make a single long length, which may have to be threaded or bent around other deck features.

Ventilators

As can be seen from the photographs, there are typically quite a number of ventilators: because this vessel was designed to work in the Tropics there are perhaps more than normal, but a century ago this was modern air conditioning!

The most common is a cowl ventilator, which on *Komet* were either fixed, manually adjustable from above decks, or controllable from below decks via a winding mechanism, which enabled them to be swivelled to catch the wind. Another fixed version is the mushroom ventilator, or 'H' vent, often seen on naval vessels.

Usually, depending on size, they are fabricated from a white-metal or plastic cowl and a wooden dowel base. Plumber's 8mm or 15mm waterpipe and copper or plastic tube angle joints make quite a good cowl if filed to shape.

Painting Small Fittings

The hull and maybe some of the major items will have been sprayed as discussed earlier, but small items and fittings will require painting separately by hand. Always remember that enamel paint can be used on top of acrylic/cellulose spray paint, but not the other way round.

When choosing a colour, aim for something a little darker than perhaps the full-sized ship used. The 'real' colour, particularly if it is a bright vivid shade, will look wrong, and far too garish. Just as there is a scale speed and a scale time, so there is a scale colour to consider.

INSTALLING ELECTRICS

Always work with the idea in mind that at some point, an item may have to be removed, so the more care and thought that goes into this theme, then the easier it is likely to be later. The simpler the boat electrics, the simpler this task becomes. As can be seen from the earlier wiring diagram, in *Komet* the author has chosen to include a number of functions, which proved a challenge in a narrow-hulled craft with limited deck access.

An old piece of wood helps to hold small items in place to spray them. Drill a small hole to peg them in place in the wood.

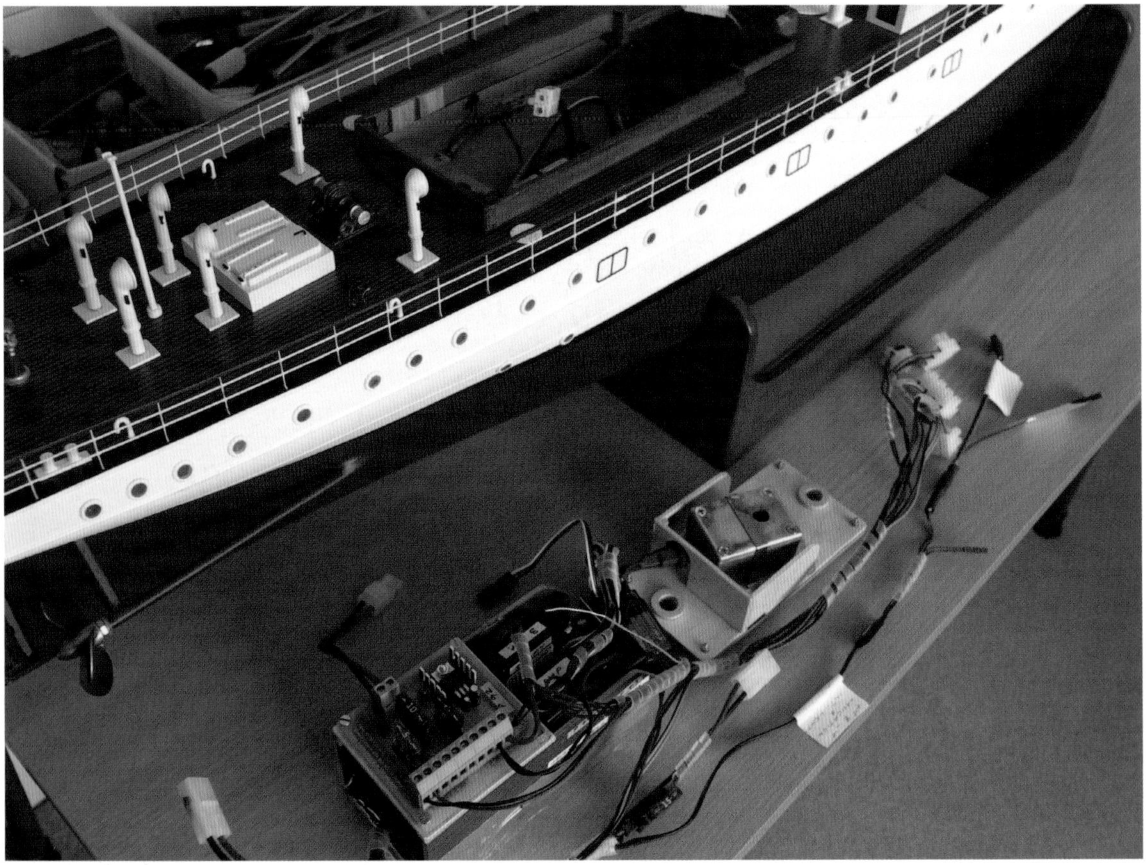

One of three electrical assemblies, made as a complete unit. Note all the wiring clips and labels. Also, all the plugs were dabbed with paint to aid identification with the mating plug socket.

The 4in (100mm) speaker installed as low as possible in the hull to keep the centre of gravity of the model as low as possible. In the foreground are the terminals for two batteries, leading off to the distribution board, with an additional board designed to stop one battery discharging into the other.

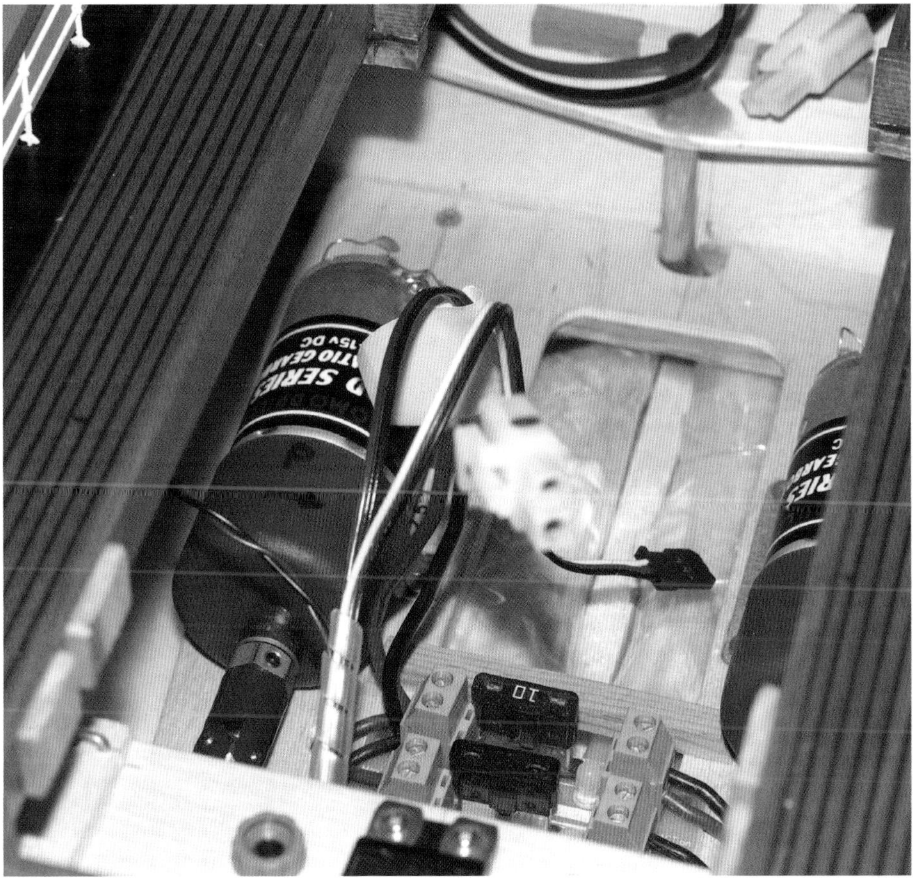

Drive motors towards the stern of the model. The brass tube, centre top, is a locator for an external detachable ballast weight slung under the hull.

STABILITY

As discussed in Chapter 2, the shape of a hull can dictate the stability of a vessel, and *Komet* is a good example of this fact. The hull is very narrow and rounded with no external keel. Apparently the original yacht was so unstable that it was rumoured that she could roll on wet grass, and was extremely uncomfortable to sail on, unless one had a very strong stomach.

With this in mind, every effort was made to reduce weight where possible, unless it could be placed low down in the hull. In practice this proved to be insufficient, and later, internal ballast was removed, and a false keel made to bolt underneath.

Where ballast is necessary, then lead shot or roofing sheet lead can be used, if the idea of making a mould and melting some old lead is not a practical solution. If using shot in a polythene bag take care that the bag is robust enough – picking a kilogram of lead or steel shot out of the bilges with a pair of tweezers can be very tiresome!

The actual positioning of any ballast, fore and aft, along the keel should be carefully considered. Assume a model requires 1kg of ballast: if this is placed centrally, then there is more tendency for the bow and stern to rise and fall further in waves on the lake, effectively pivoting about the centre of gravity. Yet if it is possible to have two $\frac{1}{2}$kg ballast weights, one at each end, there is less tendency to rock backwards and forwards, fore and aft. This may be more important in a model with an open deck that can ship more water.

External detachable ballast weight, fitted after initial trials to get better stability.

Whatever type of ballast is used, remember that young people are more susceptible to the toxic effects of lead than adults, and they should not be exposed unnecessarily to it. Lead shot nowadays is often not lead at all, but made of other materials, such as steel; as it is merely being used as ballast, it is only the weight that is a consideration.

There is another 'scale' consideration, in that often rudders have to be made larger than in real life, and keels may also have to be made heavier and deeper to offer more stability to the model. When taking a set of plans to 'scratch-build' a model, this is a serious consideration, but any modifications to the hull shape are likely to be underwater when sailing anyway, so do not detract from the visual aspect of the model under sail.

To stabilize loose shot to make it more secure, once the actual amount of shot is known, it can be mixed with a two-part resin, which once set, can be filed and shaped to exact size. Alternatively, build up shaped pieces of sheet lead as a sandwich to achieve the shape required, gluing them together as necessary.

FINAL TESTING AND SAILING

Komet was tested at home to get the keel weight and trim correct before finally going to the lake. Everything can easily be tried out, although it is a good idea to warn the neighbours beforehand,

Komet *being tried out in the test tank. The household bath is usually more than adequate to test smaller models for correct trim and ballast – larger items need something more. This was originally made to test out large submarines. (See Chapter 9.)*

The first 'sea trials' – or more accurately, lake trials – after everything is bench-tested at home, and all batteries fully charged.

She floats – perfectly.

as the sound system can be heard 500 metres away!

It might not be as easy as this to find somewhere to float-test a boat for the first time, so consider carefully where it is launched. Many ponds are very shallow at the edges and the propeller or rudder could be damaged if the boat is dropped into the water without care. Or an unstable shoreline could mean that you accidentally fall in. Certainly a flowing river is a bad idea if the engine fails, and whilst a local canal is tranquil water, can the boat be reached if it fails or drifts to the opposite bank? Heavy models require some strength to launch, especially to the lower back muscles, so consider all these points sensibly.

Then comes the first sail, a proud but apprehensive day, when all the months of work come to fruition: everything has been tested and apparently works, and other club members come to appreciate the model – but as yet, there is always that question: will she sail properly? Finally, she is off on her maiden voyage, and the thrill and satisfaction cannot be fully described: you have to experience it yourself.

Off she goes under her own power.

Chapter Eight

Building a Scratch-Built Lifeboat

This project is to build a model of the Torbay Severn Class boat – the RNLB *Alec and Christina Dykes,* number 17-28.

HISTORY

The RNLI dates back almost 200 years, with around a quarter of a million services. Torbay has had a lifeboat for about 160 years, with a long list of 'shouts' and awards for bravery. The early boats were open and pulled by ten or twelve oarsmen. Until 1922 the boats seem to have had a 'tennis ball' history of being alternately stationed in either Torquay, or Brixham on the opposite side to Torbay. Since then, a permanent position in Brixham has been the most practical solution. Almost 1,000 lives have been saved over the years

The Alec and Christina Dykes *coming back into Brixham harbour after a training exercise.*

by the various volunteers at this station, a brave and impressive record.

The Severn Class lifeboat is the largest type ever made, later designs being a little smaller. A question often posed is about the numbering system, which can be puzzling. The number '17' refers to the length of the boat in metres, and the second number refers to how many of that particular class of boat had been built. These are called 'AWBs' or 'all-weather boats', as opposed to the smaller inflatable boats and RHIBs (rigid-hulled inflatable boats) used closer to shore, termed 'IRBs' or 'inshore rescue boats'.

Originally the length was measured in feet by the RNLI, so an earlier boat in Torbay, the *Marie Winstone*, an Arun Class boat, had the number 52-19. There were also some Arun-Class boats with different stern mouldings, which measured 54ft. The *Edward Bridges* was 54-03, stationed in Brixham in 1975. Converting 54ft to metres works out at 17, so the evolution of the Severn from the Arun Class becomes clearer. In general, the term for the class of boat – Severn, Arun, Tamar – derives from the names of rivers around Britain.

Lifeboats are made to operate in rough seas, and if necessary to 'self-right' when capsized. They have a broad beam, which makes them ideal for radio control, although the large superstructure can interfere in a model when it is windy. They also have a shallow draft to operate in shallow water, which means that no ballast was necessary in the model, and great care had to be taken in the choice of battery and final weight distribution.

Many model boat clubs will hold fund-raising exhibitions and open days for the RNLI, and it is an ideal introduction to models and radio control. Anyone thinking of this theme as a model should visit a local open-day exhibition, if possible.

Lifeboat Kits

At the time of building this model there were very few lifeboat kits on the market suitable for radio control, apart from one for the Arun Class, and a much larger version of the Severn Class,

A RNLI open day hosted by Etherow Model Boat Club. Number 17-28 is on display on the left of the photograph, together with lifeboat models made by other club members.

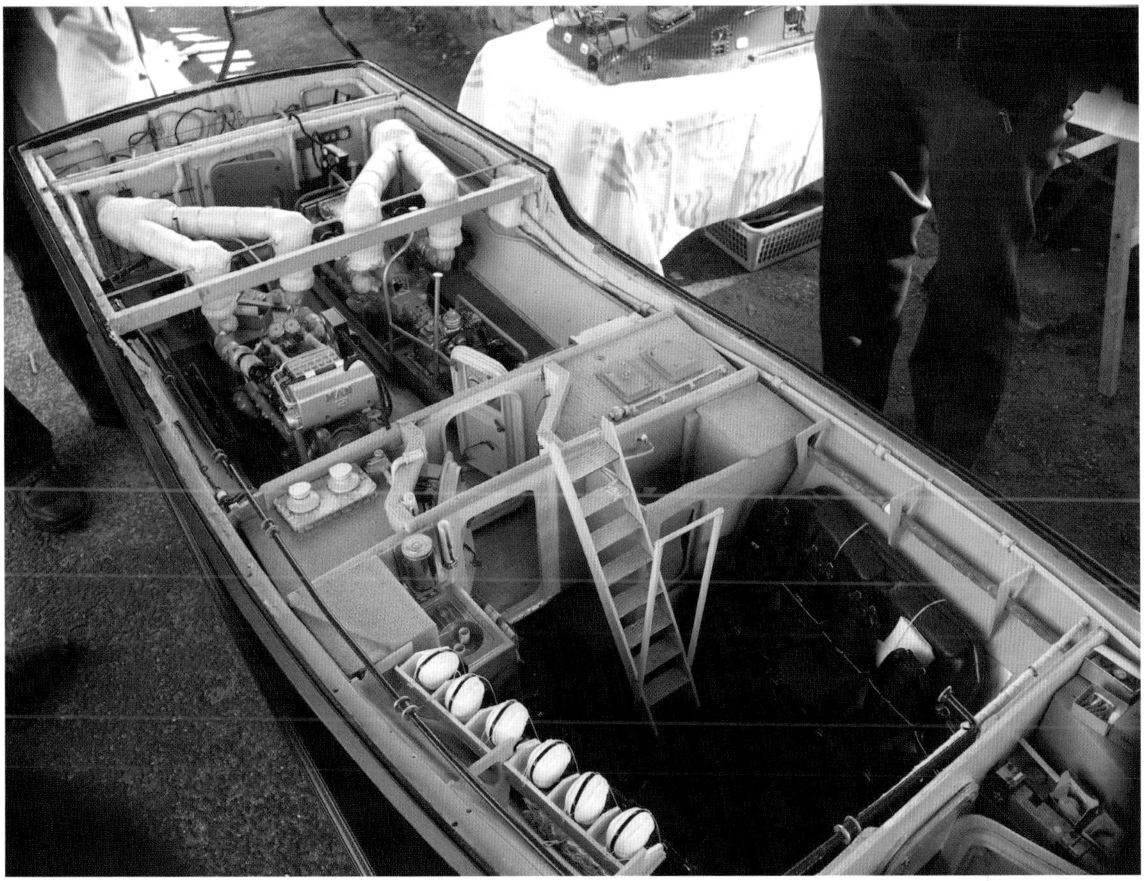

An amazing detail view of the engine room of another Trent Class model at 1:8 scale. It was built by Ron Paddison and won the gold award from the RNLI. It represents the pinnacle of model boat engineering, and no effort has been spared in recording every tiny feature of the full-sized original.

both of which today are sadly no longer available. However, there are now model kits for the newer, slightly smaller Tamar Class boat. There are also little styrene plastic Airfix kits, but these are not suitable for what was envisaged at the time.

The outcome was to consider building a scratch-built model as the only practical alternative. As the author had recently completed another scratch-build of an old Brixham sailing beam trawler called *Vigilance*, the full-sized version of which still sails out of Brixham as part of their 'Heritage Fleet', it seemed a natural progression to tackle the local lifeboat. *Vigilance* was the last sailing beam trawler to be built, in 1926, at the Brixham shipyard of J.W. and A. Upham.

Uphams also built prefabricated motor torpedo boats during World War II, and this is another ideal subject for the modeller. Anyone really interested in the subject of motor torpedo boats in World War II should read *Dog Boats at War* by Leonard C. Reynolds, published by the History Press. MTB-628 was stationed at Great Yarmouth, as part of the 55th flotilla, their insignia being the rather distinctive finish in the photograph.

It is worth mentioning a simple fact of life regarding a scratch-built model. Naturally it will be built and finished as it would have been at a specific point in time. However, a number of times the author has experienced the exasperation of building a model, only to find when next time

An earlier scratch-build by the author of Vigilance, *the last sailing beam trawler to be built in 1926, at the Brixham shipyard of J.W. and A. Upham. Later, in the 1950s, they built the* Mayflower *2, to commemorate the original sailing of the Pilgrim Fathers to America.*

Uphams also built prefabricated motor torpedo boats during World War II, one of which was MTB-628, another model kit choice by Deans Marine, adapted by the author. The 'jaws' painted on the bow is a genuine decoration that was painted by the crew at the time, on each boat of that particular flotilla.

the full-sized boat is observed that it has been repainted a different colour, or something has changed in the superstructure. Accept that this happens, and don't change things simply to keep up, because next week it could change again.

OBTAINING INFORMATION

Living close to Brixham at the time, it was easy to go and photograph the lifeboat whenever she was at her moorings; however, that was never going to give enough real information. There are many books by, and about, the RNLI, and *A History of the Torbay Lifeboats* by Alan Salsbury, published by Halsgrove Publishing, of Tiverton, offers some superb background.

However, the RNLI headquarters in Poole are the best source of information, and offer very good information of every class of boat they have made. Shop around online for more information, books and/or drawings that may be available.

Scale

Most of the drawings used were already to the scale required at 1:20, although for some reason the hull profile was 1:25; this was scaled up at the local print shop to match the other drawings. This gave a convenient overall length of 33in (85cm), an easily handled size that fitted into the car, and wasn't going to be too heavy and unmanageable to carry.

Should it be necessary to re-scale drawings, then this can be easily worked out before talking to the local print shop, using the following formula:

Required new length divided by the original length.

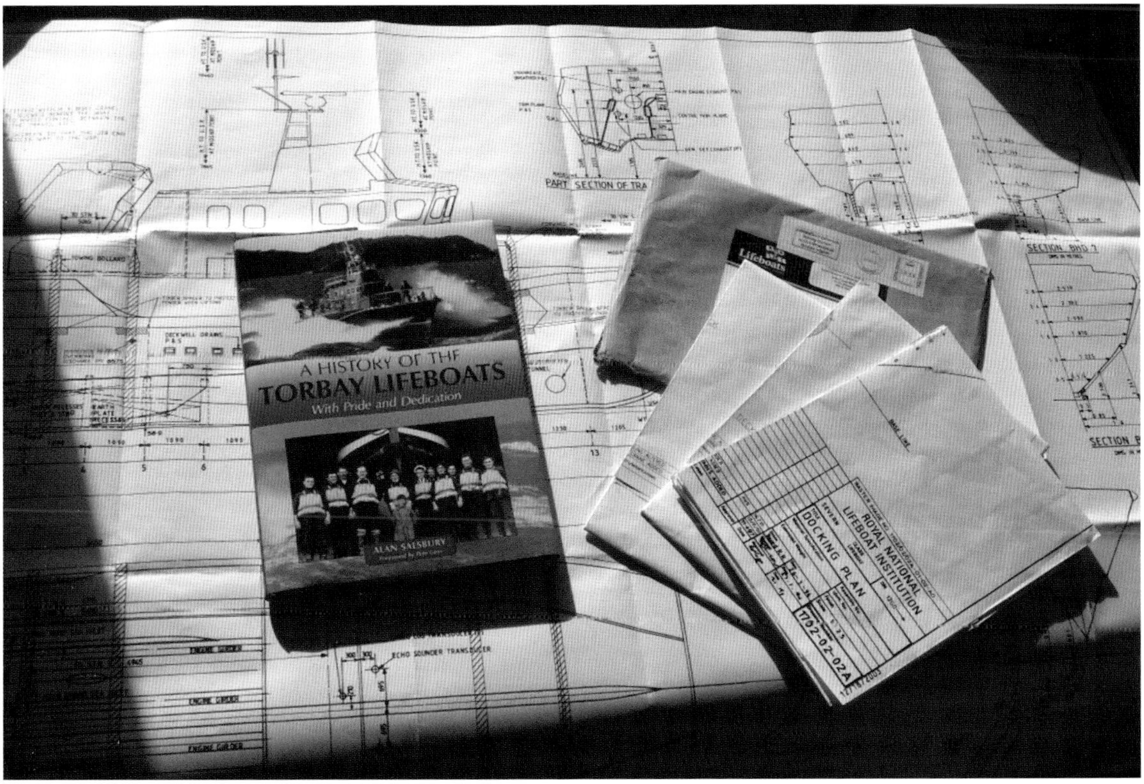

A display of the many drawings obtained as a set for the Severn Class boat, together with reference material, a vital background source.

A wall display, offering more detail hitherto not known about.

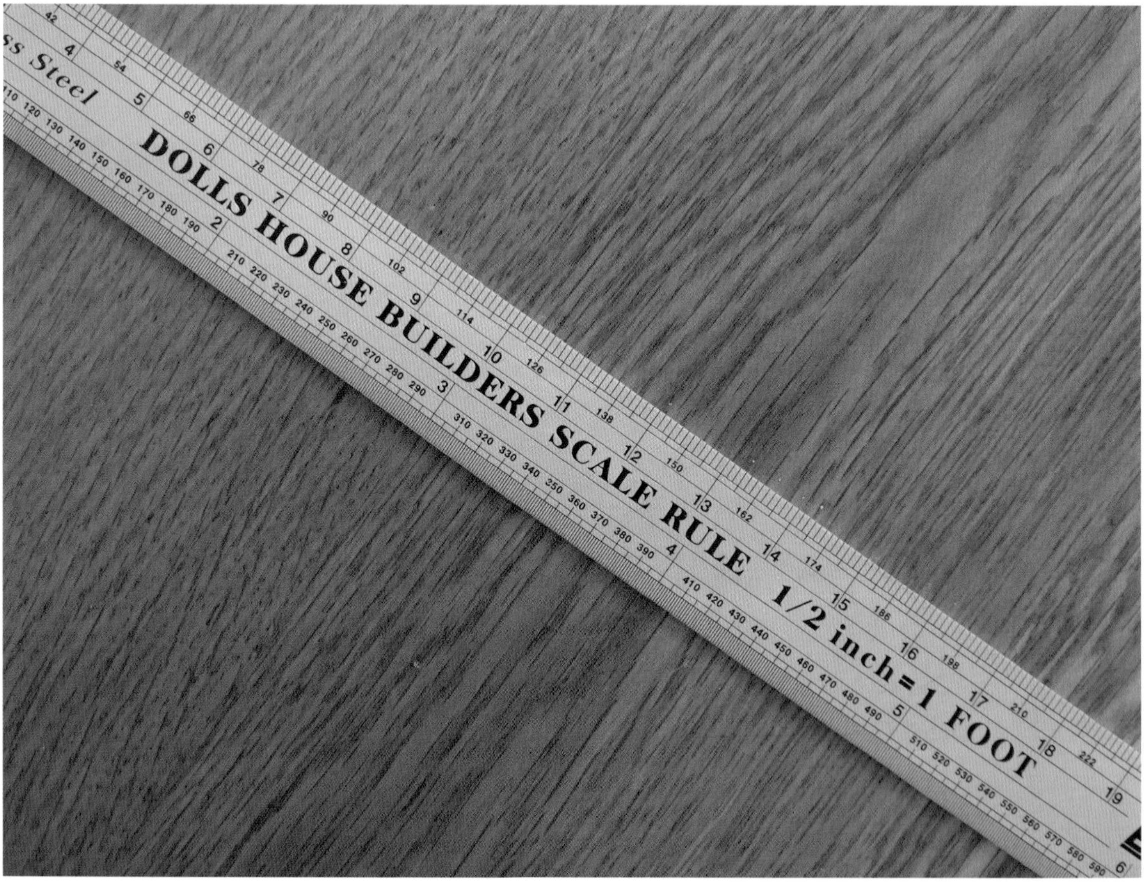

A useful modelmaker's rule available to different scales, which can help in converting measurements off the drawing to avoid mistakes. Some are for model railways or military figures, so check to see if there is one to suit the scale of the model being considered.

Say the drawing shows an overall length of 36in, and it is now required to be 40in, then 40/36 = 1.1 – in other words, the drawing will have to be enlarged by 10 per cent.

People are often confused by the various scales quoted on model kits – 1:06, 1:24, 1:48, 1:96; typically, older imperial measurement kits were a function of 12in to the foot, with scales that would be divisible by twelve. Kits from overseas and more modern UK kits tend to be metric, so are 1:20, 1:50, 1:100 and so on.

CHOICE OF MATERIALS

There are many ways to construct a model boat: it can be carved from solid wood or a plastic kit, more often from GRP fibreglass, or blown vacuum-formed styrene, paper, cardboard or foam – but the oldest method is termed 'plank-on-frame', and is similar in many respects to the old-fashioned manner of making full-sized wooden boats.

This is still often the chosen method when a mould or pattern of the hull profile is not available and the modeller is starting from scratch: thus it is a 'scratch-build'. Sometimes it is possible to buy just a bare hull, so the model becomes a 'semi scratch-build' – this is an important distinction if it is proposed to enter a competition, as it will have to go in a separate category.

Typically a good quality plywood should be chosen for the main bulkheads, which provide a cross-sectioned profile of the shape of the hull – usually a 3mm thickness is adequate. For planking large areas or superstructure, 1.5mm is used. For strip, 1.5 × 6mm spruce is used along the hull bottom. Always soak each strip in water to make it more pliable when it has to be bent to a curve along the hull. A good white PVA waterproof wood glue will give the best results.

Many planks will have to be tapered towards the bow and stern, so make up a simple jig on a baseboard with a couple of square strips glued to it, such that the plank is held vertically, rather than flat. The edge can now be filed, or sanded, or even pared down with a knife far more easily, as it is held firmly on edge.

BASEBOARD CONSTRUCTION

The idea here is to build the hull upside down, starting with a large, flat, rigid wooden baseboard. Chipboard or MDF is not suitable as it is too hard, as it is likely that panel pins will be used to hold parts in place whilst the glue dries and it is preferable not to bend them as they are knocked in. They then either damage the wooden bulkhead, or are difficult to remove.

The end result will be a dead flat, square hull – but beware of using a wooden baseboard that is warped; if a flat piece of wood is not available, firmly screw it to thick MDF (which is usually flat) and then the work surface will itself be flat, hopefully.

Bulkhead Position

Mark out the position of a plan view of the deck (inverted), together with bulkhead positions on a piece of paper, cover it with greaseproof paper to stop adhesive sticking the model to the baseboard, and stick everything down with masking tape. Small locating spacers are then nailed down to hold the bulkheads in place – they merely need

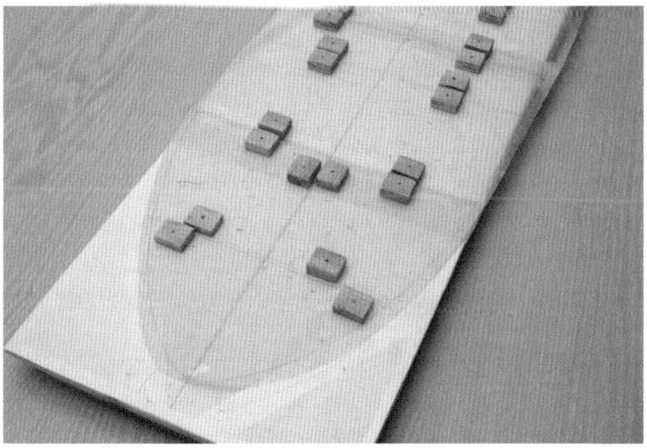

A flat wooden baseboard, showing the hull outline and bulkhead positions, overlaid with greaseproof paper for protection from any glue overspill.

to be kept upright with a set square whilst gluing parts in place.

On the full-sized lifeboat plans, all the original bulkheads are shown in their correct constructional positions with the hull profile at that point, but for the model some of them are not in the precise place necessary. Space is needed amidships to fit batteries and so on, and the bulkheads interfere with that at times, so some redrawing and repositioning is required, or they can be left out.

After drawing out each bulkhead on paper, not forgetting to adjust the outside edges to account for 1.5mm skin planks and deck, they can all be transferred to a sheet of 3mm plywood. The easiest way to do this is to use fairly thick paper or card for each bulkhead, and trace round the outer edges, or pin-prick through on to the plywood; then draw in the actual profile with a pencil on the ply, where necessary.

Take care in positioning each piece before starting to cut out the parts, and in this way, there will be the minimum of wastage.

CUTTING OUT

Patience is needed here, to carefully cut each shape from the sheet, filing and sanding down as required, to get a perfect outline. Always use a fretsaw so that the cut is on the outside edge of the pencil markings by about the thickness of the saw blade. That way there will be the minimum of filing and fitting to size later.

Some of the main components, first drawn out on paper and then transferred to the plywood sheet, prior to cutting out.

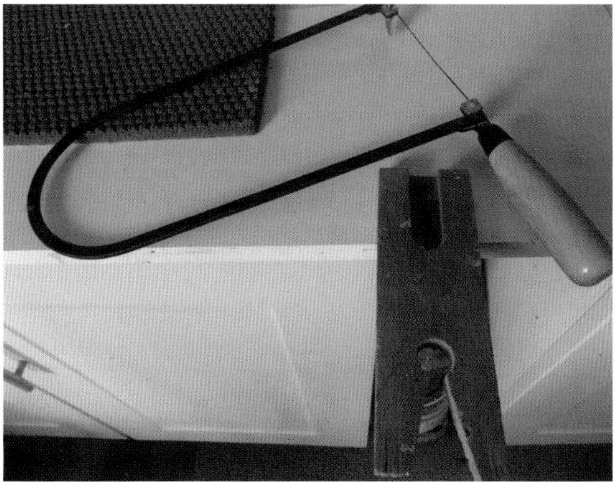

A fretsaw for cutting out intricate shapes, and a bench hook, clamped to the work table, which acts as a support during the sawing process of thin plywood. A blade with fine teeth should be used, which will help to prevent the material tearing as it is cut.

Helpful Tip

When using a fretsaw remember that the teeth on the blade should point downwards, so that the cut is on the down stroke of the fretsaw frame. Where there is a hole to be cut out in a workpiece, drill a small pilot hole and thread the bottom end of the blade through the hole – tighten up the blade and then carefully cut out the inner hole space.

The keel and the two sub-keels were also made from 3mm ply, which was doubled up to give greater strength. Cutting out is a lengthy process, causing sore muscles at times, and making the newly initiated modeller appreciate laser-cut kit parts perhaps – although there are companies who will do this for you at a cost, if the chore becomes too onerous.

Building the Hull

Once all the bulkheads and keels are in place and firmly glued together, then start at the centre main keel and plank outwards with strip material. Do not start at the sides and work in, as there will

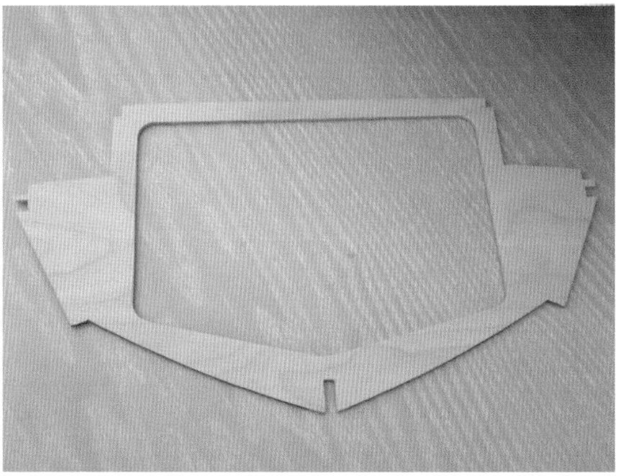

One of the frame bulkheads cut out and ready to assemble on to the baseboard; note the slots for various other longitudinal members.

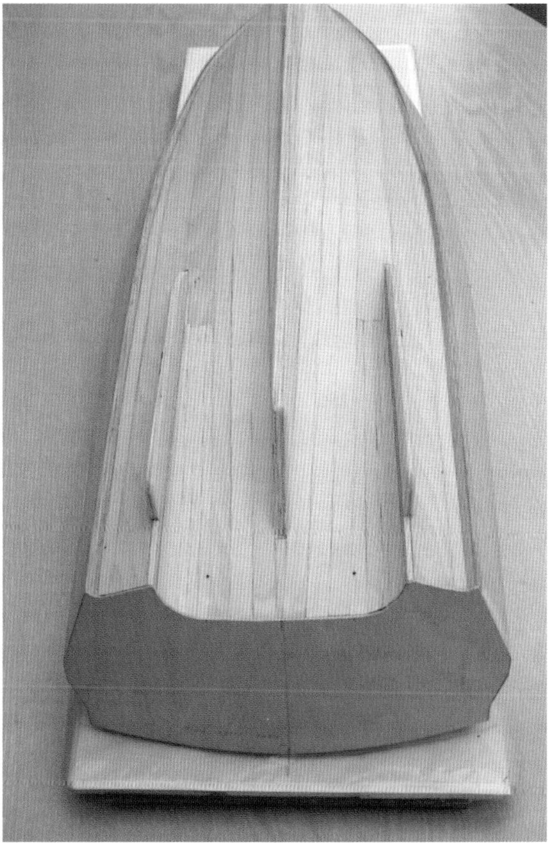

A view of the underside of the model with all the planks now installed on the frame, prior to removing it from the baseboard. Always plank alternately, one plank each side of the keel: that way there will be less opportunity for the hull to be out of true.

be discrepancies by the time the keel is reached, which could throw the hull out of true. Try not to use nails and pins through the planks, as they will all have to be filled in later to make the hull watertight. Use suitable clamps, rubber bands and tape to hold each plank until the glue cures.

Usually when planking a model there will be a point where it is almost impossible to use clamps to hold the plank in place whilst the glue dries. This can be resolved sometimes by using the outside offcut for that particular bulkhead from the plywood sheet and holding that in place over the plank where it needs to be clamped. Clearly it will have the same profile as the bulkhead.

Soak each plank for half an hour or so, after making sure it is a snug fit against its neighbour (this may involve chamfering the edges where they butt up together) leaving the minimum of gaps, which will otherwise have to be filled in later. Glue all the contact points before fitting, and then wipe off any excess glue with a damp cloth before it dries. Remember to plank alternately on opposite sides of the keel, because that way there will be an even stress centrally so that the hull does not twist during construction.

Halfway between the deck edge and the keel is a solid 5 × 5mm spruce stringer, where there is a step in the hull to make the craft more stable. This had to be steam heated in order to bend it to the hull shape required, due to its natural stiffness. In addition, saw cuts made halfway through the wood at the sharpest bend area assisted with the final shape.

The stern was made from 1.5mm ply with another ply skin over the top, as the ends of all the keel and stringers were embedded into it. Also, it was easier to form two thin sheets of plywood to the required curve of the stern, and stick them together, rather than one thicker sheet.

Finally, much of the filling and sanding of the underside was completed at this stage, before being removed from the baseboard, as everything was held in place securely.

The hull can now be carefully lifted from the baseboard, and checked by eye that it has not warped. In the unlikely event that it is possible to see some deformation, this may be rectified either by using a light spray of water over the inside and outside and then applying a light pressure, and/or weights until it dries out, to try to set it back to a true shape. Alternatively, when the deck is fastened to it, then the hull should correct itself naturally.

At this stage check all the internal joints, even holding the hull up to a light, to ensure there are no hidden gaps in the planking, which will have to be filled in. The internal stringers were 3mm square spruce, with additional cross bracing to offer extra support to the deck later. The bow area was filled with expanding foam as an added safeguard – it would be blocked in anyway, once the deck was in place.

The hull now removed from the baseboard with all additional stiffeners and internal supports in place. The bow has also been foam filled for additional buoyancy in the event of the boat accidentally sinking.

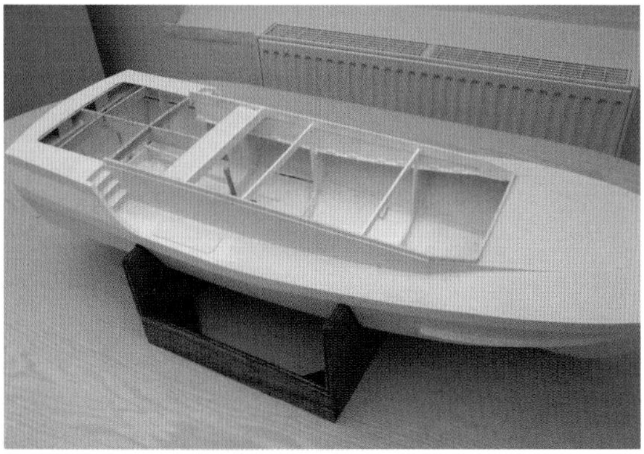

A stand has now been fabricated from 10mm plywood, so there is a rigid base on which to place the model for further work. The hull has been primed and filled where necessary, with a final undercoat on top.

The lower deck area has now been fitted and it is possible to see the curved walkway down each side. Before painting, all surfaces were given a final rub-down after any cosmetic filling had been done. It is a good idea to spray a grey primer or some contrasting colour before the white undercoat, which will make any blemishes that need rectifying stand out more clearly. As the area is sanded down, once the grey colour starts to appear, you know not to continue further.

FITTING PROPELLERS

At this point before undercoating it was necessary to drill holes through the hull and fit the two propeller tubes and shafts. Great care needs to be taken here as quite long elliptical holes have to be cut into the bottom of the hull, to get the shallow angle required. Shaft housings with oiling tubes were used – these can just be seen with a little yellow dust cap in the centre of the lower photograph. Extra oil or thin grease can be added sparingly if ever thought necessary.

Either Araldite or some other two-part epoxy filler will be needed to reinforce the area around the propeller shaft holes and the rudder shaft holes, so ensure that only the minimum amount of the wooden hull planking is removed beforehand and that these areas are accessible from inside to apply the epoxy.

The mounting board for the two motors is also in position after getting the correct angle and packing it in place. The mounting holes for the motor brackets are shown just above the yellow ESC manufacturers' label.

All the stern detail has now been fitted. The trim tabs would be hydraulically operated on the full-sized boat, but were purely for show here. Likewise the exhaust covers were not operable.

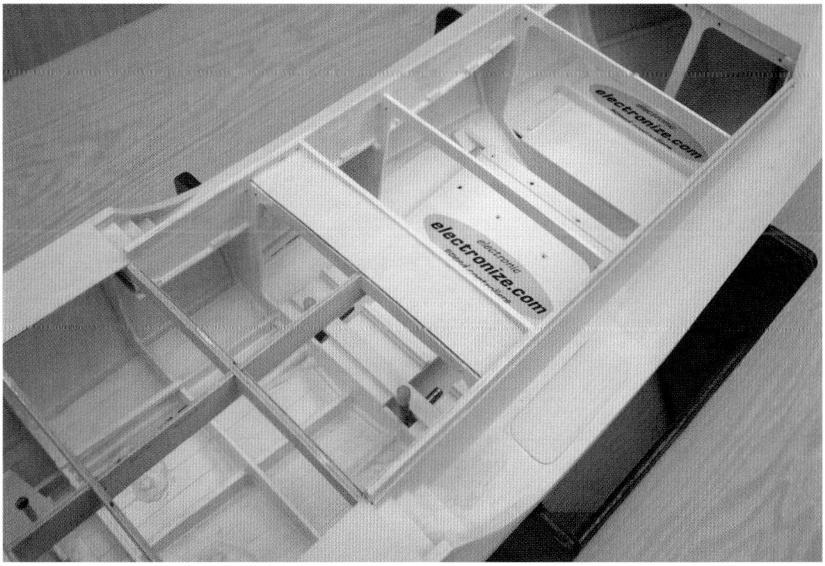

The inside of the hull now painted white to ensure no holes are visible; this also helps in locating small parts if they are dropped accidentally.

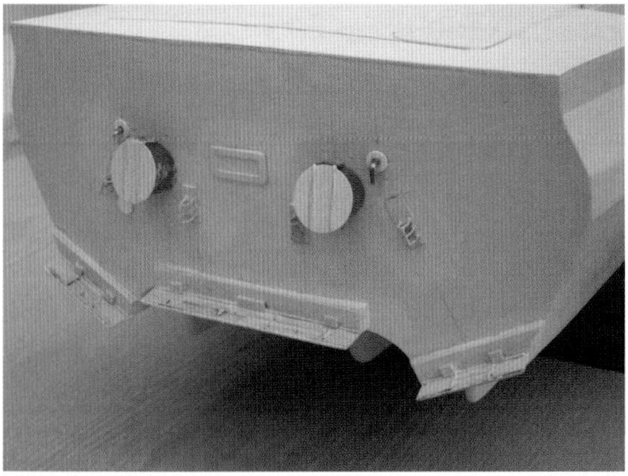

Stern detailing of various dummy parts.

An interesting lesson was learnt at this stage: after reading the drawings and making up the exhaust covers to scale, it was noted later that they were oversize. This was partly due to 17-28 being off station for a refit for most of that season, and when she returned, the model was finished and it was too late to rectify the mistake. Also, she returned with a new rescue boat and different handrailing, next to the crane.

The most valuable lesson learned here, is that when a model is chosen as a subject, then at some point in the future it may change, either in colour or design, and it is not possible to keep up with changes indefinitely. Therefore it is important to accept that the model is in effect like a photograph, and it represents a recorded instant in time – do not try to keep up with modifications, or it may never be finished.

FITTING THE RECEIVER, ESCs AND BATTERIES

When deciding on the Tx to use with this model, an existing 40MHz 6-channel unit was the most suitable: although not all the channels would be used, each motor could be controlled independently. The full-sized lifeboat has a bow thruster for better manoeuvrability, but due to space limitations it was decided not to include it. Two 12-volt 2.9Ah SLA batteries were used, due to the limited amount of space below decks.

The board is removable and slots in under the stern decking; visible are the two ESCs, the on/off isolating switch, the Rx and long (grey wire) aerial that would be threaded under the deck, the rudder servo, and the small battery for Rx power (no BEC is used here). In-line fuse holders are also shown in the power leads from the ESCs to the main batteries, which would be fitted last. The circuitry here is almost identical to that shown earlier in the book as a basic example in Chapter 4, except that there are now two motors and ESCs.

As mentioned earlier on in the book, it is a good idea to start painting from the keel up, and this sequence was again used here.

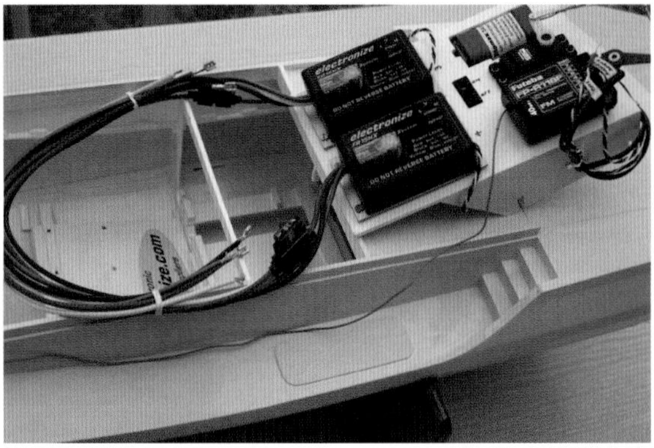

Detail showing the electronics board, prior to locating it at the stern under the deck, although it was designed to be removable if necessary.

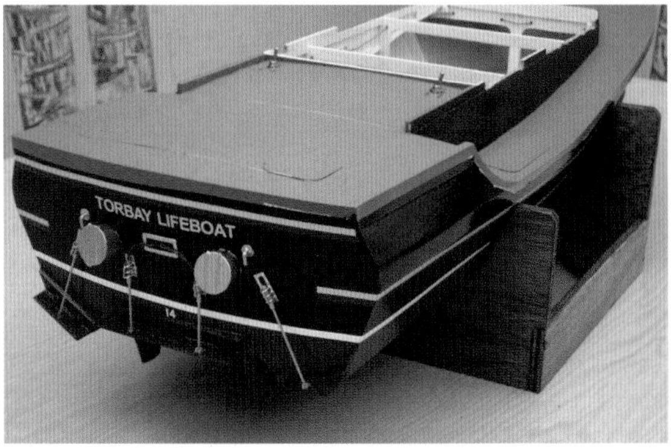

The finished hull up to deck level, but minus the rubber rubbing strakes down the sides at this stage.

All the stern detail is now finished up to deck level, with all strip decals made up from different strip colours and self-adhesive lettering. The stern lettering was made oversize on purpose so it could be read more easily from a distance. The rubber rubbing strake down the sides and stern would be fitted at a later point.

A large removable plate was used in the stern decking to facilitate access to the electrical circuit board, and also to allow access to the rudder posts and linkages. Note the two isolating switches to isolate the two drive motors from the batteries, which would be hidden in the final model under the removable top deck superstructure.

Uninvited Assistants: As an aside, it is worth mentioning that often a modeller has the uninvited attentions of children or pets, which although endearing, can create havoc, and are best avoided where possible to prevent damage to the children, pets or model!

The author's assistant, trying to redraw the model.

Just checking that everything is secure and in place!

SILICON MOULDS

Where a number of identical parts are required, it is worth considering making a mould out of a two-part heat-resistant silicon – this is not as difficult as may be imagined. The two moulds shown were made from the same two-part silicon designed to withstand the temperature of molten white-metal. Once the two-part silicon is mixed, after making the basic pattern, then the material stays quite fluid for some time as the chemical reaction slowly begins, so there is no rush to complete the task.

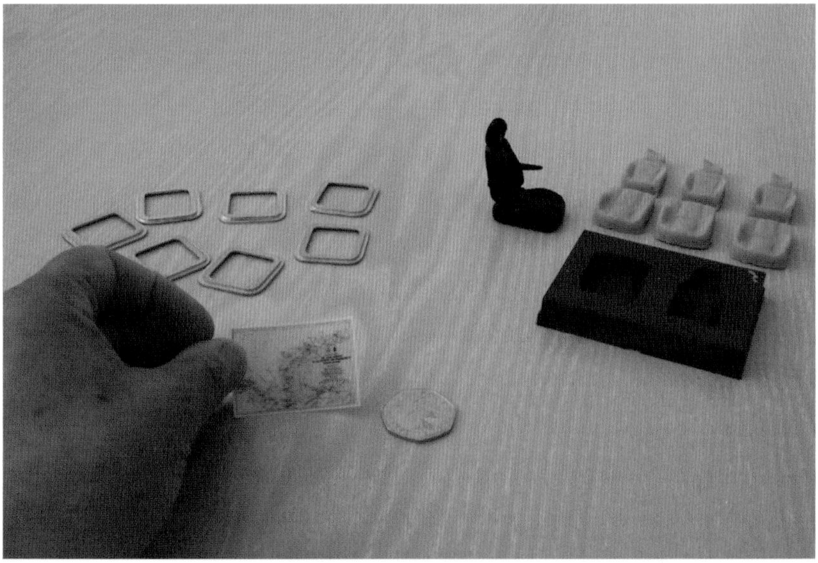

Home-made window frames cast in white-metal and seat frames in resin, using a two-part silicon for the moulds.

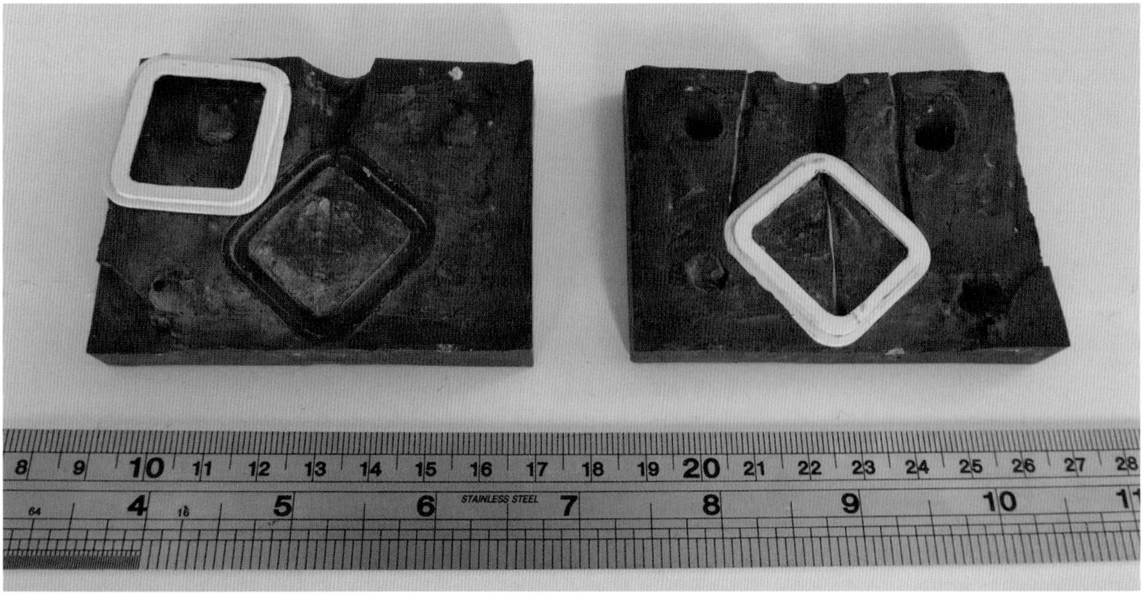

Detail of the silicon window-frame mould made in two separate halves; note the locating lugs cut into the lower frame before the top half is poured. A pattern was made from Plasticard, with the resulting finished casting beside it.

Patterns

The seats were made from two separate castings of another two-part resin material, the seat base and the upright. The two arms were made from wooden strip and glued in place afterwards. The original patterns were made using Plasticene, and were placed in the molten silicon before it set, and later removed, leaving the mould shown. A small amount of the mixed resin was then poured into the cavity, which once set could be finally shaped on the back surface later.

The windows were made using 1mm Plasticard for a pattern. A container was then half filled with silicon to produce the lower half of the mould, and the window pattern placed on the surface and lightly pressed in.

Once set, four locating holes were cut with a sharp-pointed modelling knife into the silicon, taking care not to move or damage the pattern, which was still in place. A light dusting of chalk was then applied to stop the two halves of the mould sticking together, and silicon was poured over the bottom part of the mould, tapping lightly to remove any air bubbles. As can be seen, the surface finish of the final mould is quite rough, but each half matches perfectly so this is not a problem. A final pouring hole for the molten white-metal is then cut with the knife, plus a small cross-channel to allow gas to escape and the molten metal to run more easily.

A word of caution: although white-metal has a low melting point, it is still very hot and will burn if in contact with skin: therefore ensure that the molten-metal ladle has an adequate handle and pouring spout, also that gloves and safety glasses are worn in case of metal splashes during casting, and that young children and pets are kept away.

Trying the partly built topworks on to the hull for correct fit. It was necessary to ensure the superstructure fitted perfectly so that it would not become detached under sail.

A step further on, with all the various panels now in place and the detachable roof in position. Later the roof would be held in place by plugging the handrails together at the rear, and by a latch at the front disguised as a flashing blue light fitting.

THE SUPERSTRUCTURE

The upper works were designed and made so they were removable, to enable access to the internal hull space to get the batteries in and out. The upper roof was also detachable to show the wheelhouse layout and internal cabin space, for the rescue and treatment of survivors.

All the sides and roof were made from 1.5mm plywood, which had to be transferred and drawn out from the plans. This necessitated some drawing knowledge to obtain the correct profiles for some of the front wheelhouse shapes that were not actually displayed; however, with a little care and using card cut-outs to ensure a good fit, this is not difficult, and any small gaps can be filled later, before painting.

The inside of the wheelhouse was completed before the outside was spray painted, so any external imperfections did not matter at that stage. This then had to be carefully masked off with paper and masking tape to ensure no overspray ruined the internal finish.

The main instrument panels were all fabricated from Plasticard or 1.5mm ply, but most of the actual instrumentation consisted of bought-in resin-cast dummy units, or instrument decals, available from a number of model accessory shops online. Where possible items were home-made, to avoid too much extra expense, and also as a matter of principle – if you can make it, why buy it?

How far this is taken is really down to personal taste, because most of it will only be visible through the windows. However, in this case, even the local newspaper was photo-reduced, together with an Admiralty chart of South Devon to go on the chart table, for added realism.

Prior to undercoating, much of the detail for the roof/upperworks had to be completed separately. Some lifeboats carry an inflatable – termed a 'Y' boat – at the stern, but 17-28 was refitted with a crane, and the 'Y' boat positioned as shown. This took place halfway through the build of the model, which made it impossible to check detail until she came back on station a few months later.

All models will have lifebelts of some kind. They can be home-made, or are often supplied with kits, or are bought loose. Invariably the grab-line ropes around the outside will not be in the correct place, or the bindings will be incorrect. Often they are secured in a cage, or simply rest in hooked carriers. Whatever the starting point, it is worth ensuring that they are finished correctly for a particular model. If they have the name of the ship on the side, this can be so small as to be difficult to replicate, but it is possible with a computer and printer with transfer paper.

The 'Y' boat is tried for fit, and to ensure it does not catch on the handrails. Many modellers are daunted by the thought of fitting handrails, and it really depends on the scale of the model. Building a scale naval ship at 1:250 is totally different to the scale of this lifeboat, which is ten times larger, so obviously the handrails will be ten times smaller on

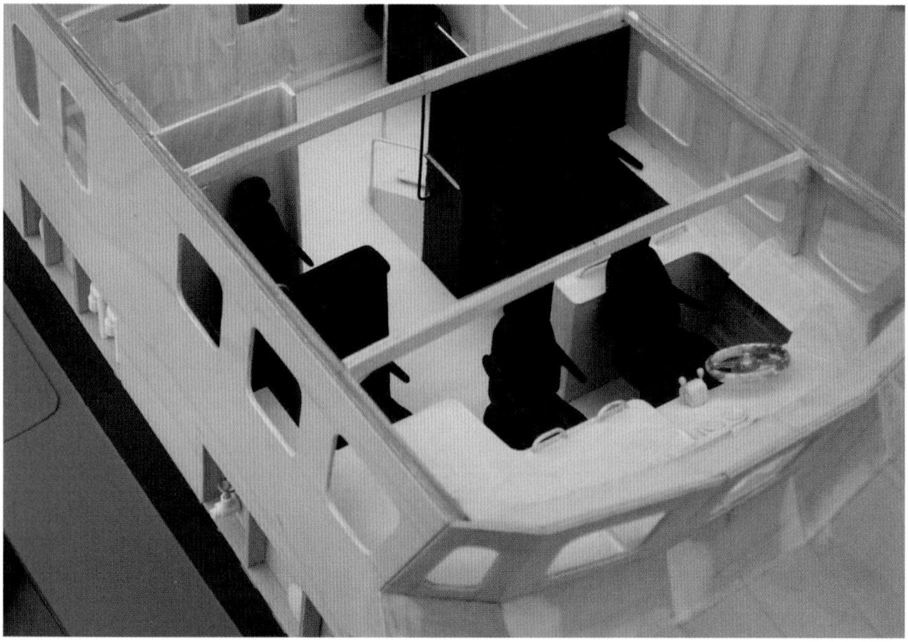

The wheelhouse is now complete, with all the resin-cast seats in place and being prepared for final painting.

The inside of the wheelhouse is finished and the external areas are being prepared for their final spray topcoat. Note how all the window areas and the top are fully masked off to protect the inside from any overspray.

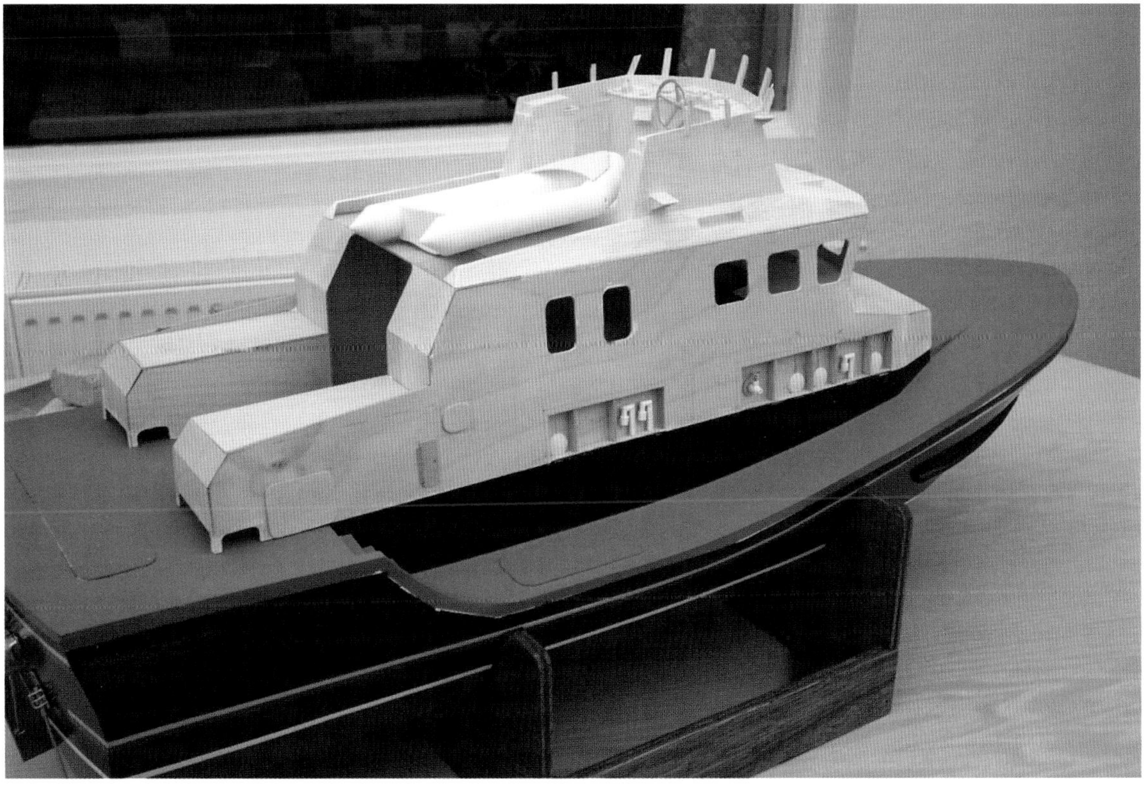

The topworks being tried for fit, prior to handrailing being fitted.

The handrailing now made up and all the joins soldered together.

the naval model and far less detailed. They are likely to be made from photo-etched stanchions and 1mm wire, and are much more 'fiddly' to construct.

With small stanchions it is easier to fit them to the deck and then carefully thread the wire through the respective holes; this is often done in sections, and joined with a small piece of tubing at the ends of the wire. With larger items such as shown on the lifeboat, the stanchion and the horizontal rail are welded together on the full-sized boat, so in order to look anything like a professional job, it is necessary to solder all the joints on the model, and make the whole thing out of tube, rather than solid rod.

The small spring pipe benders discussed in Chapter 1 were used to form all the bends, and a simple wooden jig was made to hold the separate tubes in place whilst applying solder. Where a join in the tube was required, a piece of solid rod inserted inside the end of one tube meant it could then easily be connected to the next tube and slid closed, making the join almost invisible.

A typical 'Y' boat is smaller than the RHIBs (rigid-hulled inflatable boat) used as larger stand-alone inshore rescue boats and runabouts, and is normally flat bottomed. Engine details were taken from full-sized literature, or online, to get manufacturer detail, printed out and then glued in place with superglue. The oars are carved from flat wooden strip, and decals are self-adhesive plastic strip, as are letters.

Helpful Tip

Make a simple jig for the handrail to hold parts in place while they are soldered, and slide a small piece of wire inside the tube, or drill a small locating hole where joins occur, prior to soldering.

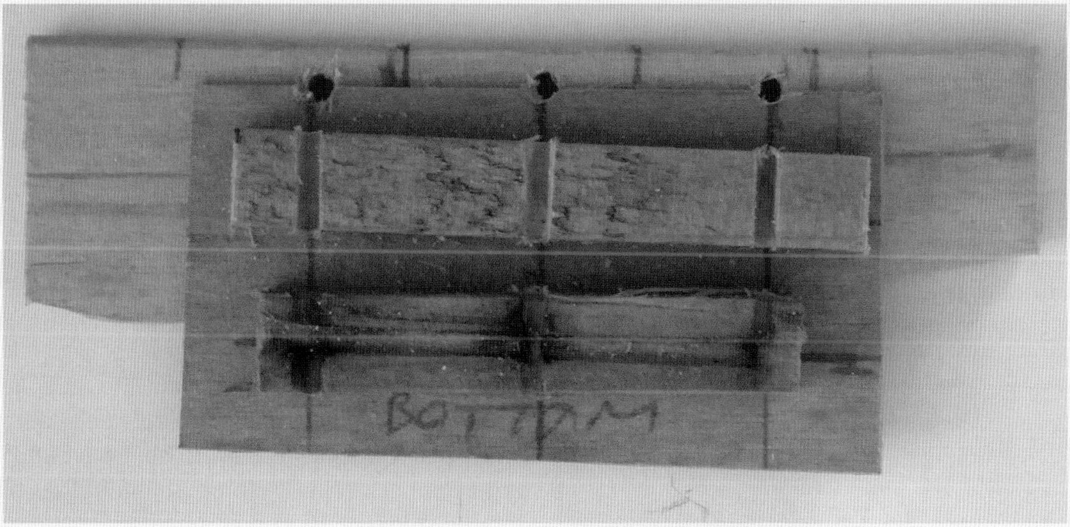

Simple jig made of wood to withstand the temperature of molten solder, whilst holding the pieces to be joined.

Detail of the 'Y' boat, now that it has been fitted out.

FINISHING AND FINAL PAINTING

Painting a model such as this requires it to be done in a number of stages. First the hull is undercoated, and then topcoated with Halford's Galaxy Blue spray paint, one of the rare occasions when a gloss finish can be used. The deck is a grey satin finish, and the upperworks are painted in Halford's VW Brilliant Orange spray. If the modeller is not able to get a satin or matt finish as a final coat, then use a clear spray satin or matt varnish finally to achieve the scale effect. If there are any windows, ensure that they are masked off to protect them from the extra coat of satin spray paint.

It is possible here to see the finished upperworks, with Y-156 omitted for clarity. The windshields require some care to fit properly, without getting adhesive on them, which is almost impossible to

The upper wheelhouse area, now painted with some of the instrumentation in place.

Another view, with both topworks mated together.

remove later. As mentioned earlier, much of the instrumentation is commercially available from model outlets, or can be home-made with a little imagination.

The upper roof/topworks had to blend in so that the minimum of joints were visible once the 'Y' boat was positioned – note the join used to hold the roof in place, just visible on the handrailing.

The crane was fabricated from Plasticard – simply use pins or brass rod where pivots are shown. It is a fairly vulnerable item when finally installed so must have some structural strength, even though in this case it was not operable.

The figure of the coxswain was made from a small doll of an old fisherman, which happened to be at the correct scale, and then sprayed yellow. The hat is from a Lego set, and the lifejacket is made from a piece of 30amp red electrical cable with the copper wire bent to shape around the figure's neck. Finally some self-adhesive black plastic strip was applied as a harness.

Everything has now been added to the topworks, with the coxswain in position, together with the 'Y' boat, with the exception of the aerials, flag and latch for the blue light.

Finally a quick check is made to ensure everything is in place inside, and has not come loose during the build. The upperworks are now complete, and only the external main deck features have to be considered.

Close-up of the finished control panel, prior to fitting the figure of the coxswain.

Making up the crane and the coxswain.

Everything now assembled and in place before the last stage of fitting out the main deck area.

Close-up view inside the wheelhouse, showing the chart table and instrumentation detail. Most of this is hidden when the roof is fitted, but can still be seen through the windows, if necessary.

EXTERNAL MAIN DECK FEATURES

There are two whip aerials on the sides of the upper topworks, which were made to be detachable for storage. These were made from steel spring wire, which is stronger and more rigid than brass wire, although it is essential to paint it to prevent rust.

Now complete and exhibited on its display stand, 17-28 is as near to the real thing as was possible to create at the time. Note that the white-painted handrails are all made from soldered tube, whilst the black handrailing towards the bow is a solid stanchion and wire handrailing, as mentioned earlier in this chapter.

The nameplate for the people who contributed to the boat's construction, 'Alec and Christina Dykes', after whom the boat is named, was made by printing off the text on Lazertran paper using a computer and ink-jet printer. All the other decals and labels were from BECC, who provided excellent service, because at the time the RNLI had just redesigned all their logos, and the new design was quickly made up for the model.

This model was made using a three-channel Tx and Rx. In hindsight it could have included a flashing blue emergency light, a siren, side navigation lights, maybe a searchlight, and a speaker with a sound system, but weight was a problem. Maybe next time, with a larger model?

HELPFUL TIP

As a safety precaution it is a good idea to put a dab of epoxy resin on the tip of an aerial to prevent injury to eyes, as sometimes it is difficult to see it when probing around the inside of a model trying to locate a lost nut!

Ship's Fittings

Many times, when making a model, it can be difficult to find details of anchors, winches, cranes, ship's boats, rigging, rope and so on. Whilst not

The finished model viewed from the stern. Virtually all the detail was hand-made, with the exception of deck cleats and the like.

Similar view of the bow area.

really applicable to this specific model, there is an old reference book that can prove invaluable, particularly for naval vessels: old copies are around online of the *Admiralty Manual of Seamanship* – there are various editions, but volume 1 is the one to look for.

'Rivet Counters'

It is worth a quick comment here on the phrase 'rivet counters', which the newcomer to modelling may encounter at some point. Like any hobby, modelling has three categories of enthusiasts: its experts, those who think they are experts, and those who realize they are not! The author would like to think that he is in the latter category.

However, when the second category of expert views the new model for the first time, do not be discouraged if you are told that the type of anchor is wrong, or the colour was different in 1965, or 'that bulkhead only had twenty-three rivets in it, not twenty-four as you have shown.' It does *not* matter at this stage, so worry about that when making exhibition or museum standard models later.

EXHIBITING AND COMPETITIONS

As mentioned at the beginning of the book, everyone has some desire to know how talented they actually are at any given task, and the only way to measure this is by entering competitions and exhibitions when available. Whilst this is not perhaps something for the novice modeller, it is still an excellent way of improving skills and knowledge later on.

Sometimes an otherwise excellent model is spoiled by the paint finish, either because the modeller was only interested in the actual construction and hurried to finish the model, or perhaps they lost interest – either way, many, many hours of labour, not to mention cost, will have been wasted for want of just a little attention to the final sprint to the finish.

Listed below are some of the criteria that a judge will use to assess the quality of a model, and the proportion of marks that each section will have been awarded. This is not the only system – there are others, but within a small percentage, they are similar:

Overall impression (50 per cent): Are the proportions correct, is anything missing, broken, clean or dusty? The style and condition of the stand, and the labelling, will be assessed.

Detailing (10 per cent): The scale of every item: would the full-sized boat have looked like that, is the period correct for all items?

Accuracy (10 per cent): Scale lettering, colour, ladder rungs scale, rope sizes. Are there joints in the planking, rivets?

Finish (10 per cent): Use of correct paint (to gloss, or not to gloss?), type of construction – GRP or plank-on frame – weathering, clean paint edges that have not run.

Class (10 per cent): Is it all the work of the owner, is it in the correct class – kit, semi-scratch, scratch – is it an appropriate level of difficulty for the skill level of the owner?

Documentation (10 per cent): How much documentation is there, and how clear and accurate? No documentation will immediately lose 10 per cent of possible marks. Three or four pages are sufficient, with photographs.

Always remember that if a modeller is to be judged, do prepare for disappointment and/or criticism: it may be painful at first, but it can only improve the skill level – and some day there could be a rosette and a cup next to the model.

IN CONCLUSION

Finally, the photo shows the lifeboat model sailing in Brixham harbour, with the real article in the background. A word of caution here: it is not practical, or safe, to simply go and sail a model radio-controlled boat in one of the busiest commercial and recreational harbours in the country, just on a whim. Permission had to be obtained from the Harbour Master in advance, with assurances that the model transmissions would not interfere with any radio telecommunication systems from vessels leaving harbour, and so on.

The author also owes a debt of gratitude to the RNLI station in Brixham, who patiently answered so many queries along the way.

This model, and *Komet* in the previous chapter, are purely representative of what procedures can be adopted to make an electrically powered model boat. They are not meant to show a definitive method, to the exclusion of anything else, or to be the first model a novice to the hobby attempts: they are only a selection of ideas. There are many ways that you can make a model, and it is down to personal skills, experience and available facilities – the only criterion is that the experience is enjoyable and fulfilling.

Later, when the author left the area, the model was donated to the Brixham RNLI station and was used for fund-raising. As of the time of writing, it is on permanent display in the Brixham Heritage Museum, just by the traffic lights, in the centre of Brixham, together with models of all the earlier boats down the ages.

This little museum is a delight, and if ever the reader is on holiday in this lovely area, spare an hour or so to have a look around it and transport yourself back in time, and also maybe learn a little about the fantastic service that the lifeboat volunteers provide for all of us.

View of the model taken from the slipway next to the lifeboat station in Brixham Harbour. Permission had to be obtained from the Harbour Master to take this picture for publicity purposes.

Chapter Nine

Making Life Easier

STANDS

All models will need some means of holding them in place, and holding them upright, whilst they are being made – a working stand. Once complete, they will perhaps need something that is not covered in paint, dust or saw marks from the actual construction – in other words, a permanent stand, with some form of padding to protect the underside. Sadly, on some kits the stand is treated as an afterthought of no importance, which can be frustrating for the novice modeller who suddenly realizes that a stand has to be made at some point.

A 10mm plywood stand is robust and suitable for most boats, but can be more difficult to cut and shape at this thickness; if so, make up two pieces at 5mm and glue them together. Always use some kind of padding where the stand contacts the underside of the model.

If the model is to go on display or to be used as an exhibit, then the stand should be as good as the model, in both design and finish. Many modellers who enter competitions for the first time, fail to win simply because the stand is also considered to be part of the model by the judges, and is marked down accordingly if it is not up to standard.

Most yacht modellers use a simple folding stand at the lakeside, a little like a folding chair with two webbing straps across the top, rather than a seat. This is to accommodate the extended weighted keel usual with racing yachts in particular, and where a solid stand would take up too much room.

Any well produced kit will offer profiles of the sides of the stand to give a reverse view of where the stand should mate up with the underside of the hull – and sometimes even the wood to build the stand is supplied, though not always. It is a good idea to make up the profile in card before actually cutting the wood, just to check it is correct to the shape of the hull underside.

Remember that the profile is already provided with a kit for each bulkhead in the offcuts, so do not throw away waste offcuts until the model is finished, as they may come in very useful, for profiling and also for holding planking in place where nothing else is suitable. Padding is needed to protect the hull paintwork with something like self-adhesive foam tape or similar, so do not forget to allow for the thickness of the padding.

If something like a plastic kit is chosen, then there will be no plan as such, only the hull itself, unless further research is undertaken: there are many books on the subject, such as *Flower Class Corvettes*, by John Lambert and Les Brown, published by Seaforth Publishing. This Revell kit is often chosen to convert from a simple plastic kit to a working radio-controlled model.

Display stands for static museum-standard models can be taken to extremes, and are used to enhance the appearance of the model, the only limitation being the imagination of the modeller.

A folding strap stand, typical of those used for deep keel yachts.

A more robust, practical stand, typical of GRP-hulled models, made from 10mm external grade plywood, and then varnished, as it will always get wet when a boat is retrieved from the water. Often it is made as a shallow tray so that other items can be temporarily stored inside it.

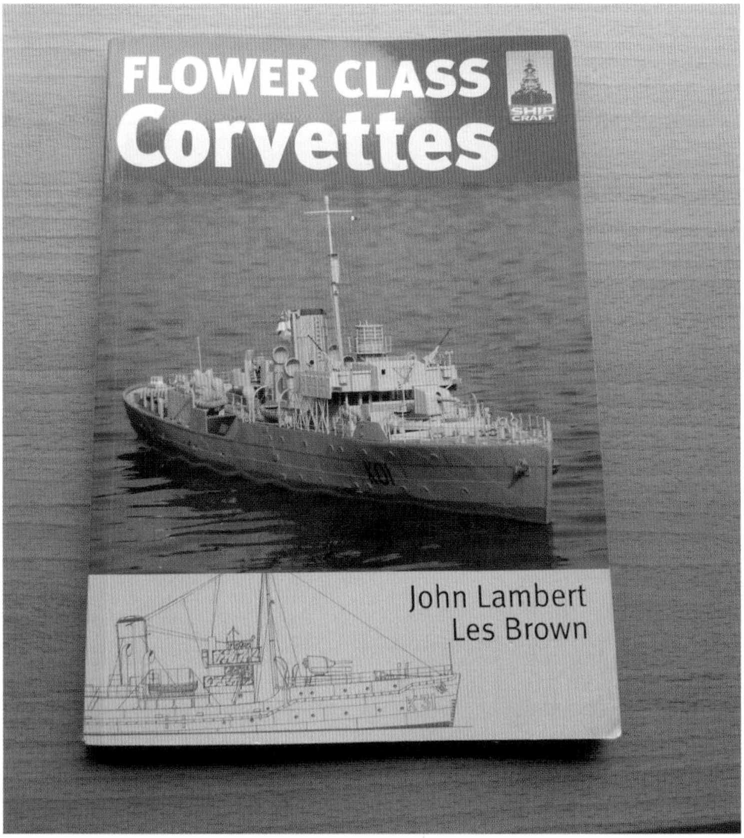

Another source of information. Always look around for books on the model being made: invariably someone will have written about them somewhere.

Not many plastic kits are large enough to adapt to radio control; this one by Revell is an exception, and many modellers have used it as a kit.

A glass-cased museum-standard display model, here shown to illustrate the elaborate decoration that can be used to gain more atmosphere in the display.

These are usually protected in a glass case so do not require to be as strong or weatherproof.

Some modellers fabricate a spares toolkit and stand-cum-seat – the stand on one end, the seat on the other – with drawers for spares (or sandwiches and a flask) and a shoulder strap for carrying, similar in many respects to a fisherman's basket.

CARRYING THE MODEL TO THE WATER

Heavy models, even without batteries – which are often left out and fitted on site, rather than being carried in the model – can be extremely hard to carry. Short slings like those shown are fine where there are no handrails, but are still not ideal. 99 per cent of models are damaged when they are being carried about, or being launched, almost never when they are actually sailing.

A short single-handed carrying system, but not suitable for boats with handrailing.

If it is possible to park the car at the lakeside, then the task becomes much easier, but often the car park is some distance away, and either the model has to be carried clutched close to the chest, or better still, on a trolley.

Launching Trolley

Using 10mm ply as a base, the trolley illustrated was made to carry a number of models – the central crossbar can be slid along and relocated to clamp a variety of stand lengths, with enough space all round to carry batteries, or other bulky items. A notch in the stand gives the model additional security from unnecessary movement whilst in transit.

The unit was designed to be nose heavy, with the axle just beyond half way back, so that the hinged front legs could be deployed when stationary, and secured in place when transporting the model. All parts are detachable and can be quickly screwed in place using wing nuts, so the model will fit into the boot of a car. As there are no springs or suspension, the tyres are only partly inflated, which offers some compensation when pulling the trolley over rough ground, in order to protect the model.

The shaft is a piece of screwed rod, and wheel bearings are not needed. The shaft is simply held in place with threaded lock-nuts on each wheel, which are detachable.

Various positions and locating holes for screwed wing nuts, so that the centre bar can be repositioned for each boat stand.

A home-made trolley for transporting some of the author's fleet, which are too heavy to carry by hand over long distances.

The whole thing can be taken to pieces for easy packing away once the day's sailing is completed. Generally, the model and stand will still sit on the baseboard in the car on the way home, which stops it potentially moving about.

GETTING THE MODEL INTO THE WATER

Launching Slings

Launching slings come in many shapes and sizes and are designed to actually get the model from the lakeside into the water, which may not be as easy as it sounds. A model can easily weigh 10 to 15kg, and lowering this at arm's length can throw considerable strain on the back muscles. Anyone with a weakened back should carefully consider this. Lakes with a water level much lower than the standing area are particularly difficult to launch from. Sometimes even waders are worn where the modeller has a slipway or beach to launch from, meaning it is necessary to wade into deeper water to launch the model into sufficient depth.

Two slings are needed, one to go about a quarter of the way from the bow, and the other a quarter of the way from the stern, making sure it is clear of rudders, propeller shafts and propellers. The simplest form is a piece of stout rope, or better still a pair of large vehicle fan belts.

An important consideration is that the slings clear handrailing, in particular, also masts, booms,

A rope sling showing a plastic tube for protection and to offer a level of 'stiffness' and greater control.

About 1m of length will normally be sufficient in order to lower the model into the water. Note the copper pipe 'spreaders' to ensure that the rope does not knock parts off the deck area.

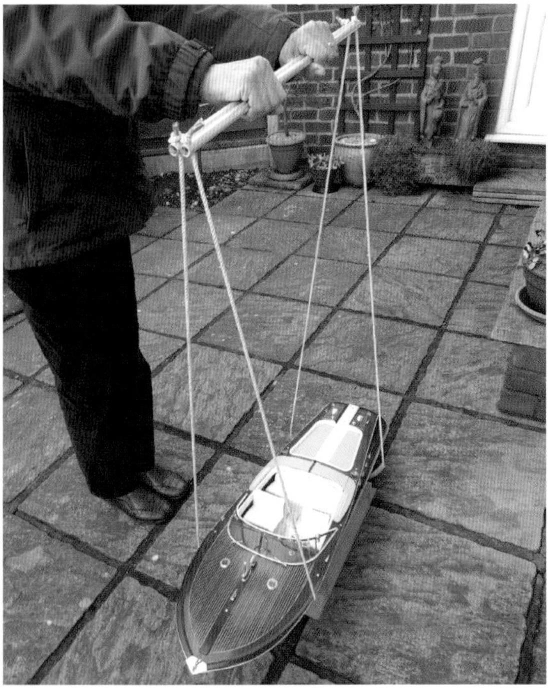

Another version, where the space between the fore and aft slings needs to be known to avoid damaging the underside of the model. Note that the ropes tend to converge, so care must be taken not to damage delicate deck components.

radar topworks and so on, as it is all too easy to bend upper deckworks when the model is lifted and the slings narrow as they take the weight. Fan belts tend not to deform too much and do not damage paintwork, so are ideal.

If using thin modern synthetic rope, many of which float, it will be difficult to get it beneath the hull when retrieving the model from the water; by using a short piece of hose, which will also protect the hull, the problem will be solved.

Combined Launcher

Another solution to getting a larger model into the water is to use a modified two-wheeled shopping-bag trolley. Remove the trolley back to expose the frame. Many of these are collapsible, so fit a base that will take the stand for the model, or make up a combined stand from exterior grade plywood that can be fixed to the trolley.

The model can then be wheeled to the water and launched directly into the water whilst still sat on the trolley.

THE TEST TANK

The obvious test tank for a model would be the household bath. However, not everyone has access to such a thing, so alternatives should be considered. An old tin bath is ideal, as is a garden pond, or any other large watertight container. The essence of the exercise is that the boat remains

All the parts cut out for a home-made test tank. One of the drawbacks of making large models is that they are too large to fit in the household bath when testing is needed. Anyone fortunate enough to have a pond in the garden could perhaps use that as an alternative.

Dowels are inserted to hold the end pieces in place.

The side stiffeners are now clamped after gluing and nailing them to the plywood.

The dowels are cut to size and made to be removable, so that the ends and sides can be stored away separately.

Close-up of the corner; note each corner was numbered separately, so the sequence of reassembly in the future would be clear.

The inside corners of each end were filled with a wooden strip to ease the tension on the polythene liner when it was in place and full of water.

close to the modeller, for adjustment, movement of ballast, attaching batteries, and so on.

Often the modeller has to take the new model to the boating lake to test it out. The author's own club has a rescue dinghy for the retrieval of 'dead' boats, while other clubs have a radio-controlled rescue boat with a large padded 'Y' frame on the front to catch a stray model and return it to safety. But consider what would happen to the model if it decided to go 'rogue' and park itself in an inaccessible part of the water – or worse still, sank after all your hard work. Better to try and test some of the systems under control in a tank.

The finished end plate, next to the side pieces.

The frame with the final sides in place; each side was built in two halves.

The half side-panel stiffeners overlapped so they could be pinned together with another dowel.

The test tank fully assembled and ready to have the polythene liner fitted.

The tank disassembled and ready for storage.

The tank illustrated was effectively designed around a model submarine that was about 7ft (2m) long, so it was unlikely that anything larger would be needed for future models. Also, it is difficult to get water out of a bath except down the waste plug, but here the tank is assembled next to a rainwater butt and all the water comes out of that. After use it is scooped out with a bucket and returned to the butt, so very little is wasted.

This meant that two sides of the tank could be a convenient 4ft long, and were easy to get at that size, as a half-length, as most plywood is sold in 8 × 4ft sheets. So an 8ft long tank with clearance around the submerged submarine would be ideal.

The tank in use. Testing the control of the submarine to flood its tanks and submerge, and ensuring that the ballast weights are in the correct position, is vital for a submarine. It should be noted that the outside of the tank had to be supported with a few bricks to counter the pressure of water pushing them outwards, mainly because there is no fixed base to the tank.

SPARES

Whatever spares are thought necessary, it is a foregone conclusion that the one necessary item required when something breaks down is not going to be at hand: this is a hard lesson to learn and one that only comes with experience.

A range of small spanners for tightening propellers/universal joints is a must, also a small adjustable wrench, fuses, small screwdrivers, small Allen keys, superglue, rubber bands, string, hand wipes, a few thin strips of lead flashing for balance/ballast trimming, Tx and Rx crystals if using 40MHz – in fact anything that can be put in a simple tool-carrying case, dedicated to model boating.

From experience, any other modeller on site will help out if there is a problem, but it is better to be prepared and not have to rely on that.

A plastic carry-all toolbox – from memory it only cost around £6, and has proved its worth many times over.

Spare fuses, superglue, small watchmakers' screwdrivers, Allen keys and small spanners, especially those that fit the propeller locknut.

Spare insulating tape, string, a rubber bulb on a tube for sucking water out of the bilges in an emergency, dry rag – in fact anything that may come in useful.

WHAT WILL IT COST?

Asking how much it will cost to build a model is like asking how long is a piece of string: it will cost what the novice modeller can afford to spend. However, at today's prices, and assuming that the model and components are new, rather than second-hand or from an online source such as eBay, then the following will hopefully offer some guidance as baseline figures.

As well as the materials from which the hull will be made, you will need a radio transmitter and receiver, a battery, a servo for the rudder, an ESC to control the motor, the motor itself, propeller shaft and propeller, universal coupling, wire/plugs/fittings, and adhesive and paint: the likely minimum cost of this will be around £220.

A beginner's kit would be in the order of £50 to £100, and this will include most things necessary, other than the items listed above, plus paint and glue. There are naturally much more expensive kits on the market, so this would be for a simple kit without too much embellishment.

There will be three choices for the hull. The first option is to purchase a blown, or vacuum-formed styrene hull. This will be thinner and will need more internal bracing with wooden bulkheads, but will be much quicker to build. The second option is that the model could start with a GRP glassfibre hull. This is much stronger, but more expensive, unless the hull is home-made. Lastly, and more traditionally, it could be made out of wood using a plank-on-frame construction, which will take the longest to build and will require more skill. The costs might be as follows:

- Ready-made vacuum-formed hull and plan: £50/£70. Total cost for everything: around £270.
- Ready-made GRP hull and plan: £90/£120. Total cost for everything: around £300.
- Plank-on-frame plan: £15. Total cost for everything: around £290.

Whilst these are very approximate figures, it becomes clear that there isn't that much difference between them. However, the purchase cost for a typical kit for the more advanced modeller is on average £300/£400, going up to £1,000 – and this is without the £220 for fitting out, as itemized above.

Making a Hull out of GRP

For those who are really dedicated to making a highly detailed hull, then the process of making a hull out of GRP becomes more attractive. First, plans and hull profiles are needed to make a 'plug'. This is effectively the finished hull, so all external plating in thin card, rivets and so on, needs to be included if a highly detailed finish is required. It then needs to be thoroughly sealed, and finally sprayed with a silicon release agent, which is important to stop anything sticking to it.

A gel coat, followed by a glass mat, will produce the actual mould. If there are a lot of details that could hinder the final release, then the mould will have to be made in two halves that split along the keel, later to be bolted together to give the final shape of the mould to make a hull. This is really only worthwhile if a number of hulls are going to be made. It is not proposed to deal in depth with this subject here, as there are numerous books and videos on YouTube and similar, showing how this can be achieved in detail.

Thinking Sideways

In order to keep costs to a minimum, then a new mindset is needed. Before discarding anything, imagine if it could be modified to use somewhere on a model boat. Waste-water piping and many plastic fittings are excellent for funnels or ventilator pipes, or maybe a 'pop' bottle can be made into a submarine (it has been done). Plastic push-out pill dispensers make good light covers when cut out. Margarine tubs and yoghurt pots make up wheelhouses, but test them to ensure they can be stuck with the adhesive being used.

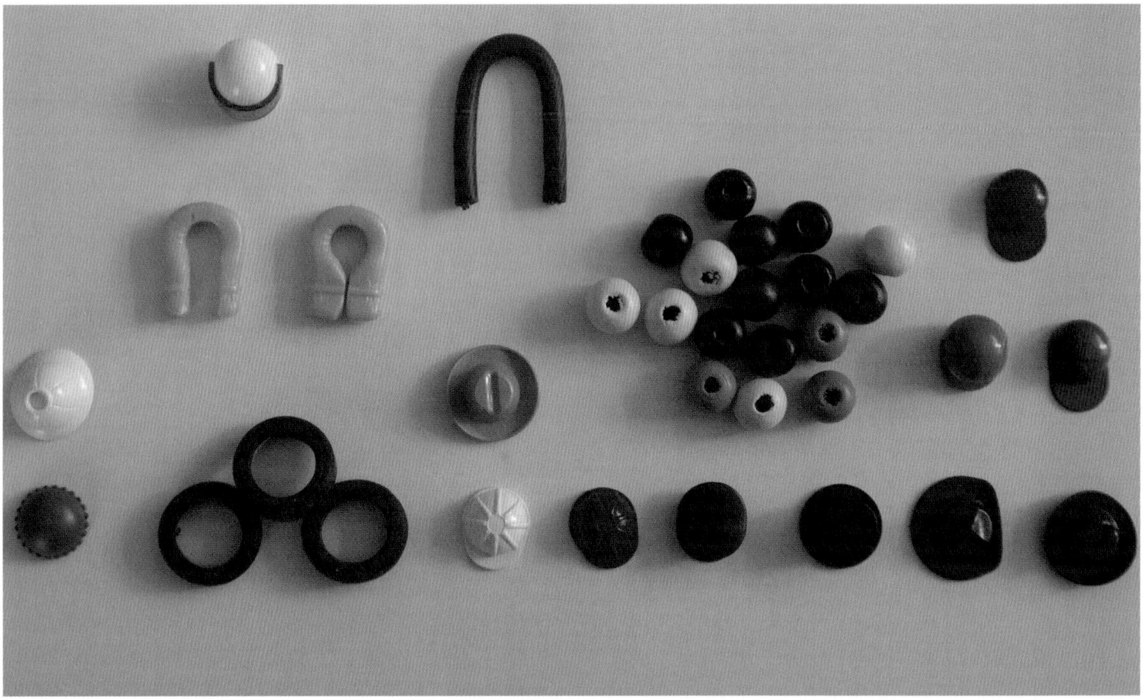

Save anything that may be adapted: bits of electrical wire to make lifejackets, other parts from Lego, tyres for fenders from old toy cars, and wooden beads, which make excellent buoys.

Sticks from firework rockets, wood offcuts, plastic offcuts – the list is endless, and only limited by the imagination and adaptability in the mind of the modeller. It is even possible to make up a papier-mâché boat hull from newspaper, provided it is well varnished to waterproof it before taking it on the water.

RULES OF THE ROAD

We live in a society governed by rules at every turn, and this cannot be avoided even on the lake. Most of the rules are actually modified versions of those that govern full-sized craft at sea to avoid collision.

As was said by Harry Day, a World War I fighter ace: 'Rules are for the guidance of wise men, and the obedience of fools' – words that are paraphrased by another fighter ace in World War II, Douglas Bader in the film *Reach for the Sky*. It is much easier to study the rules and obey them, many of which have been developed over years of experience. Find out the accepted procedure on the water you intend to use, and abide by the guidelines – it is simple courtesy and common sense, after all.

There is another pertinent quote, much older, from W. Shakespeare's *As You Like It*: 'The fool doth think he is wise, but the wise man knows himself to be a fool.' What is important is that a novice modeller considers other lake users, be they other modellers, or members of the public who happen to be there at the time.

If there is a yacht race in progress, do not drive through the middle of it, as yachts broadly need the wind to move, and may have to tack suddenly as the wind changes. Always aim to steer to the stern of a yacht rather than go in front of it. If overtaking, leave plenty of room.

If another vessel is heading towards your model, slow down and stop until you are certain where the other vessel is going: if passing head-to-head, pass port side to port side. If your vessel is faster ensure that the wash does not swamp another craft nearby. At a distance this may not always be clear, as sometimes it is hard to tell the direction of travel.

BASIC TROUBLESHOOTING

Problem: the motor won't start:

- Is it switched on? Check the switch.
- Is the ESC also switched on? If there is a separate switch, check that switch.
- Is the battery charged?
- Are the battery terminals properly connected, and more importantly, are they connected the correct way round? Red/brown $+^{ve}$ to $+^{ve}$ and black/blue $-^{ve}$ to $-^{ve}$.
- Similarly, are the motor terminals connected, and the right way round?
- Same comments for the ESC.
- Are any other connections loose, not connected, or incorrectly connected? This is the most common cause of problems.
- Are there any dry joints of soldered connections, where the terminal was dirty or not properly prepared and tinned with solder before soldering? They often separate later.
- Are any connections corroded? This is more likely to happen on older, well used models that have been thoroughly wetted at some point. It is a particular problem where sea pools are used.
- Are any wires broken, or burned through to earth, or short circuiting a signal?
- Is any wiring insulation missing? The same problems as the point above.

Problem: the propeller is not turning:

- Is the propeller free to turn? Make sure nothing is tied around the propeller shaft, such as string or weed.
- Are the motor and propeller turning the correct way to drive the boat forwards? If not, reverse the connections on the motor. Do not reverse the wiring anywhere else.
- Is the propeller loose on the shaft? Check the lock-nut is tight.
- Are both the propeller shaft lock-nut and that on the universal joint tight, and is the Allen screw tight where it is attached to the motor shaft?

Problem: the rudder is not operating properly:

- Are the servo wires disconnected from the Rx, or not pushed in properly? Any item that is plugged into the Rx may suffer from the plug not being pushed in far enough – this is a very common malfunction problem.
- Supply to the Rx is not switched on, or is disconnected. If it is a separate battery supply, are the batteries flat? If there is a BEC, is it connected properly?
- The push rods, or the connections between the rudder post and servo may be disconnected, loose or damaged. This is more common where there is only one rod that has to pull and push. Where two rods are fitted, one pulls whilst the other pushes, and this is much less likely to fail.
- The rudder is jammed within the tube that carries the rudder post. This is a common problem on older boats where a steel shaft has corroded.
- The servo is broken: check the movement with the push rods disconnected.
- The little retaining screw has come off, and the servo arm has come off the splined end of the servo shaft. This is unlikely as it is normally quite a tight fit, but is worth checking.

Problem: no control:

- The Tx is apparently not transmitting to the Rx. A new/different Rx is being used to an older Rx in the boat, such that the two are not bonded.

They may actually be incompatible – hopefully this will have been checked before arriving at the lake. Read the operating instructions for the Rx/Tx being used, and follow the bonding procedure.
- The Tx is not switched on.
- The Tx batteries are flat, or the terminals are corroded.
- The aerials are damaged.
- The Rx aerials are not properly deployed. An old 40MHz aerial may be cut or coiled up – it must be extended. Modern 2.4GHz Rx have one or two short aerials, which should be at 90 degrees to each other if there are two.
- The Tx sticks/knobs/switches are not in the neutral/off position before switching on.
- With older systems, the Rx is switched on before the Tx, such that it starts responding to 'ghost' signals, or another Tx.

It is good practice to get into the habit of always removing all batteries after sailing; also remove any water or damp that may have splashed into the boat.

It cannot be stressed enough to ensure that the polarity of all connections are checked and are all right. If they are not, or if there is any doubt, then something could be instantly destroyed at switch on!

Care After Sailing

The easiest way to store up problems for the future is to neglect a few simple tasks after sailing, when the model is put back on the shelf, until next time.

Apart from obvious things such as taking out the battery and recharging it, check to ensure that everything is dry inside the hull: if there is any water, thoroughly dry it out, also leave all hatches and removable upper deck works off to allow air circulation – use a hair dryer, if necessary. Try to find out where the water came from, and aim to stop it happening again.

If anything has been damaged or knocked off, repair it now rather than leaving it until later, otherwise it will be forgotten until the next sail and by then will have been lost, misplaced, or the adhesive will simply not have time to cure properly after a repair.

Many models are stored in a place such as a workshop or garage, where dust accumulates, so try to protect the model as much as possible. Model boats by their very nature have many hard-to-reach nooks and crannies, and dust can disfigure the most pristine of models.

Covering the model with a sheet of polythene will normally reduce this problem. A heavily dusted model can be cleaned to some extent by careful use of a clean, very soft make-up brush. Another solution often quoted is to leave the model outside during a heavy rainstorm – however, this will naturally be dependent upon the design and materials of the model. Do not try to use a hosepipe, because it is quite likely that it will damage the model.

INFORMATION AND SUPPLIERS

If you search online, there are many companies that will supply your various needs. There are many more than are listed here, and a quick search will locate them, but as a starter the following may be of help:

modelboats.co.uk: For the latest news and information on the various model kit suppliers, and components, then I suggest you go to *Model Boats* magazine, a must for up-to-date articles and equipment, plus everything from sailing ships to nuclear submarines.

expotools.com: An excellent source of all modelling tools and materials.

component-shop.co.uk: For anything electrical, including also good advice.

mfa/comodrills.com: Good for tools, motors and much more.

Sylcreate.com: Everything in silicon and resin for making moulds and casts.

Mobilemarinemodels.com: the tug specialists, and more.

Deansmarine.co.uk: A long-established kit manufacturer.

Cornwallmodelboats.co.uk: Another long-established, dependable online shop for kits and materials.

Howesmodels.co.uk: One-stop shop for the modeller.

Davemetcalfboatmodels.com: A great range of kit hulls.

Sarikhobbies.com: Another excellent kit supplier.

Fleetscale.com: An excellent range of kits.

Modelfittings.co.uk: Everything for the dedicated modeller who wants to embellish a model further.

Mtroniks.net: An excellent range of ESCs for all types of boat.

Deluxematerials.co.uk: Adhesives and finishing materials.

Macsmouldings.co.uk: Fantastic range of resin fittings, and more.

Modelboatbits.com: For everything in fittings.

Skipper.co.uk: Hundreds of working plans for model boat construction.

IN CONCLUSION

Hopefully, apart from making many new friends and having the satisfaction of building and sailing your creation out in the fresh air, you will be invigorated by the range of new skillsets you have mastered, and the greater knowledge of materials, tools, adhesives, paint, electrics, radio control, to mention but a few, that you will have acquired.

The suggestions, ideas, procedures and tools described in this book are the result of many years of modelling by the author and the knowledge gained along that journey. They do not represent the only way of approaching a task, nor the only item available.

Like any hobby or sport, there will be differences of opinion – if ten experts are locked in a room and asked a question, there will likely be ten different answers or solutions. This does not mean that nine are wrong, only that the answers will be coloured by the experiences of each expert. Thus it is hoped that the enthusiast new to model boating will use the ideas herein as a guide, and not as a rule, cast in stone.

Yes, there will likely be challenges along the way, but that is the key to real achievement: mastering the challenges and gaining confidence, and the feeling of satisfaction, is what it is all about.

Yet this is only the 'tip of the iceberg', because with your new knowledge and skills, a whole world of enjoyment awaits you – enjoy it for years to come, and the best of modelling.

Index

Related Titles from Crowood

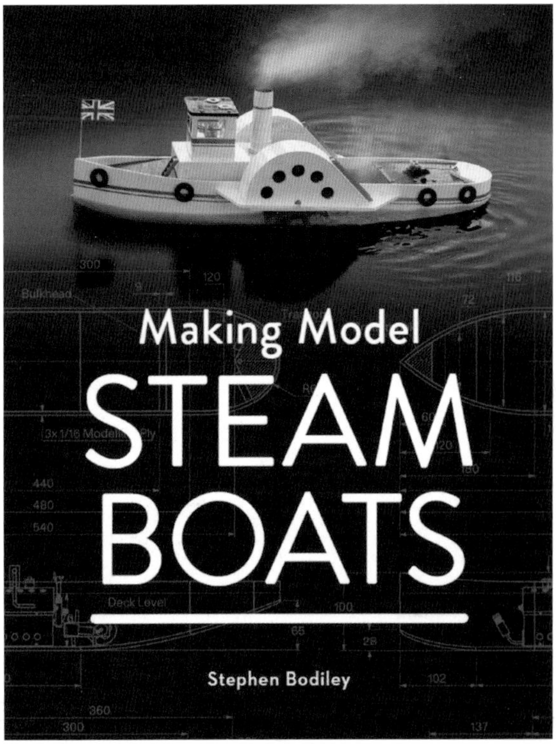

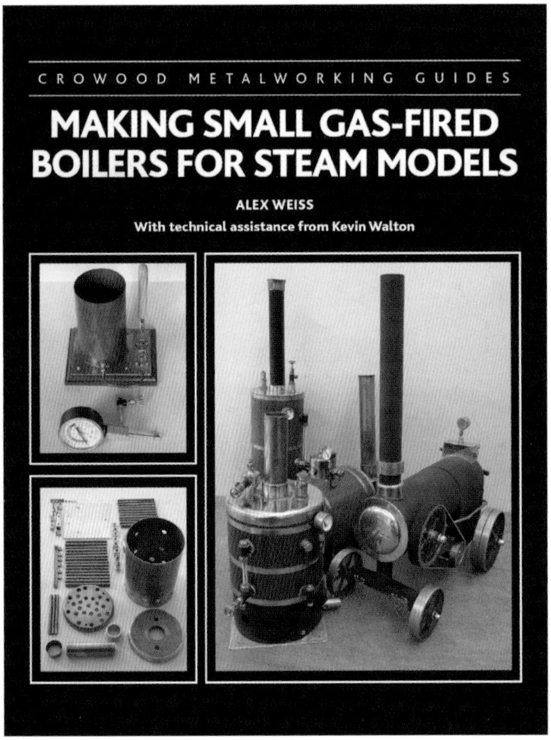

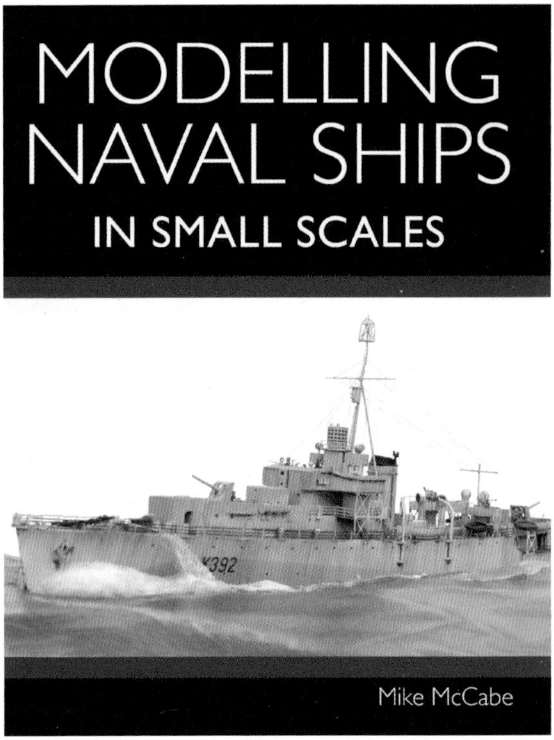